Photographing Children in Natural Light

Art and Techniques

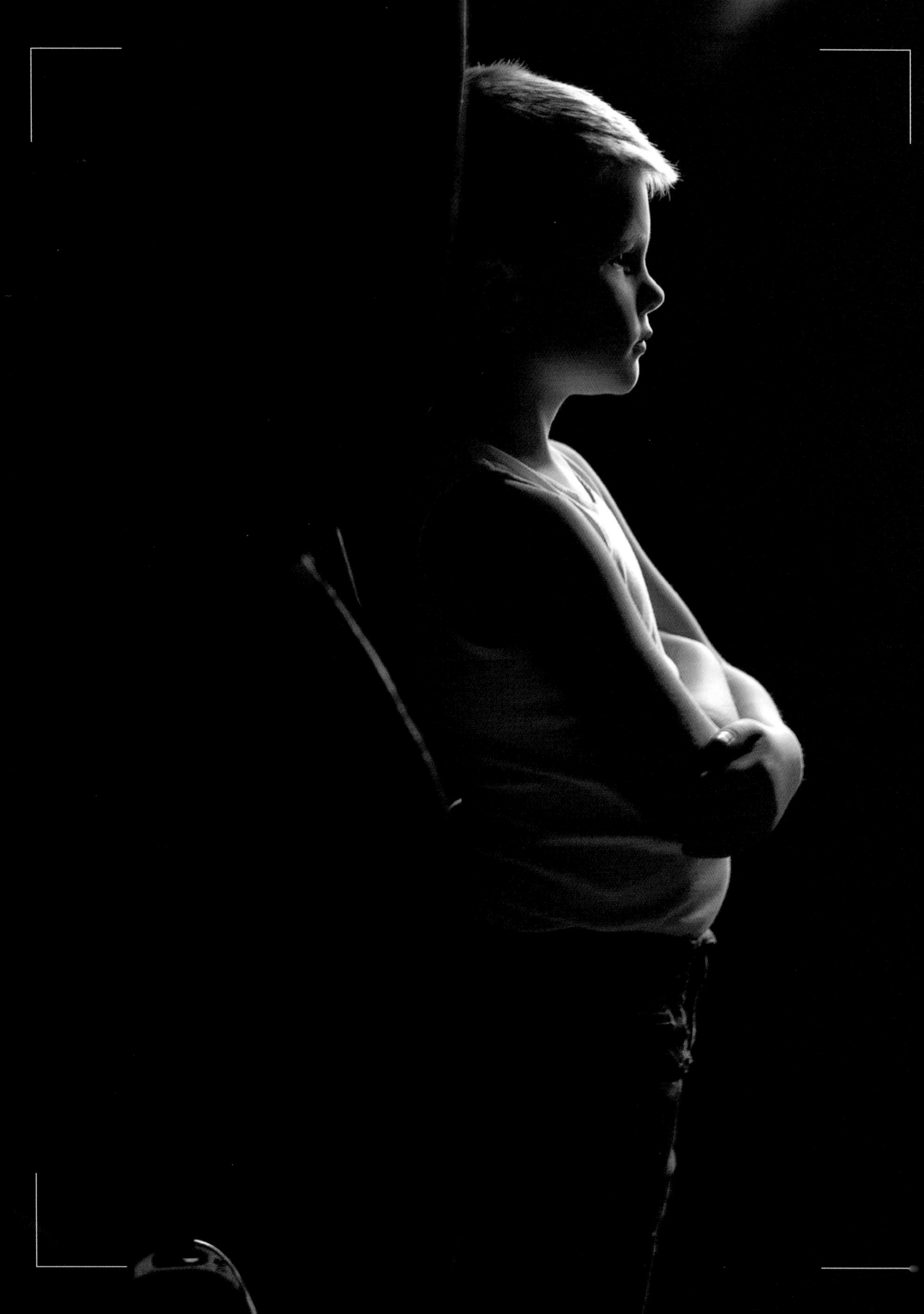

Photographing Children in Natural Light
Art and Techniques

Bella West

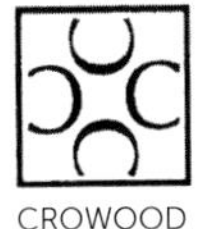

CROWOOD

First published in 2014 by
The Crowood Press Ltd
Ramsbury, Marlborough
Wiltshire SN8 2HR

www.crowood.com

British Library Cataloguing-in-Publication Data
A catalogue record for this book is available from the British Library.

ISBN 978 1 84797 711 3

Graphic design and layout by www.peggyandco.ca
Printed and bound in Singapore by Craft Print International

CONTENTS

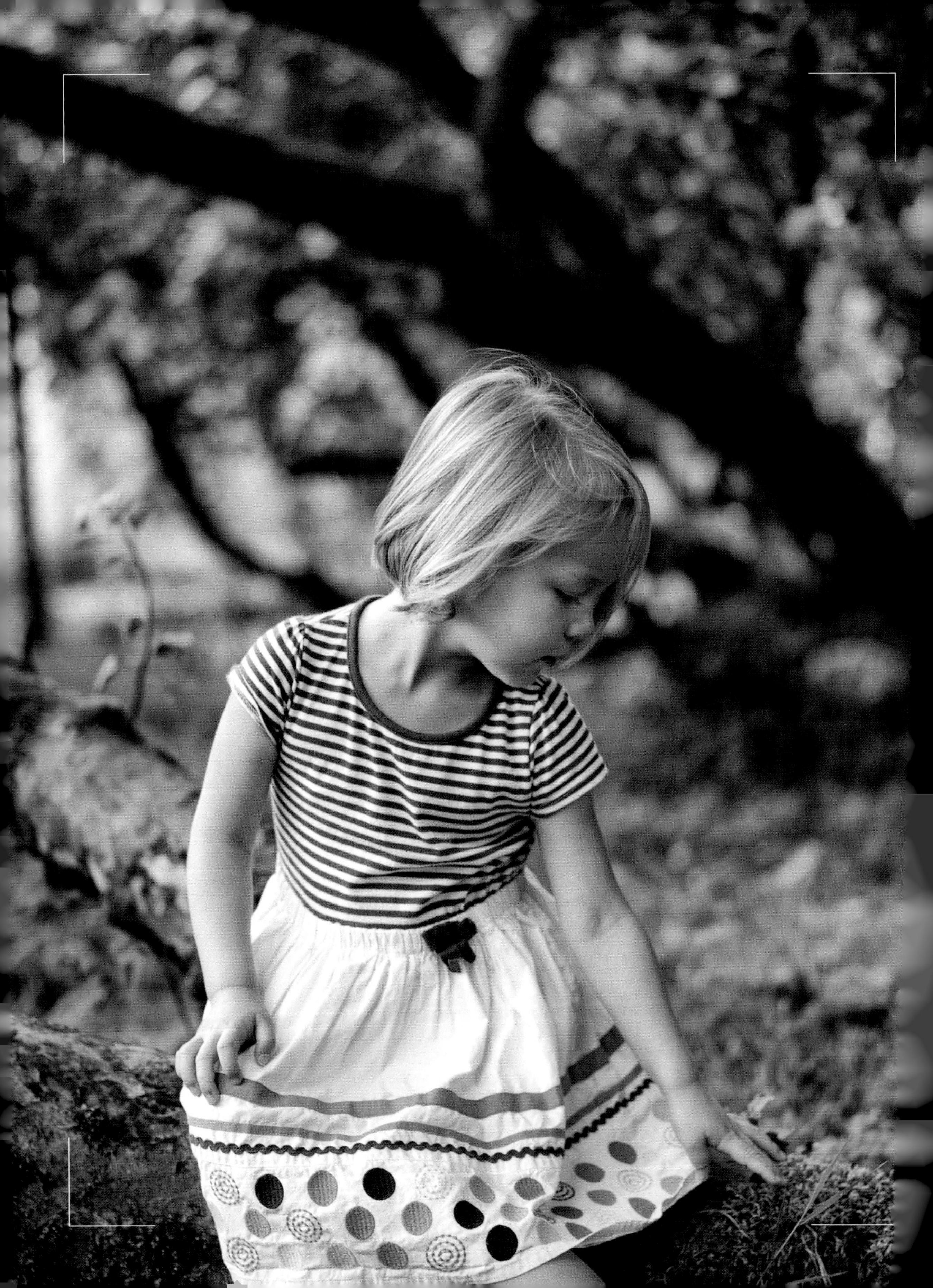

Foreword

I am truly privileged to be invited to write this foreword as the chief executive of one of the world's leading qualifying bodies of photography. For the last decade I have been spearheading the pursuit of quality, professionalism and creativity in photography, and Bella West has helped guide that process.

The British Institute of Professional Photography has exacting standards when assessing photographers' work. It's a progressive structure and is aimed at supporting photographers to become the best they can be. Being self-critical and selective are difficult achievements and Bella has not only worked through this process as a photographer, but has developed into an outstanding assessor, lecturer and trainer herself. In 2013 she accepted the Institute's invitation to chair our Wedding & Portrait Awards, a national awards scheme for professional photographers. She guided the judging panel through discussions and dissention effortlessly!

Bella West has built her reputation on an assured manner, quality and timeless style. She learned the hard way – working up through the ranks of sports photography to a position as one of Europe's leading portrait and wedding photographers. It doesn't surprise me in the slightest that she continues to 'pay it forward' by training and guiding photographers of all levels to be the very best that they can be.

This book is an intelligent lesson in the skills, artistry and control needed to be a credible portrait photographer, written by a photographer whom many attempt to emulate, but whose creativity lifts her into a league very few of us (even those of us with twenty years' experience!) can hope to be a part of.

I sincerely hope you savour the creative simplicity of Bella's lighting and composition and are able to take these skills forward in your own photography. I know I hope to!

Chris Harper FBIPP
Photographer and Chief Executive, British Institute of Professional Photography

◄ By setting the scene, finding a location with sympathetic light, we can observe children's natural curiosity and personality to bring together sensitive portraits that are timeless and exude profundity.

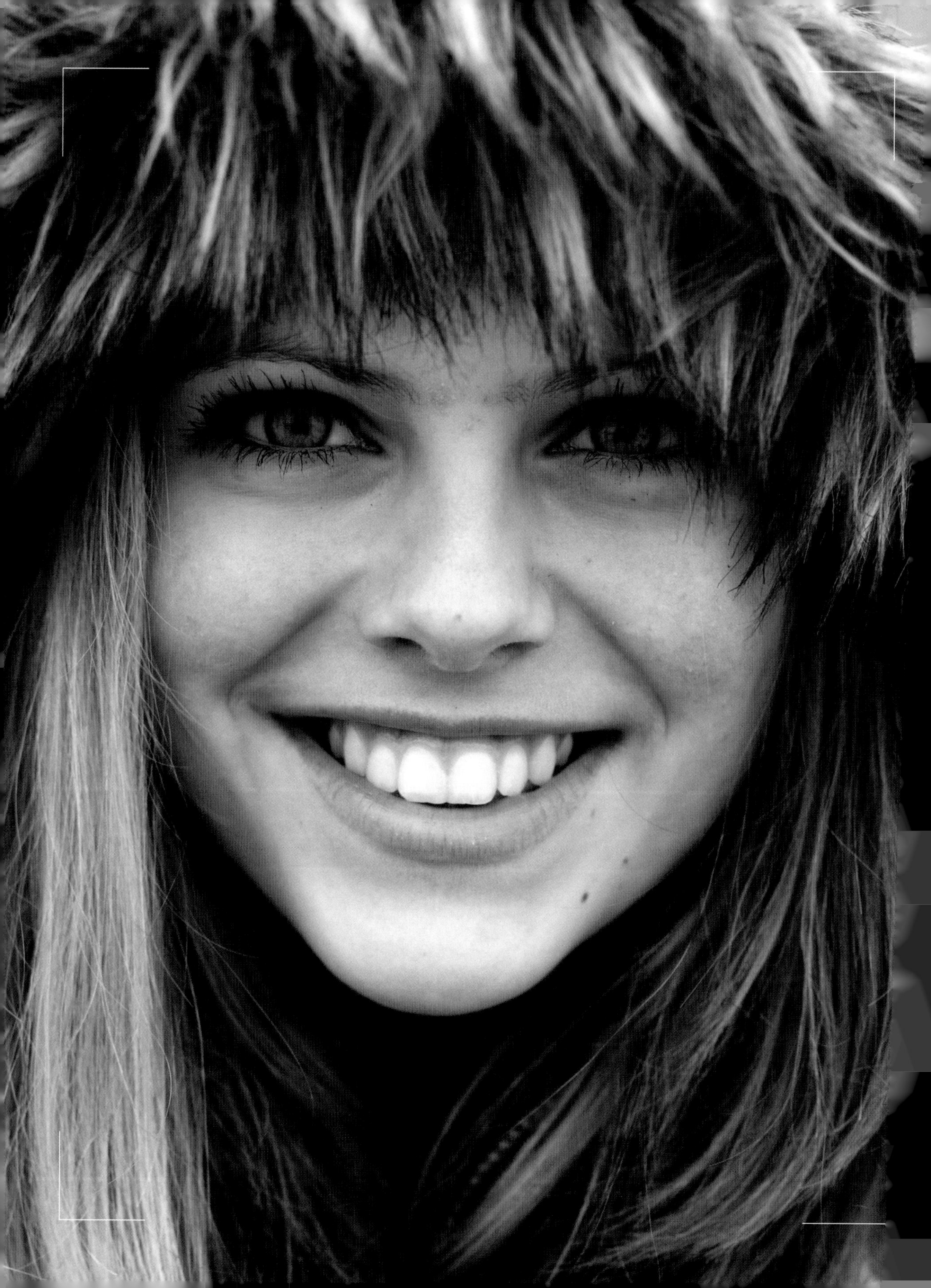

Introduction

This book is directed at photographers wishing to take their portraiture to a new level, whether taking photographs of their own children at various stages of their childhood or dipping a toe into the professional world in order to earn an income. The content addresses all the elements that contribute to strong and saleable portraits. It will encourage readers to use the environment to create something very special for themselves or their clients from the most ordinary of locations or the most challenging of lighting conditions – by using the elements. Creating a special connection between photographer and child is fundamental to the finished feel of your portraits.

What this book won't do is teach you an eye; that has to come from you. It will, however, help nurture a skill and make you more aware of possibilities and how to implement those ideas in your head. You will look at new ways of finding inspiration through your own environment, daily life and life experiences – and be inspired to draw from the ordinary.

The digital medium has opened up photography to the masses. It has become highly accessible and the opportunities for creativity are endless. It is a new education in itself for young and old – implementing methods in camera throughout the execution and through to the final printed piece. It has encouraged us to take risks through experimentation and personal projects, which in turn teach us our own creative limitations and that of the camera.

◀ Fig. 0.0
There is a skill in being able to engage with the subject in a way that brings out their natural expression and allows them to feel at ease with you, thus taking a portrait from being a 'snap' to a professionally commercial image. Knowing when coming in close is going to work through utilizing textures, or creating space and allowing the image to breathe, invites the viewer to read a portrait in order to create an emotive response from them.

Those photographers who used to use film on a personal and professional level will understand this huge transition in both technical innovation and, to an extent, in the way that we take pictures, allowing them in a certain measure to dictate our creativity. A new door has now opened, giving us opportunities for experimentation, personal creative development and, through access to art via the web, inspiration beyond our wildest dreams. This surely is a positive and should be embraced.

Have we, however, almost become slaves to the camera and computer? Perhaps what we have lost in this transition process is the mystique that photography once held: the unknown capabilities of the camera. Post-production was limited by today's standards, with the exception of dodging and burning, chemical manipulation, and pushing or holding back development to create the desired effect. The skill of the photographer was paramount to the success of an image or collection of photographs. Have we changed the way we see a picture before we take it? Are we thinking perhaps of what can be achieved post-production rather than the essential make-up of an image within the camera – the lighting technique, composition (to a point), attention to detail, and so on? Has it made us lazy? And does it matter?

For the purists amongst us, first and foremost we are photographers. We endeavour to create and capture moments in their most native forms. This book is about just that. We will touch on post-processing, colour management (you are the lab technician now, too), but essentially we will be looking at the fundamental make-up of a portrait using the environment (natural light in most cases) and some old-school techniques which will help you to understand how to produce skillful, honest portraits, whether it's for family prosperity or maybe as a first step to becoming a professional photographer.

Development and subsequent refinement of a style need to be encouraged in order for the photographer to progress and gain personal satisfaction in his or her work. Recognize what moves you as an artist. This inspiration can be sought in different ways and sometimes originates from the least obvious sources, such as the environment, our children, fashion, films, life experiences and art.

As professionals or semi-professionals who charge a fee for our work, striving for that 'one moment' is probably not our greatest goal. We need to be seen to be creating something beyond the snapshot, with the aim of keeping a portrait natural yet with a strong professional edge and on a consistent basis. There should be artistic value to a photograph. Unlike perhaps a painting, a photograph is exact, precise and should be an honest representation of a child at a particular time in its life. This applies to all genres and styles of working – there is a market for them all. Photographers who prefer to work in a more documentary, fly-on-the-wall fashion need to have strong compositional skills and an ability to place themselves rather than their subjects in order to create natural portraits in beautiful light. Portraiture should not be restricted to one contrived way of working. However, in order to create powerful imagery which contains impact and longevity, all the elements need to come together. So if you are working in this style, don't think that a documentary image is made up solely of great expression and being quick on the shutter. Composition, shape, tonality, expression and timing are just a few of the areas you will need to consider and implement into your work in order for it to graduate from being a snapshot into a professional portrait and thus enable you to command a reasonable fee.

If you asked the general public, could they tell you what it is that sets a professional image apart from a snapshot? What is it within a commissioned portrait that gives it the edge over a snapshot? Do they know the difference? In a recent survey amongst both professional photographers and the general public/parents, it became clear that the trained eye is very much recognized. This is important to know so that, as professional photographers, we can refine our skills and push creative boundaries – more so today than ever before given that the public has access to the same technology as the professional. It appears that it really is down to a photographer's skill as opposed to the equipment used.

The public was asked: 'When you look at a professional portrait, do you know what it is that takes it from being a snapshot to being a commercially valuable product, something you are prepared to spend good money on? What is the element within the picture that makes it different from a snapshot?' The responses were:

- 'The portrait is usually more artistically pleasing, great composition, etc. And I would expect a portrait to capture something more than the visual representation of the person. How the photographer does it I have no idea!'
- 'It's the moment captured – in terms of intensity of emotions (whatever they are) as well as the longevity of the moment.'
- 'How do you bring that "whatever it is" out of someone (who is most likely feeling a little uncomfortable and nervous about having their portrait taken) and then capture it in a beautifully placed image? That is a skill that places the photographer apart from the guy taking snapshots. And also what sets talented photographers above others in their field.'
- 'Attention to detail, getting the lighting, pose, background, exposure and printing just so.'
- 'Light and perspective.'

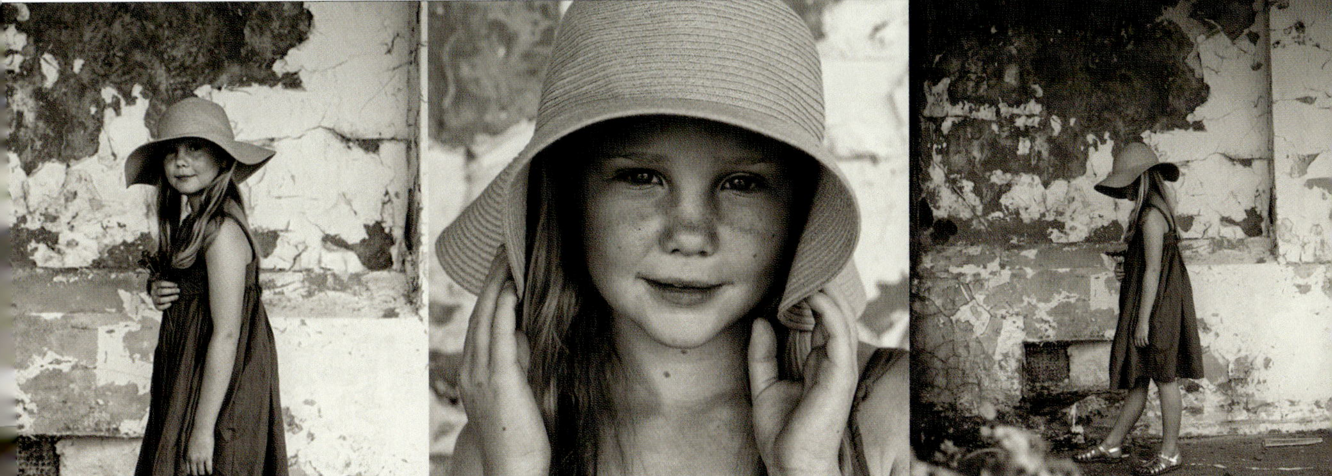

- 'It's something in the photo that is unexpected. It may link to the person whose portrait it is, or it may be something that clashes with what you would have thought you would see. It's that thing that makes you sit up or have some sort of emotional reaction – I don't think it matters if it's positive or negative; anything is better than a flat response.'

- 'I'd expect a pro portrait to look natural, relaxing, stunning in colour (or black and white if chosen), tidy and clear of its chosen focal subject whilst at the same time clearly planned. I think the above sounds on the surface contradictory but makes sense in a good portrait. Ultimately they do say a lot about the photographer in that they show their ability to do the above, whatever level that ability may be. A snapshot of the same subject I would expect to be more "cluttered".'

- 'For environmental portraiture where the same light and background would be available to all it is how the professional uses that light and background and sees it so very differently to that of the client that is again synonymous with the pose and emotion they wish to evoke from that portrait.'

- 'A snapshot is almost entirely subject-focused. With a professional image it's a two-way street.'

This last comment reiterates what a professional portrait of a child taken in natural light isn't. To bring these elements together takes an eye and imagination, but the implementation requires skill. The value of our work is determined by a number of parameters and all the elements must come together to create equilibrium. The fundamental make-up of a portrait taken in natural light contains the following elements:

- An idea born from an experience, inspiration or just a whim – without the idea or concept, there is no image, whatever the genre.
- A willingness to open your eyes to what is around you.
- Recognizing what you enjoy visually and emotionally.
- Being inspired by people, places and life – these will help you create your own ideas and design within your photography.

Light and Exposure

Marrying light and exposure effectively and understanding the control required in certain situations is key to the overall 'feel' of your work. A sound knowledge of how to adapt to natural light conditions in order to create the images in your head will ensure cohesion between idea and photograph. This may be soft atmospheric or hard graphic – how you use the directional light will be significant to the message your images give to the viewer.

A firm understanding of your camera's capabilities is fundamental, as well as being familiar with its metering system, so that you can control the light coming into it and make changes 'on the hoof'. Children don't hang around and we need to be there to anticipate and to be reactive to changes. You will be working in both high and low key situations and often, especially outside, the light can change dramatically within seconds. Using a manual metering system, as opposed to Automatic or Program, will give you control and *you* will be dictating the exposure rather than the camera.

Being consistent in the way you use light will add to your own recognized style, together with the way you present your work, and the content and feel of your portraits. In turn, you will find it easier to market yourself to a specific client base. This applies to all genres from documentary and fly-on-the-wall to contrived and classical.

Posing and Placement

Creating space around your subject may give you further options for placement in areas which are perhaps not the most obvious. The success of how obscure you make this is often led by the quality of light on the child.

The contrast between the softness of the girl in Fig. 0.3 and the rigid architecture around her can work well, especially when you feel a picture is becoming too 'serious' or contrived. It can bring life to your work and retains that all-important feel of being a child at a carefree time in its life.

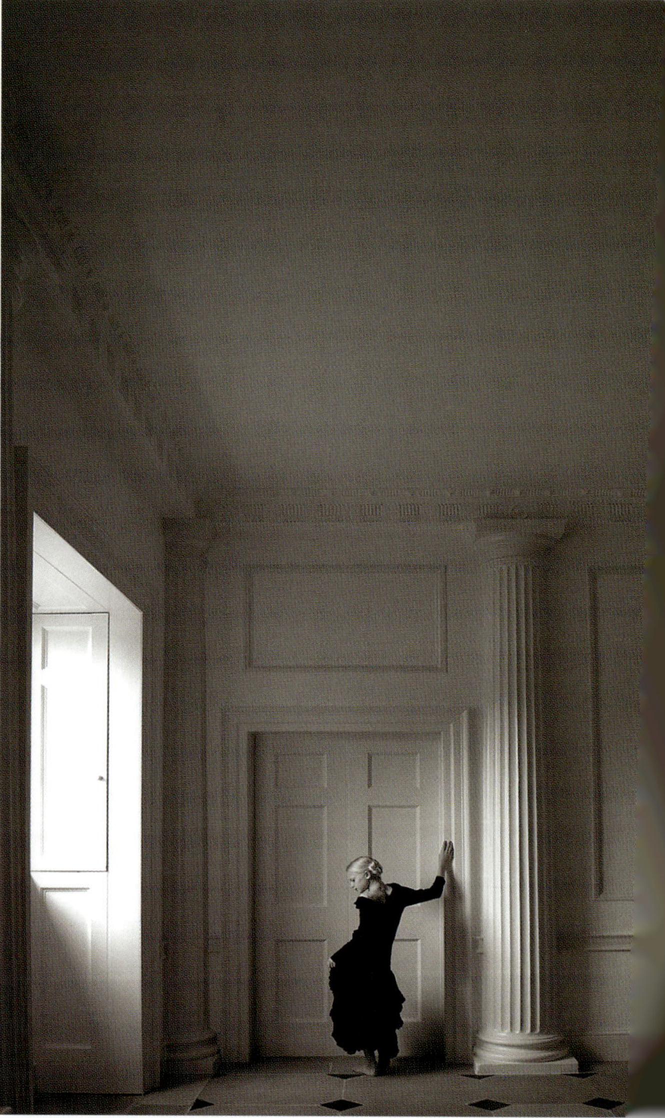

▲ Fig. 0.2
With the placement of your subject, you can define the overall feel of the image and create a narrative. The location and composition you choose will draw the viewer's eye to your subject. The complexity or simplicity of a portrait can come down to where you place the child in the image – it can be as simple as that.

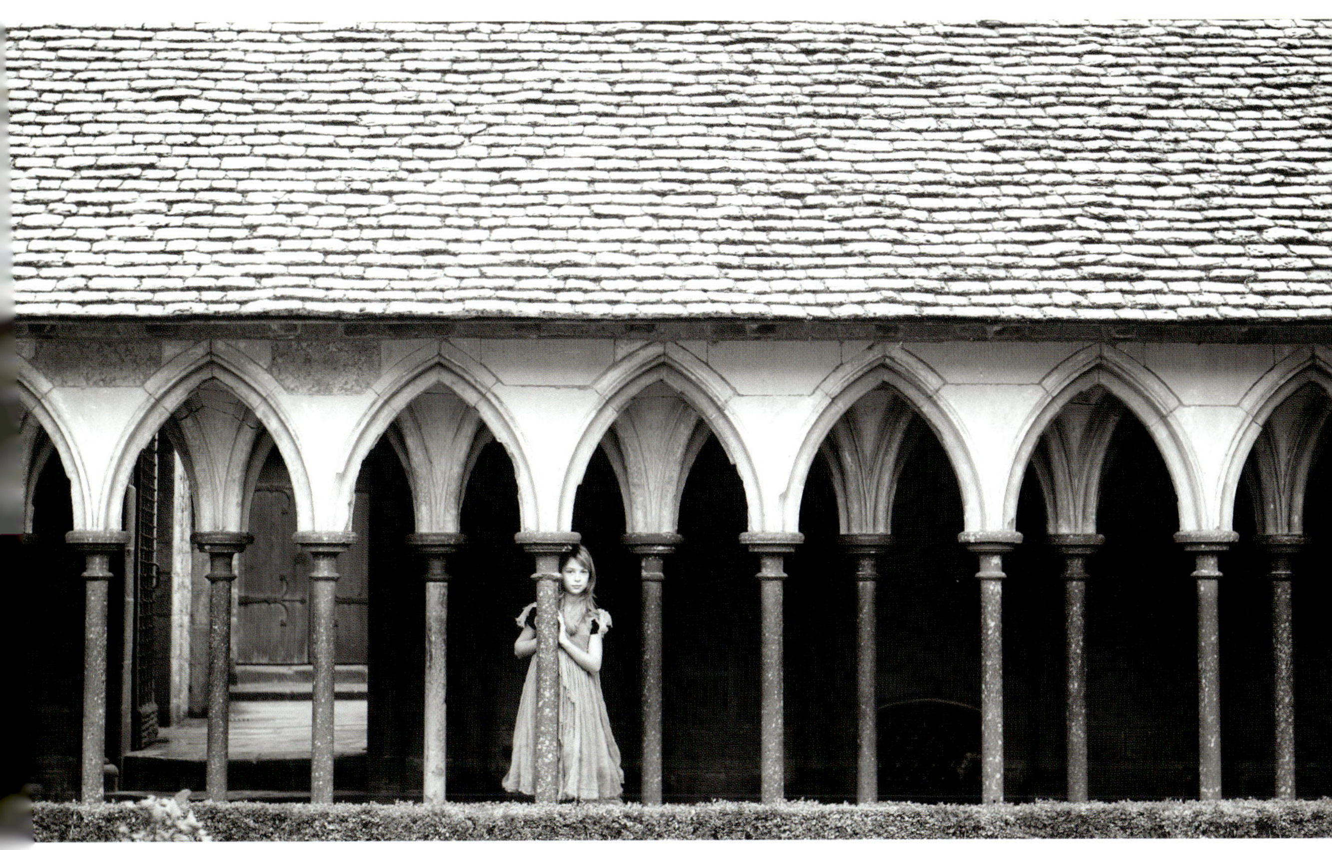

▲ Fig. 0.3

In this image the photographer has chosen to place the little girl almost centrally – perhaps to provide a range of cropping options. However, the area to the left of the image in front of the door would have been another possible position given the directional light from the doorway. The graphic uprights also lend a contrasting movement within the cloisters to this area, embracing the architecture yet introducing a softness.

Composition and Perspective

Having an open mind to how to compose your image, where to place your subject within the viewfinder, as well as where to place yourself, will give artistic perspective and strength to your portrait by opening up a narrative and encouraging a further dynamic to the picture which goes beyond the subject. Decisions are often split second, for example allowing more space around your subject to incorporate the environment or coming in close for a beautiful head study.

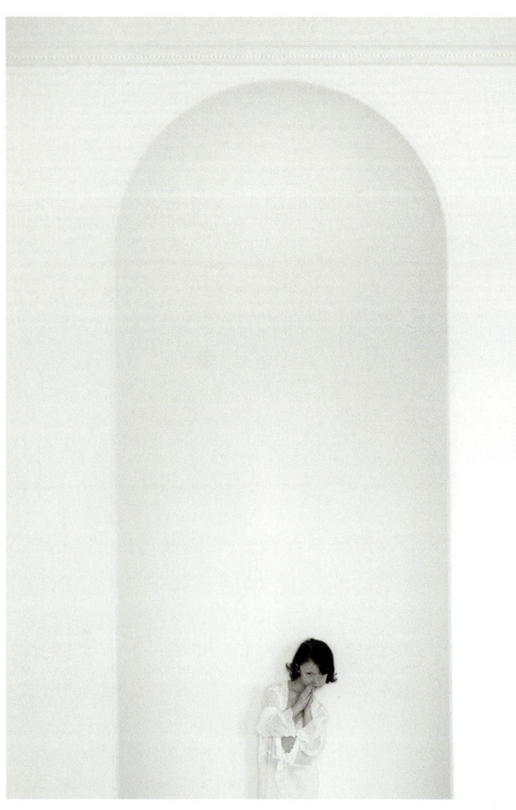

▲ **Fig. 0.4**
Having at least a vague idea of what you want to achieve from a location can give you a springboard; being open to adapting to various compositions and being bold will add artistic value.

Communication, Expression, Emotion

Communication is the final defining element. The communication you have with your subject will wholly determine how the viewer feels about the image. The many factors that contribute to a successful portrait can often be let down through an expression which is perhaps not convincing or doesn't fit the feel of the intended final image.

Emotional value is ultimately the engagement between the viewer and the portrait – on both counts, it is the emotion within the picture which evokes the response from the viewer, whether it is a parent, grandparent, or complete stranger. Understanding what gives your photograph lasting power and giving time for your subject to take on his or her own character will impact on how your images will be seen in, say, thirty years' time. Will they still create discussion and hold emotive value? This emotional response is the result of a successful photograph – whether it's a snapshot or a professionally polished print. The difference between the snapshot photographer and the professional is that if you are looking to earn an income from your portraits, you need to be able to produce that emotive value on a consistent, daily basis and not rely on a lucky moment. You need a formula in your working method to create depth of feeling in your work.

An emotional response may be one of warmth and euphoria or perhaps even sadness, but the photographer's aim is to create something that carries strong emotive value. This doesn't necessarily come just from the expression – emotion can be evoked from early morning light, a particular location, movement, the elements, anonymity, a glance or just a beautiful black and white print of someone very special. A portrait can have the power to anaesthetize the viewer with its depth and emotion; it can make one question the location, the age of the subject, the time of year, perhaps the social meaning – and maybe sometimes the ethics of an image.

Take Sally Mann's compelling environmental portraits of children. Some viewers remain open-minded and understand her serendipity and honest vision, whereas others find her work offensive or even exploitative. But there is no denying her ability to blend the majesty of an environment with the exploration of boundaries and the visual vulnerability of her subjects. Whether this response is negative or positive, it is still an emotional, subjective reaction. You can't expect everyone to love your style of work, which makes defining your own that more important.

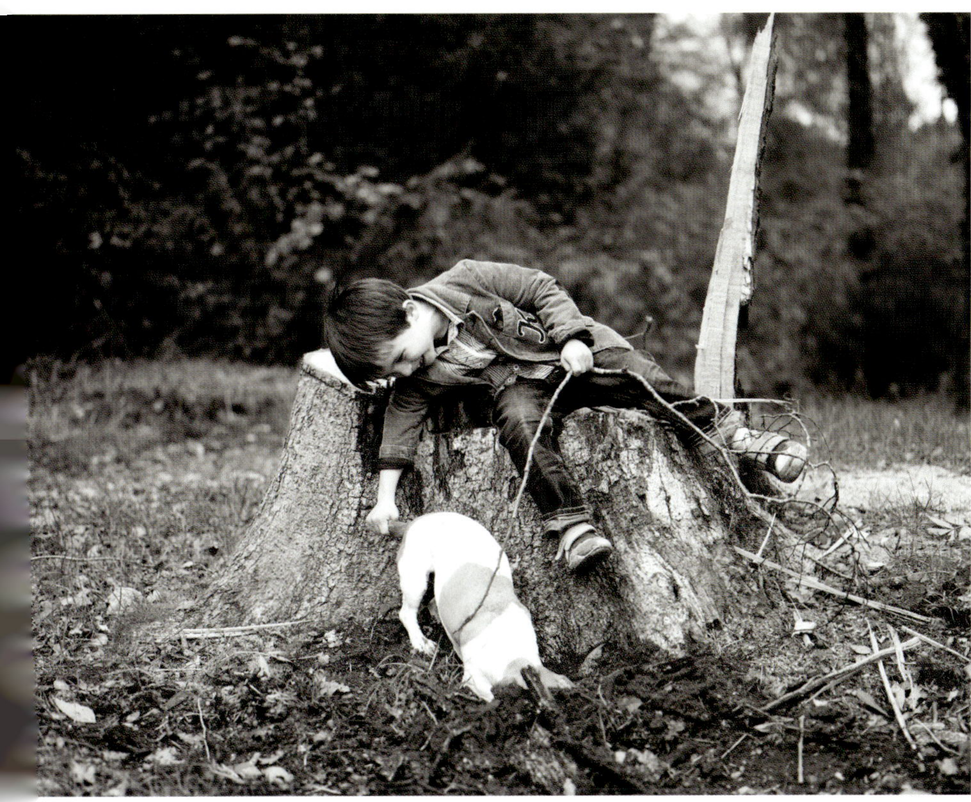

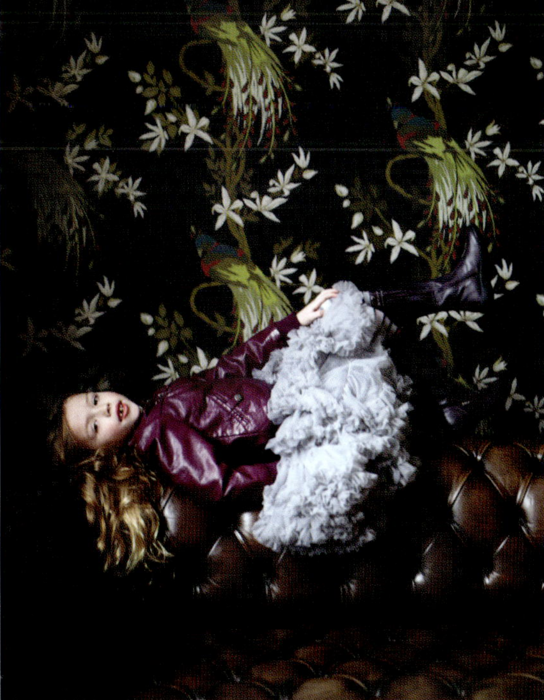

◀▲ **Figs 0.5 and 0.6**
The methods you use to put a child at ease will come from your own personality, and your own character can often resonate in the final piece. Time and experience will make you adept at what works best for you and which methods create the best response.

▲ Fig. 0.6

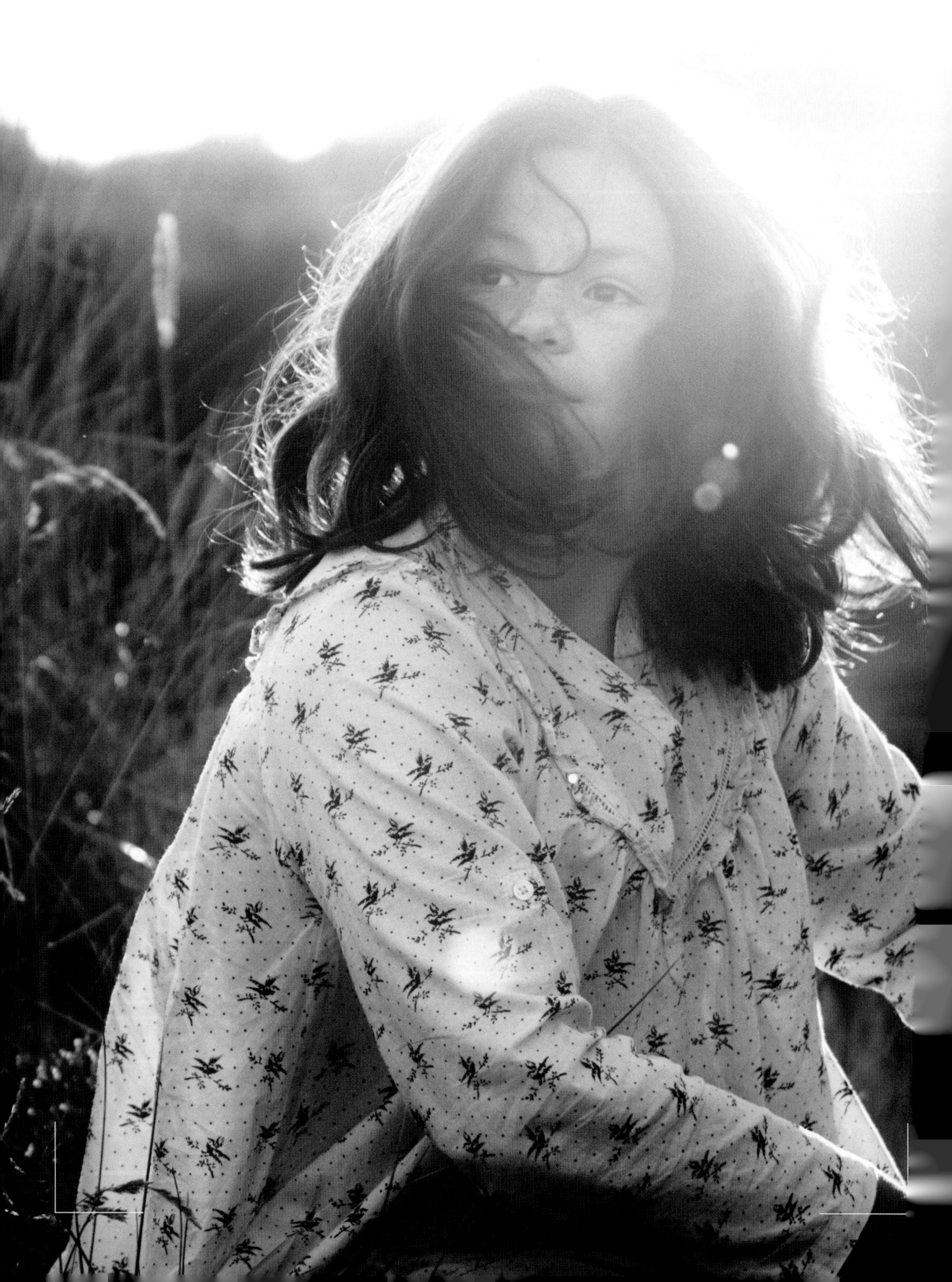

Chapter 1
Why Natural Light?

Removing ourselves out of the somewhat artificial environment of the studio into what can be an unpredictable workplace can be daunting for the inexperienced or those who have worked within a 'fixed formula'. It's no easy task, especially if you've learnt your trade, established yourself in a studio environment and are perhaps in that comfort zone of what works for you.

However, working in available light will not limit the creative once they understand what is possible and what (to a point) isn't. It provides an opportunity to create images which are both simplistic or complex in their make-up, depending on how the light is used. Whether the image is a beautiful backlit shot taken in a cornfield where we can incorporate flare and imbue a classical nostalgic feel, or whether an interior window light offers a chance for graphic drama, a different feel can be achieved at different times of day depending on the strength, quality and colour of the light. Yes, it can be unpredictable, and it is a challenge to bring all the elements together, but the results are individual and there are no boundaries in terms of creativity.

That wonderful hour when the sun rises and later when it sets has been indoctrinated in us as being the best time of day during which to take beautiful portraits and, when handled well, we can indeed produce something special at those times. However, in reality this isn't always possible and, given that the light comes in many guises throughout the day or year, we must use what is available at these times to create something specific.

You may not want that soft backlit shot; you may be looking for something more harsh. There are no rules as to when the best time is for you to shoot, but you do need to understand the effects of these given times in order to implement the ideas and learn how to control 'wayward' light. If you are selling your images in a professional capacity, it is essential to grasp what your market demands with regard to the feel of your 'product', as well as find out what is the most flattering light for a particular style and what, crucially, is going to sell.

Studio versus Location Lighting

One of the advantages of working in a studio is that you can position lights as you wish, which of course you can't do with the sun, so when you're outside you need to move yourself and your subject, as well as factoring in a little more planning with regard to the time and position of the light source. Within the studio environment, we talk more about high key and low key lighting set-ups than we do for location shots. The meaning of 'key' flirts with a similar analogy in music – the 'pitch' or tonal range. High key in a studio is a sharp-lit image, holding minimal shadow detail, even sometimes to the point of being burnt out. This is obtained through use of a light background and artificial lighting/flash, in some cases using multiple light set-ups. In contrast, a studio low key image uses just one or two lights, targeting a small area of the subject and giving a more subtle view, almost to the point of effecting three dimensions through the use of deep shadows, and so on.

◄ Fig. 1.0
Understanding how the position of the sun at given times of day and at different times of the year, will help you create images that go beyond the norm of location portrait photography.

In Fig. 1.1, despite the inside exposure being balanced with the exterior, overexposing by a stop has lifted the image and given it a soft, whimsical feel. We don't necessarily need all the detail within the image – of course, going by the rules, we would want to retain all the detail, but there are times when we need to use stronger exposure to create a mystique, anonymity and atmosphere. When you're making images to this effect, by over- or underexposing, it has to look purposeful rather than lacking in control; this also applies to other methods, such as using movement or harsh light to accentuate the graphic.

The lighting ratio is the ratio of light levels from the brightest area to the darkest part of the subject; the brightest lit are lit by both key and fill. In Fig. 1.3 the 'kissing' light is where the light, to the human eye, just kisses the face and graduates into darkness, with a high light ratio between the face and the back of the head (contrast). A spot meter reading was taken from the face. In order to exaggerate the definition and to define that spotlight effect, the camera was then set to underexpose in order to gradually create a natural vignette and ensure beautiful detail in the face while eliminating detail in the hair. If the detail in the hair had been required, a reflector to the left could have been added or the shot exposed for longer – but the latter would then have compromised the detail in the face by overexposure. A reflector to the left would be the preferable solution. A shallow depth of field has also ensured that the eye is directed to the face and there is no distraction from the surrounding area.

The downside to underexposing and retrieving detail from an image file is that you may create noise within the shadow areas. This can of course be a creative choice and you can use this as an element in your work.

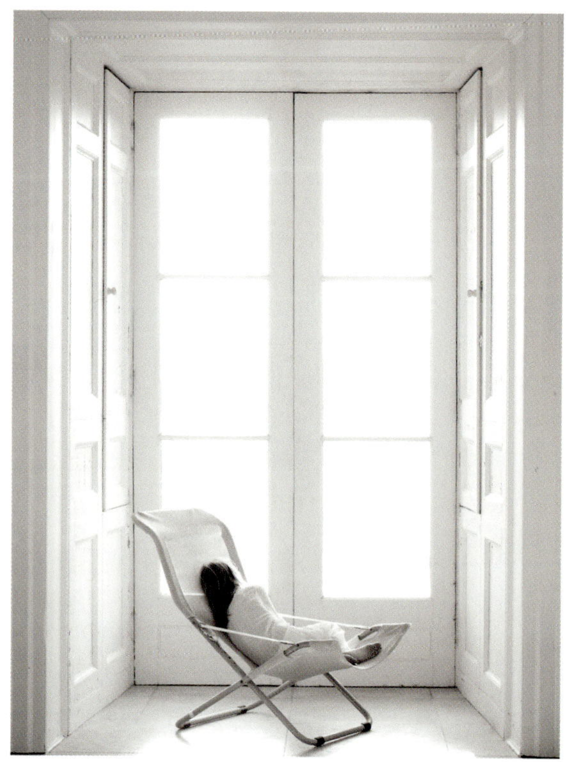

▲ Fig. 1.1
High key on location: the lack of tonal range creates a high key effect by using the white walls to envelope the strong sunlight flooding through the window, with an added reflector to balance the softness of the light to the fore, shrouding the subject. The only real mid tone is in the child's hair, perhaps similar to a pencil drawing.

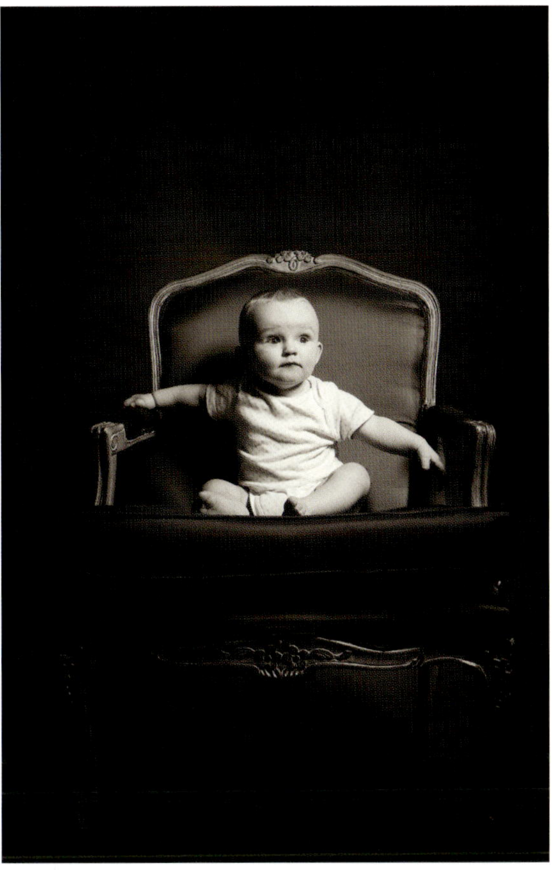

▲ Fig. 1.2

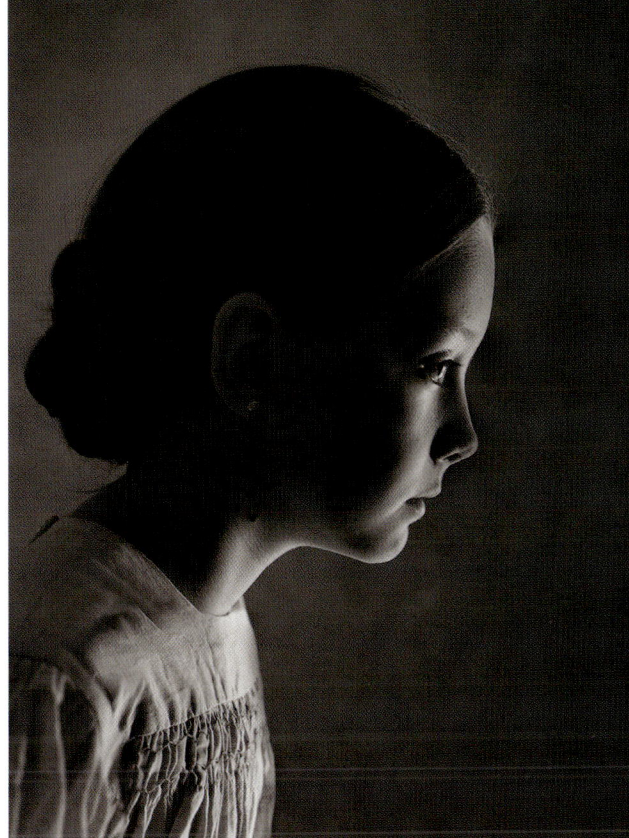

▲ Fig. 1.3

Figs 1.2 and 1.3
Low key studio portrait (Fig. 1.2), using one light on the front; the background is lit with a small spill with a honeycomb. (Photo: Saraya Cortaville)

In contrast, Fig. 1.3 is utilizing window light on location, in an otherwise dark room, with no fill-in to lift detail in the hair.

There are often compromises to be made when there are such extreme contrast ranges. You need to decide which part of the image is the most important. Although we aim to achieve the best possible results at camera stage, having post-processing options in your mind when you are shooting may make this decision easier. Both the high key (Fig. 1.1) and low key (Fig. 1.3) location images are quiet and sensitive, yet lit and exposed in different ways.

Disciplining oneself to view a location in terms of what is achievable with the given light in that location is part of training the eye to work with the imagination and to have the fundamental skills to achieve the desired effect. So the thought processes with regard to lighting in the studio or on location are the same, but on location they can be used to different effect in order to incorporate the environment and the narrative we are looking to project.

▶ Fig. 1.4
This photograph demonstrates natural directional light. The quality from either side of the cloisters swathes the child in soft daylight, with added reflection from the white stone floor, thus there is no need for additional reflectors.

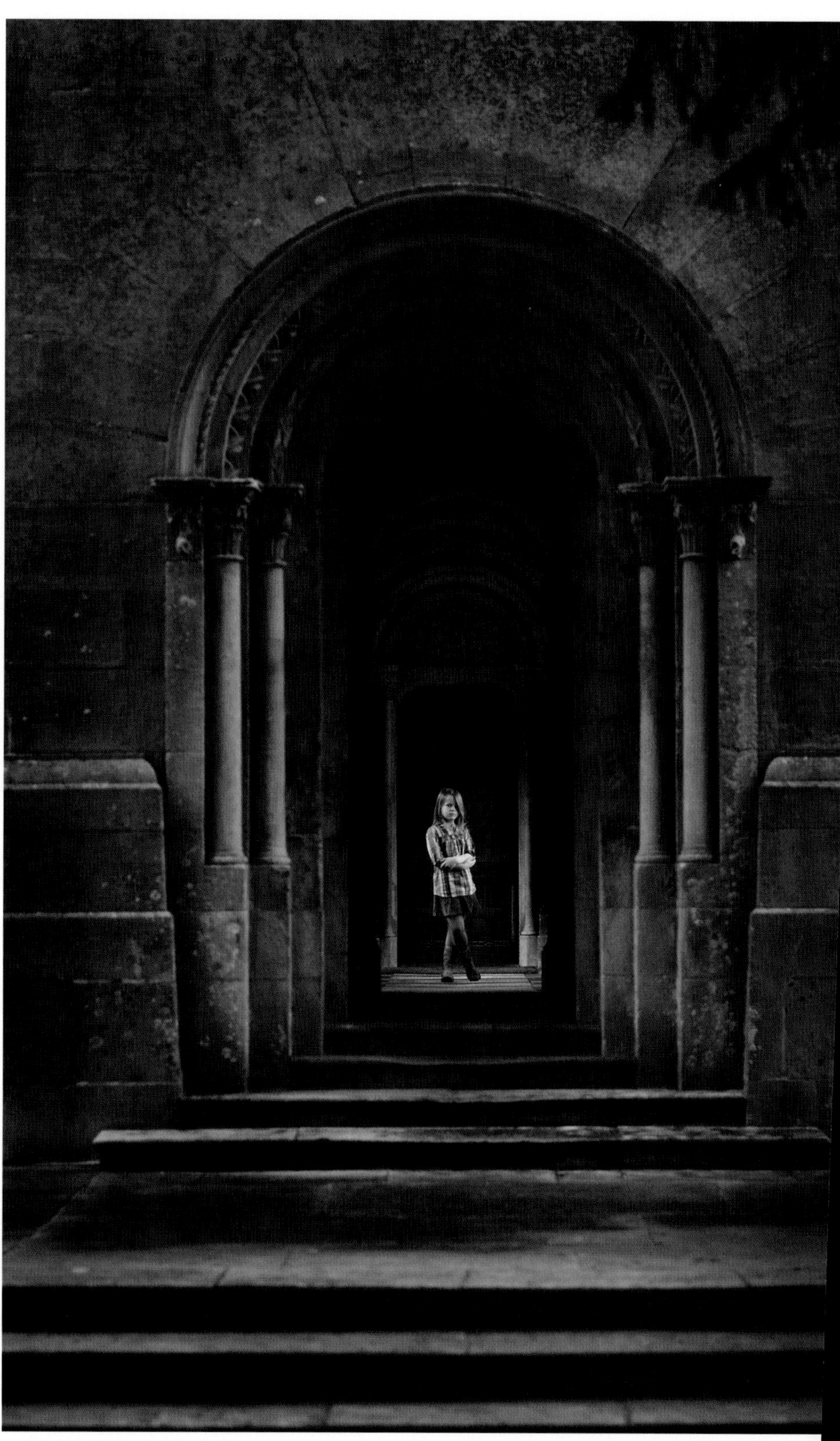

Light from Different Angles

Given the capabilities of modern DSLR cameras, we have the opportunity to produce both high and low key images to a professional quality. High ISO ratings enable us to push our cameras, particularly in very low lighting, giving us the opportunity to make pictures with depth and feeling in almost any conditions. By using directional light – a definitive light source – we can add shape and form to a portrait, enhance or detract areas of an image that are perhaps less flattering, and manipulate or mould a figure or subject in a particular way.

In Fig. 1.4, the lighting is perfectly balanced between the exterior and the child inside. This image was shot on a manual spot metering mode; a light reading was taken from the child. If the exterior had been much darker (up to two stops), the child may well have been overexposed if this had been taken on an automatic mode. We can afford to stop down a further half stop if necessary in order to bring back even more detail, but slightly overexposing the image in its entirety at the shooting stage ensures that we have more detail throughout the file which can then be bought back in the RAW conversion.

Once you have the set-up as seen in Fig. 1.6, you have the basis for your canvas and your building block has been created. You can then experiment with posing and composition, and push your creativity within that one area, utilizing the location in various ways.

Introducing backlighting, with the sun behind your subject, will offer you imagery which is sympathetic at most times of the day, though a different approach is required depending on the strength and direction of the sun. Understanding when and where the sun is at a location prior to your shoot will make your job easier. For example, if you arrange your shoots at midday in summer, the sun will be at its most powerful and highest in the sky. If you have no choice but to shoot at this time, you have two options.

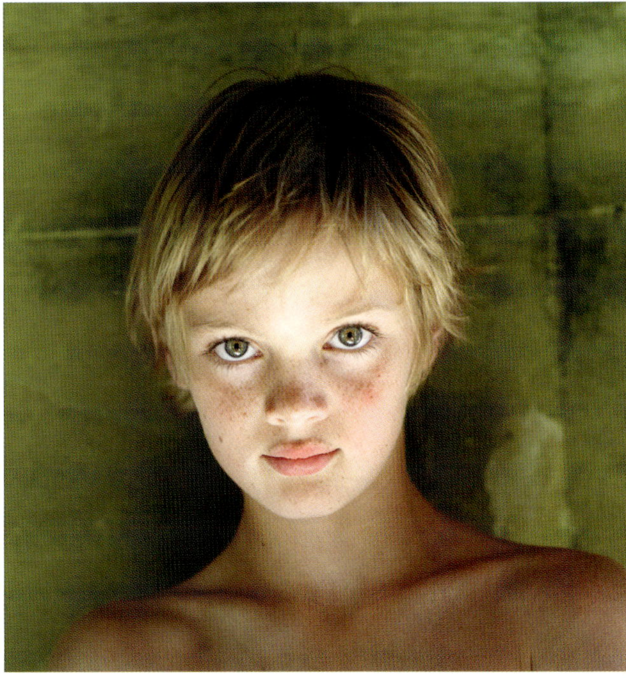

▲ Fig. 1.5
Having a broad directional light straight on to your subject will ensure good, safe exposure, but can result in widening the facial features and presents a more one-dimensional feel with lack of shape from any shadows. If you have no option but to use broad light, select a longer focal length lens and a shallow depth of field in order to differentiate subject from background.

Firstly, and more preferable, is to find some shade, yet keep the sunlight behind the subject, thus still keeping that lovely rim of light around the edge (*see* Fig. 1.9). A wide contrast range between background and shade will, of course, create a strong shadow; we can add some reflector light to balance exposure to the face along with careful placement.

The second option, in midday sun, is to take your exposure from the shadow area – the face. This may of course compromise other areas such as the hair light blowing out. If you are serious about overcoming this, you can opt to use a diffuser above the subject to shield that harsh light, cocooning the subject in the shade. If you aren't used to working with an assistant, this may be the time to employ someone as you will need a reflector in the foreground to bounce light back and another to control the diffusing.

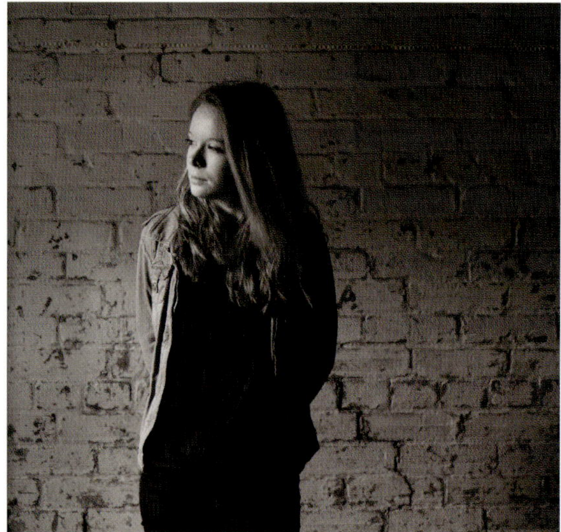

▲ Fig. 1.6a

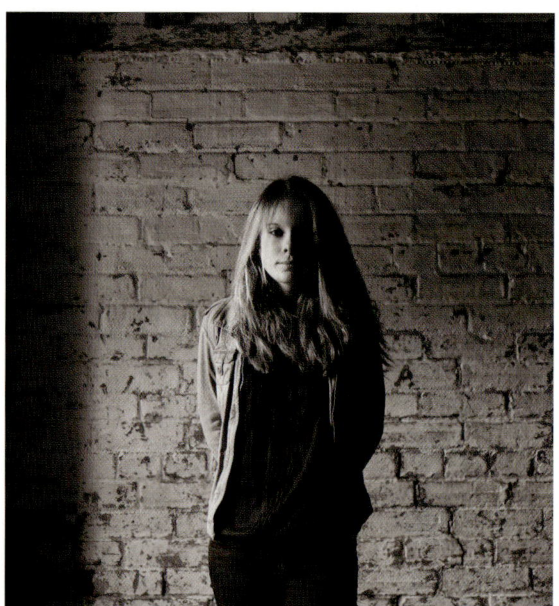

▲ Fig. 1.6b

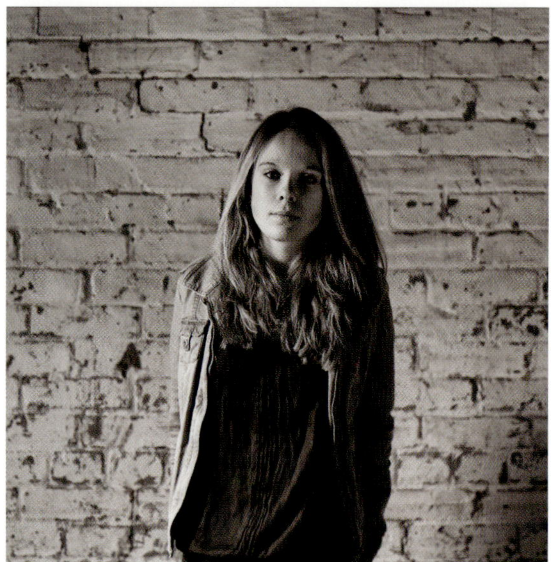

▲ Fig. 1.6c

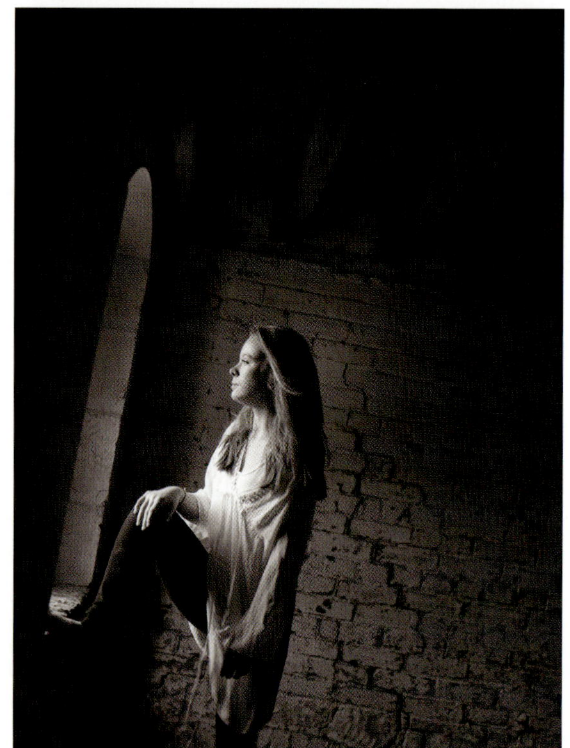

▲ Fig. 1.6d

Figs 1.6a–d

a Turning the subject so the window light skims across the face (short light) to give a more flattering shape.

b In contrast, split lighting is a classic lighting treatment and is as graphic as it sounds: a window light, positioned 45 degrees from the subject, illuminating the side of the face with little or no fill on the other and very little detail in the shadow area.

c Subject in same position, with reflector to 45 degrees right, thus picking up detail in the face to soften the features.

d Dramatic window light, taking the subject closer to the source, but a Lastolite diffuser simply placed against the outside of the window dampens the light and thus lessens the contrast between the tones.

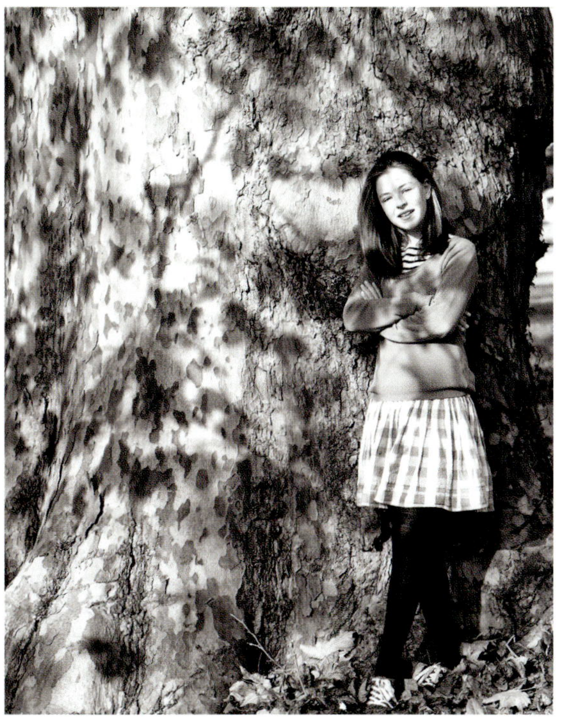

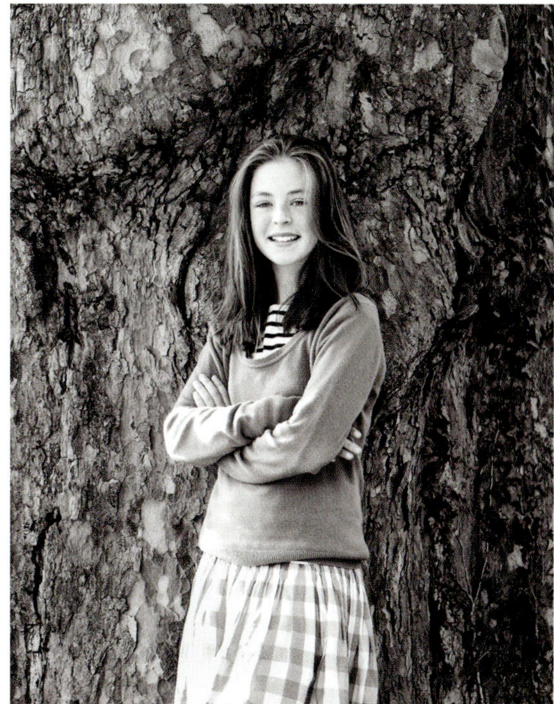

Figs 1.7 and 1.8
Despite the dappling causing a pretty effect, light falling directly onto a child's face not only obviously causes the child to squint but can be unflattering to the face and skin tone, as well as causing unattractive shadows, particularly around the eye sockets. By simply taking the child around to the side of the tree, the problem is overcome. You can see the original harsh light to the left.

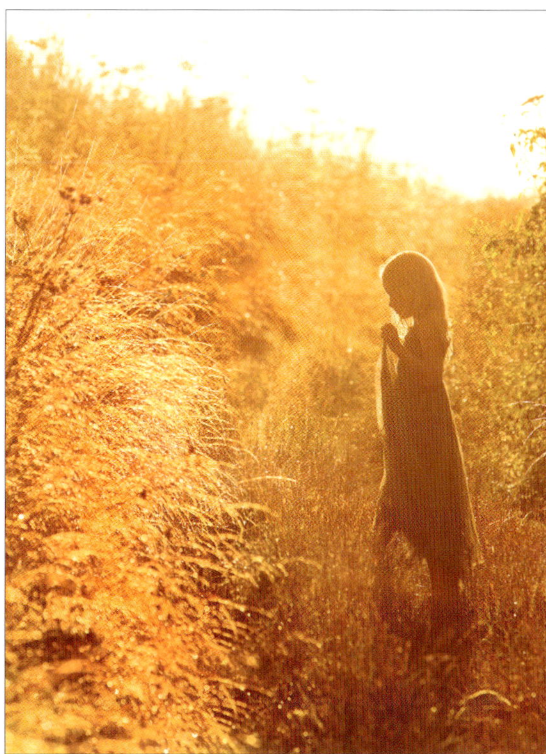

Fig. 1.9
Backlighting throws the subject into shadow and lends a beautiful glow to the field around her.

But how do you deal with this if you are just shooting candids and want minimal disruption/communication between you and the child? This is a time to carefully choose light and time of day over location. By positioning yourself in the right place for the light and encouraging the child to play within that area, there's no reason why you shouldn't get beautiful, backlit candid portraits as long as you expose for the face. You can compose as you wish, and use movement and expression within this space – though there may be times when you will have to expect some compromise in the highlights.

Natural Light in Art

Inspiration as to what actually defines the 'quality' of natural light can be found in many forms and is worth taking time to study. Visiting art galleries and reading up on the works of Old Masters – where the artists had no choice but to use what was available to light their subjects – will reveal the beautiful softness of window light, or show the dramatic skies and harsh light that can add drama to a picture. You may well be surprised by what is possible – to the point where you might question whether it is indeed just available light that you are seeing.

When studying art pieces, take note of where the light source is coming from. Bearing it in mind when experimenting and when using reflectors and diffusers, you will find you can control or bend natural light on location as easily as you can in a studio under controlled artificial lighting techniques.

You may be familiar with the term 'Rembrandt lighting' – a perfect analogy of what quality light is. A particular painting may not be to your taste, but an understanding of how it was achieved married with your own camera skills will give you the tools to run with ideas and perhaps use this technique within your work but in your own style. A traditional quality can therefore be applied to a scenario while actually resulting in something quite contemporary or edgy. The experience of looking at paintings can help us apply the look and feel to our own work – not copying or plagiarizing it, but applying the basics in order to create the most flattering image.

Embracing the value of natural light, and recognizing the versatility of what is possible, is something that all photographers should factor into their work in order to create images which not only have strong quality of light within, but also use the location as a major part of the picture. The uncertainty which the inexperienced photographer feels when placed in the natural environment perhaps comes through a lack of sound knowledge of exposure and the camera's ability to capture light in any given situation. This applies especially to photographers who have been studio-based or reliant on flash to light their subject; removing that safety net can be unnerving. By using manual exposure we can adjust our camera to work alongside the current natural light to effect, as opposed to working on a relatively static exposure situation within a studio setting. The results have a far more organic feel, and offer the freedom to make adjustments to create the desired effect. Natural light, and the quality of it, does not select where it falls. We will be looking at selecting light over location further in the book, but never dismiss a location solely through visual aesthetic; in contrast, a location is only as good as the light that falls on it.

As with a studio portrait, creativity is defined by the photographer's imagination and ability to marry idea with technique. Working on location gives us endless opportunities to use what is available to us with regard to natural light, while working in harmony with texture, graphic, colour, architecture, tone, depth of field, movement and form. And of course, we can choose a new and different backdrop every day!

Take a look at the work of such photographers as Edward Steichen, whose location work in the early 1900s, often taken in natural light, is still iconic and strong today. Steichen worked under great technical limitations, having to bring together beautiful light and strong posing and placement in the locations he

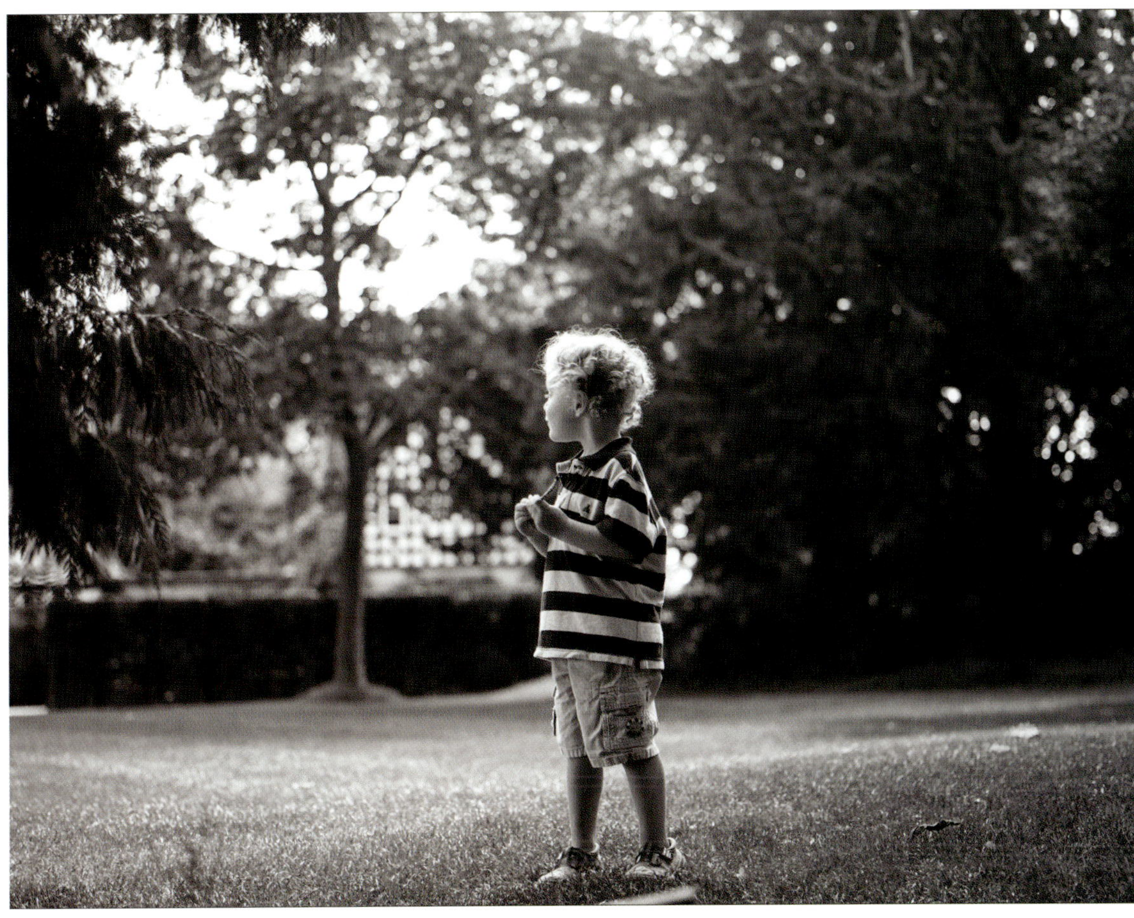

▲ Fig. 1.10
Shooting in the midday sun when the sun is high in the sky requires careful placement. The child here is positioned just inside the shaded area, but not too much to lose the contrast detail. Without the rim light coming through from behind, the portrait may be flat and require the photographer to use reflectors to bring life back into the portrait. Taking the child back further out into the sun risks losing the detail in his hair (especially as he is so blonde) and causing heavy shadows under the eyes. We can overcome this by shading the top light with a Lastolite diffuser – a perfectly reasonable solution if you are building a portrait in a controlled fashion.

made use of. The simplicity of his portraits, above all, is what gives his work the iconic longevity and value that it still holds today. His work would certainly grace any wall in a twenty-first-century gallery.

Steichen seems to have embraced boldness; he went beyond the limitations of what was available, rather than shying away from it. We can learn a lesson from this. Placing ourselves in challenging situations with regard to lighting and location can often encourage us to create something less obvious and more interesting. It presents us with opportunities to use movement and low key lighting with depth and feeling. It's an exercise in looking at the ordinary. Being 'unique' is an unnecessary pressure to put on ourselves, and Steichen's work makes this clear. Very little is unique today; it's mostly been done before. However, the way in which we apply our imagination and skill to our work is what gives us individuality as artists, if that is what is desired. Applying gimmicks and fads to a portrait 'because we can' is not a creation of imagery that comes from our own head and heart. Be careful and selective in this – taking something away from a picture rather than adding strong symbolism can often make a portrait stronger. The old adage 'less is more' still stands.

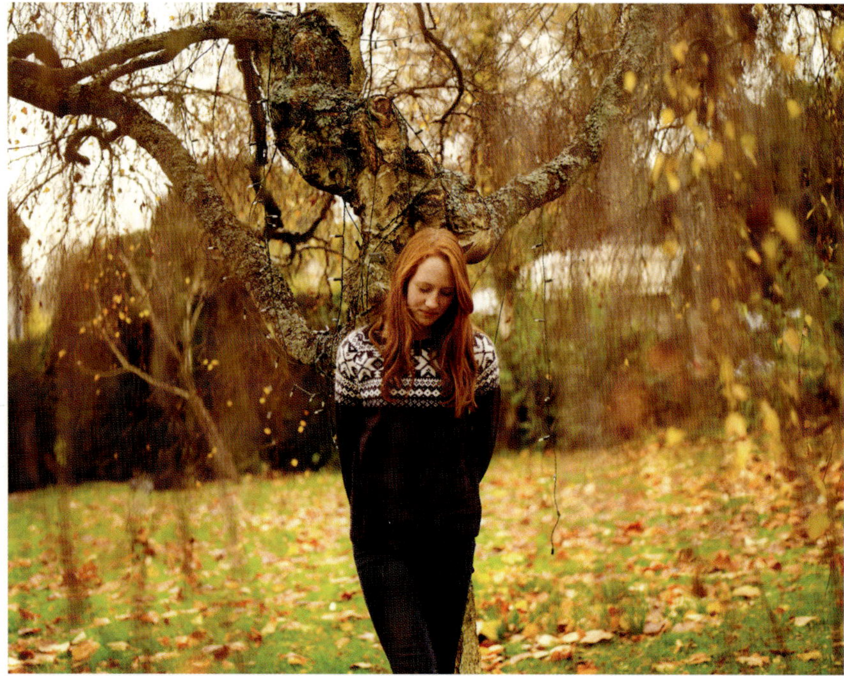

▶ Fig. 1.11
Working outdoors not only offers the benefits of working with natural light, but also opportunities to use features of the landscape to enhance the composition, as here where the branches of the tree provide a soft frame for the subject.

Working in natural light gives us endless opportunities to develop the ideas we have in our heads. This is not to say that flashlight cannot create mood and ambience, but it does not perhaps contain the spontaneity and natural feel that gives a child's portrait that wondrous nostalgic essence – the questioning, interested feeling the viewer has when wondering when a picture was made. In some way, flash can remove the powerful natural tool of connection and quietness that we have when working with available light, while keeping the environment as familiar as possible for the child.

Working with Children

Of course, one of the greatest advantages of working with children within the environment, as against the studio, is the experience for the child. Rather than being in the alien environment of a studio or in front of lights, we can allow children to run in fields, on the beach or just in the back garden, which is a far more familiar place than a studio. It gives the photographer the opportunity to interact with the child and to build that all-important rapport and connection. Certainly when photographing children, the advantage of working in ambient lighting conditions gives the photographer the freedom of space. Provided we position ourselves appropriately for the light, we can encourage the child into this area, which gives us our canvas to work on. Shooting on location removes the formality of a studio portrait. This does not, however, take away the value of good design; it's just a different type of study.

Additional assistance can be sought through reflectors, but the aim is to keep the ambience of the portrait wholly natural, thus avoiding the use of flashlight which will often remove the overall softness of the light. Even in a strongly backlit situation we can avoid the use of fill-in flash by careful selecting the location and time of day, and through balancing exposure with the use of reflectors.

Working within the home environment also lends itself to a more pleasurable experience for the child. With familiar toys and belongings around them, children feel secure and at ease – to a point, you can allow them to dictate how the portrait

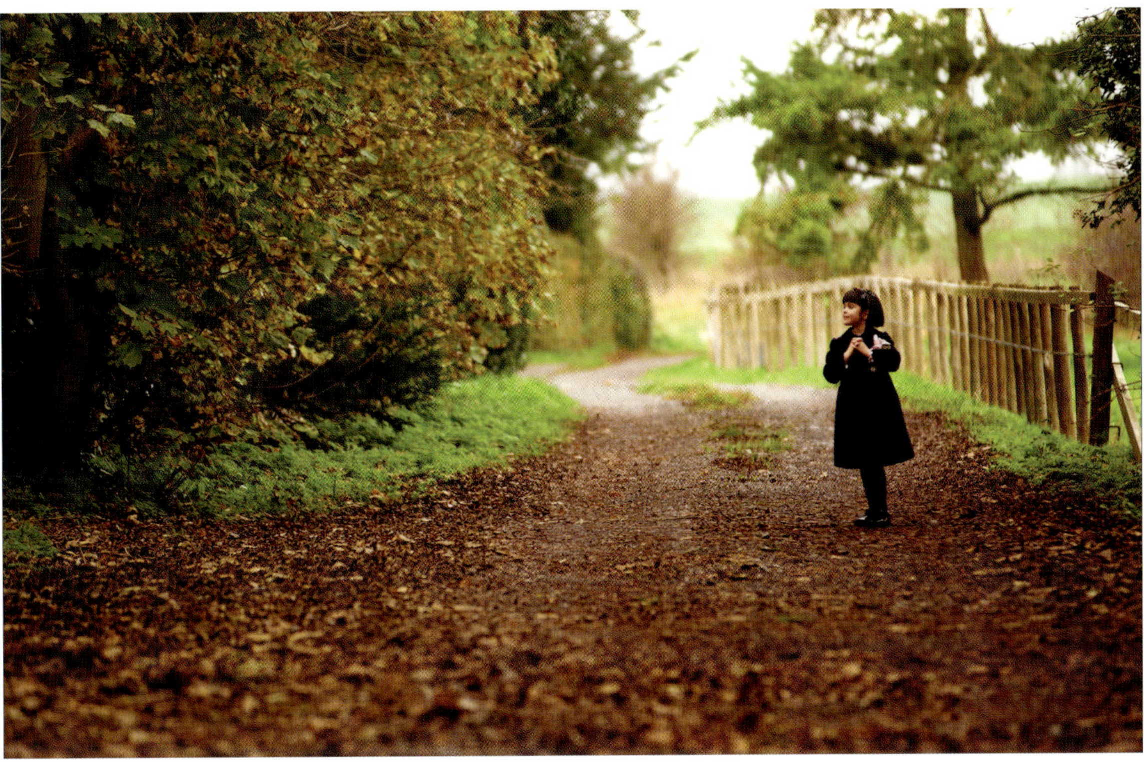

▲ Fig. 1.12
Using the environment as your canvas opens the opportunity to utilize texture, colour and natural space.

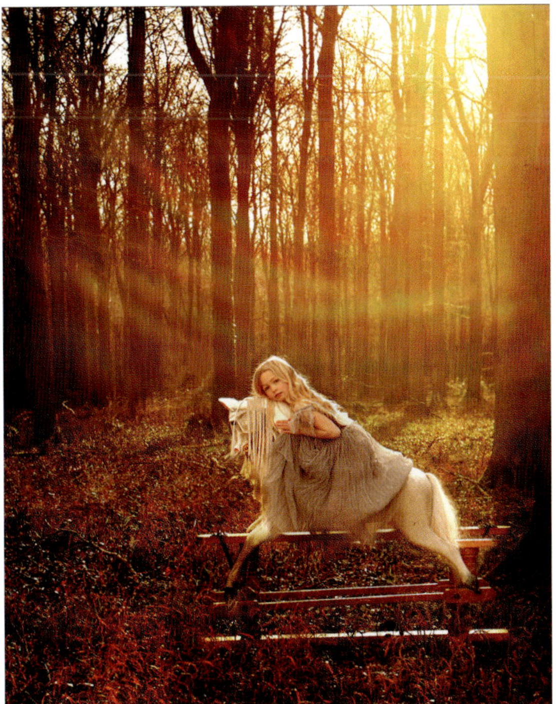

progresses. Encourage the child to show you around the house, use any opportunity to play with him or her, and strike up a dialogue before you start shooting, rather than taking the child to an unfamiliar place. It can make the shoot easier for both you and the child if you allow the child the freedom to take some control while keeping it fun and relaxed.

◄ Fig. 1.13
Working within the environment does not necessarily command the use of a strong structural or architectural backdrop. Look for colour and shape within the most ordinary of locations. By selecting the best time of day you can create something very special from the least obvious.

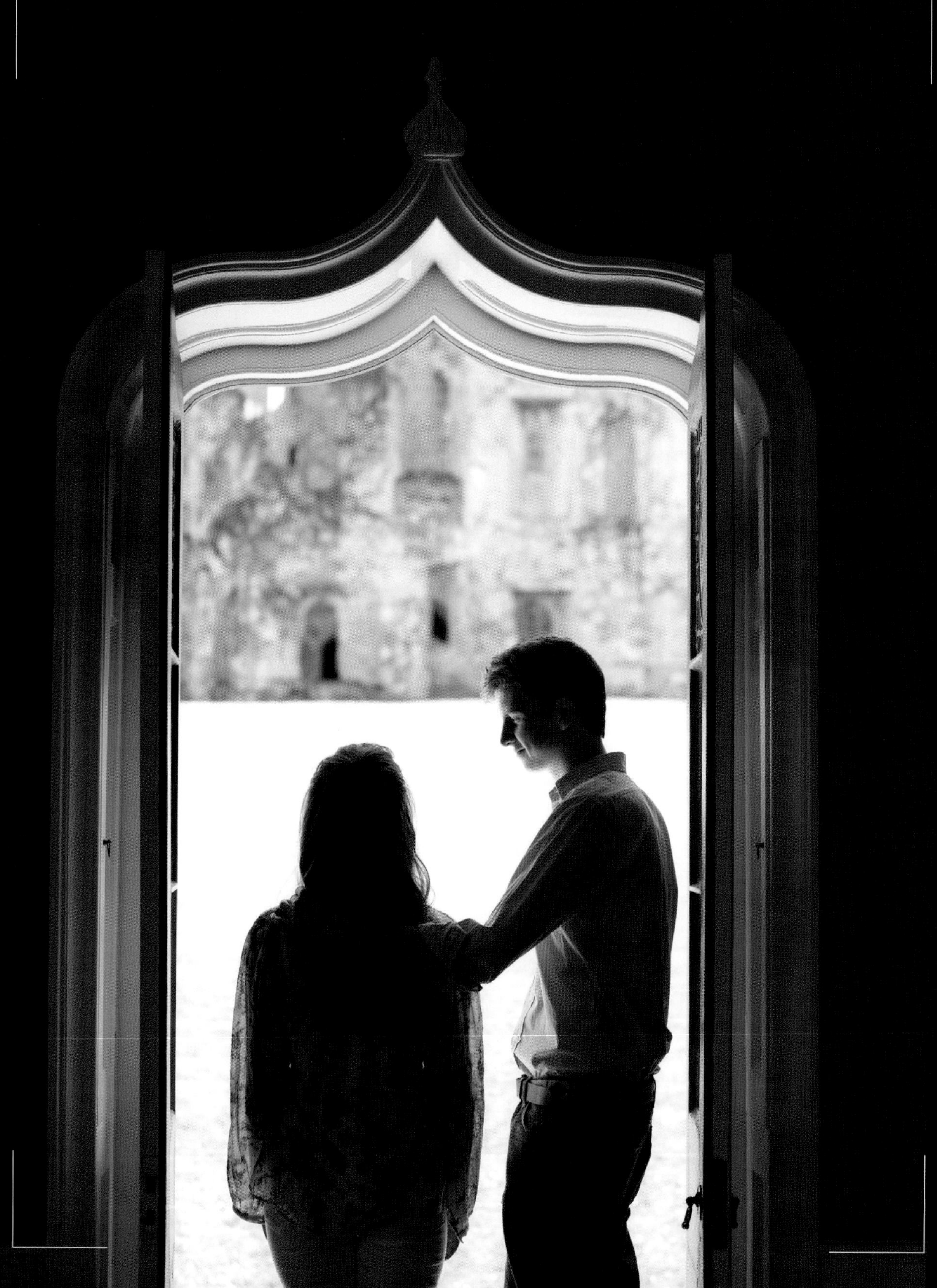

Chapter 2

Kit

Current camera models are now infinitely superior technically compared to those that were used when Arnold was at the height of her career. They can push boundaries that would have been inconceivable to the likes of Edward Steichen in the early 1900s. Yet Steichen's own use of graphic, acknowledgment of shadow and highlight in his portraits, together with immaculate composition and placement, effectively brought together all the elements of powerful portraiture. Iconic photographers like him still created images which set the bar high by today's standards. They were not reliant on a high ISO, instead manually focusing and panning a moving subject in lighting conditions that were naturally available in situ. They were masters at creating drama, graphic and evoking emotions with their imagery while using sometimes the most basic of tools.

How much easier things are today! Indeed, the digital medium has opened up opportunities for new invention, for pushing the boundaries of creativity, and we should embrace these advances. But do we put the same care into the conception of the image today as photographers did then, or do we depend too much on the technology around our necks, thus relying on that safety net post-capture? And does it matter if we are?

Photographers were making the same decisions then as we do now with regard to posing, the lighting, composition, and so on. We are still looking for the ultimate, perfect portrait. Some people would

argue that today's cameras make this far easier to achieve, which can only be a good thing if you want to test the feasibility of an idea.

Understanding where we want a picture to go – an inkling at least of the final output – is fundamental so that we can select the tools for the job, including the kit we use to capture the shot. There is a lot to be said for those who can work a camera under the limitations of low light, perhaps with a fast-moving subject, and still produce strong imagery. It's a discipline that many might not recognize, but what it gives you is ultimate control in camera, thus removing work time at the computer. However, this is perhaps the other end of the spectrum – we should not be doing things for effect, or because we 'can'. Ultimately we should be working with our tools to produce the finest photographic images that we are able to, however that may be. If we can make that process easier for ourselves, then surely that isn't a bad thing.

◀ Fig. 2.0

The brilliance of the digital medium has allowed us to experiment, and perhaps take risks with our photography both in camera and in post-production. The essence of foundation to an image comes through an understanding of the limitations of our camera and what can be achieved through using just basic equipment.

The Limits of New Technology

A total reliance on technology and the workings of the camera is not conducive to successful photography. Indeed, despite the brilliance of technology, there are fundamental elements which have eluded the modern camera brain. This is not to say that will always be the case, but for now here is a list of what the camera cannot do:

1 Create a concept – the idea has to come from you.
2 Select and see the possibilities of a location.
3 Create cohesion between subject and location.
4 Choose the best time of day to work in that location and light the subject.
5 Communicate with the subject. Instill confidence, create emotion, feeling and response. Tell the odd one-liner...
6 Compose an image in its own viewfinder.
7 Notice a lamp post protruding from the subject's head.
8 Pose your subject effectively – he or she will not notice if a hand is clawed or the body shape is ungainly, but addressing those elements can contribute to the overall finesse and confidence of a picture.
9 Make decisions about depth of field and how much or little detail to incorporate.
10 Know when to add space, introduce natural framing and incorporate the environment.

Point 7 is something that can be fixed, but isn't it better to be disciplined enough to pick up these small annoyances? If we don't notice small details like this, we will be more liable to miss other weaknesses and not focus properly on attention to detail. And if slack attention to detail grows, we become more reliant on post-production first-aid, which removes the crucial element: that of being a photographer. This isn't to say that having Photoshop as a tool in order to remove nuances isn't incredibly useful, but if we rely too heavily on this for back-up we become lazy photographers at the shooting stage. The satisfaction of creating an image is surely just that: the creation of something very special with a fine attention to detail.

Without human input we would lose one important element: the process of creating something never to be repeated, from a holiday snap to a piece of fine art portraiture.

Understanding the limitations of your camera is fundamental to thinking about your tools and forming a partnership with your kit. Feeding information to and taking information from your camera will give you the ability to execute those images in your heads. Just as we program computers and calibrate monitors in order to record data in the most effective

ESSENTIALS FOR YOUR KIT BAG

- Two camera bodies.
- A longer focal length lens, up to 200m (70–200mm will give you flexibility) for those candid moments and a wonderful depth.
- 80mm, 50mm and 24mm lenses.
- Silver reflector/diffuser – makes of reflector and diffusers such as Lastolite fold up tight into a bag and are lightweight, making them perfect for location work. If you are photographing groups or a large area and need to add some light from a reflector, choose the larger reflector for greater, consistent coverage.
- X-Rite white balance target and X-Rite white balance checker.
- Tripod or monopod if necessary.
- San Disk cards – these are very reasonable to buy now, so invest in far more than you need. There's always the argument that using small storage cards adds to wear on camera sensors. On the other hand, if a card containing all your data from the shoot becomes corrupt, you've lost the lot. Personally, I prefer to use smaller cards.

way, a camera should be treated in a similar way – given the correct information and settings, it will perform.

Above all, if you are just starting out in photography, heed the advice to keep things simple. Work out what best suits your style and way of working and get to know your camera like a third hand. You may find it useful to hire various lens choices before deciding to spend what could be a lot of money on kit you may not use. Photography is an expensive vocation; there is a lot of pressure to buy the latest and greatest of cameras. In reality, if you haven't learnt the skills of good classical portraiture, you will just be wasting your money.

Focal Length Lenses

Different focal lengths will give you variable results and have a more or less flattering effect, so understanding perspective and the effect of focal length is fundamental. It's worth experimenting with lenses to recognize the perspectives, depth of field, and so on, that work for you. This will make selecting the right lenses for a job easier and save you taking heavy gear you don't need. Working on location, it's advisable to keep your kit to a minimum – you may have to do a fair bit of walking and don't want to be weighed down with unnecessary equipment. Having said that, there is nothing worse than being out on location and needing that one lens that you decided to leave at home. If in doubt, pack it! Certainly it is worth investing in a backpack camera bag to keep your hands free, and if you have an assistant obviously you have the option to carry more gear and he or she can also hold items of kit like reflectors.

There are pros and cons to using an assistant. The benefits are that you have an extra pair of hands for carrying gear, especially for reflector work. Assistants could also be trained to double up as your second shooter – using a different focal length lens from you, they may get a new perspective and viewpoint. They can also act as moral support

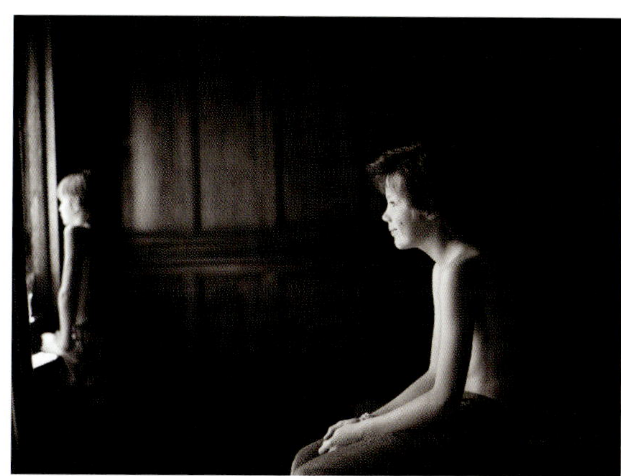

▲ Fig. 2.1
This high contrast image taken at ƒ2.8 uses depth of field to keep the foreground sharp.

(photography can be a lonely business!) and having another eye is useful when you already have plenty to think about. Some photographers, however, prefer to work alone, keeping that connection between themselves and their subject without distractions and, for the child, the assistant would be another strange person he or she didn't know.

Prime lenses (fixed focal length) are preferable for their quality of glass and tack sharpness but can be costly, so consider this if you are taking pictures as a hobby rather than for a living. Carrying a short zoom (80–135mm) or a longer focal zoom lens (80–200) may be preferable to carrying multiple lenses.

Having that longer focal length lens will also give you some space between camera and subject. This can make the shoot less intimidating, especially in the early stages, until the subject feels more comfortable. It means you can position yourself for the light and be somewhat incognito, provided you can communicate effectively with your subject. For singles and couples, shooting wide open at ƒ2.8 or below will give you a beautiful sharpness and quality, and diffusion of the surrounding area. Couple this with low key lighting conditions (you may need a monopod if you are prone to camera shake) and it is the perfect choice for creating an atmospheric study.

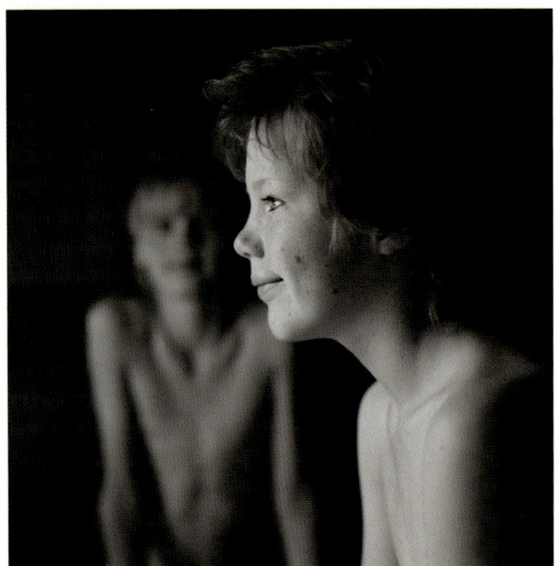

▲ Fig. 2.2a

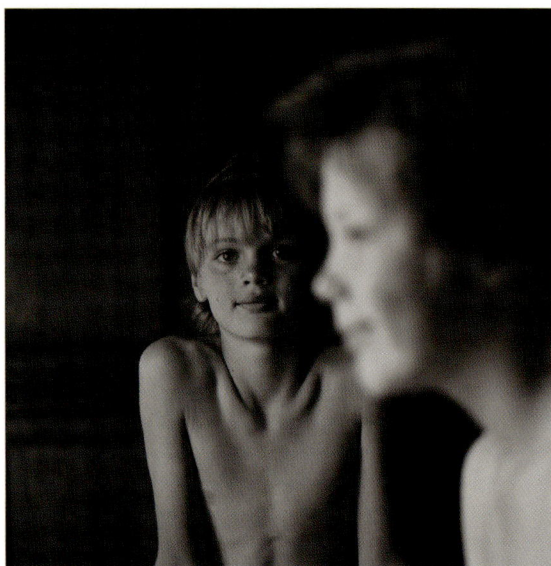

▲ Fig. 2.2b

Fig. 2.2a–b
Playing with depth of field to split focus. Working in low light in a controlled environment encourages time to slow down. Use a tripod to ensure sharpness in low light situations.

In Fig. 2.1, the child in the background, very much visible but out of the range of depth of field, is still significant. Three natural light sources were used: two direct from two windows directly onto the subjects, and a subsequent light from a reflector on the nearest child. A reading was taken of the child closest to the light – if a reading had been taken from the child in the foreground, the far child would have been overexposed. Naturally, there is less lighting exposed on the nearest child (almost a two-stop difference) so a reflector was added to the nearest child to balance the two areas. The photographer then underexposed -1 in order to bring back detail in the skin and to throw the shadow area surrounding the boys into almost complete darkness, thus creating a natural vignette.

Tripods and Monopods

Once an image has camera shake or is out of focus, nothing post-capture can be done to retrieve this completely. This emphasizes the need to slow down and pay attention to detail at the capture stage. In modern-day lifestyle photography, using a tripod has often been considered 'old school' or unnecessary – on the contrary. You should not dismiss any aid to making your work wholly professional. If you imagine that every shot you are taking is going to be enlarged to, say, thirty feet, it has to be pin sharp (unless you are using movement as a definite factor). Take the time to fix a support if necessary.

While working in low light conditions can bring great creative satisfaction for a photographer, it can also be testing when dealing with longer exposures and camera shake, even when working with state-of-the-art stabilizing lenses. There's nothing more frustrating than the realization that what looked great on your viewfinder is actually not quite pin sharp where it should be. Some photographers have a very steady hand and are adept at working at shutter speeds as low as 1/15sec, others not so – you will find your limitations with experience. Given that many of the quality glass lenses are fairly heavy, coupled with the fact that you may be holding the camera for a while in order to 'get that one moment'

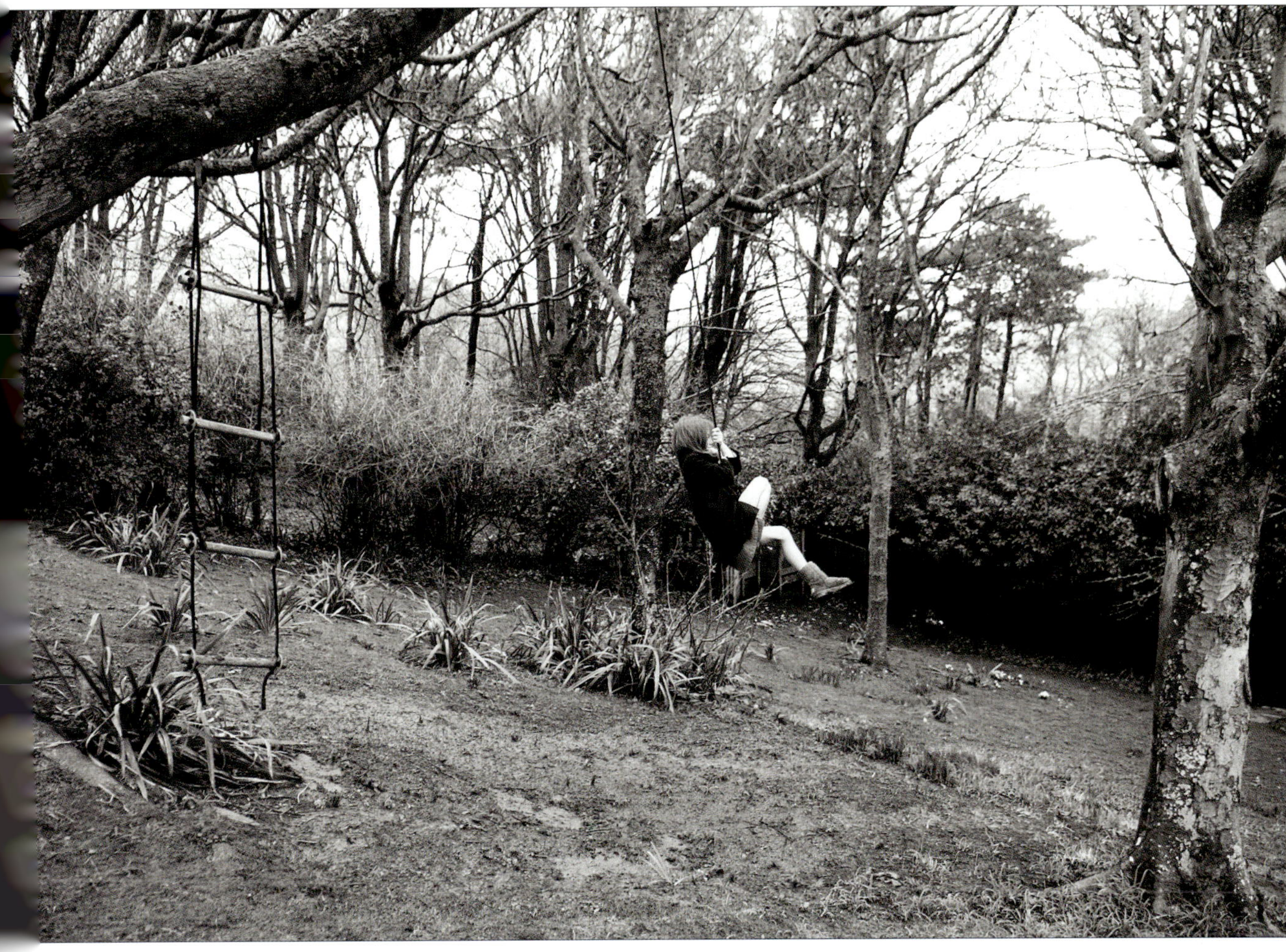

▲ Fig. 2.3
Working with a wider lens, in this case 17mm, incorporates the environment, encouraging narrative and allowing the portrait to be personal and nostalgic.

or when bracketing, it does sometimes mean that you need assistance in the form of a tripod or monopod. The advantage to this is that you can compose your image in the viewfinder and spend your time communicating with your subject without having to be behind the camera. If you have ever watched David Bailey at work, he spends more time in front of the camera, tweaking and chatting and putting his models at ease, than he does hiding behind it. As well as this, it obviously gives you the opportunity to shoot long exposures without camera shake (unless your subject is moving). Having the

camera static will also give you the choice to shoot with a smaller aperture and greater depth of field if you wish to retain detail in the background, and at a lower ISO to avoid noise distraction.

The disadvantages of the camera being fixed are of course that it leaves you unable to be spontaneous. You may miss one of those magic moments which happen naturally and quite frequently when working with children – we talk about observation later in this book and the importance of being aware of people and situations around you. Selecting two cameras, one on your shoulder for more candid shots and the other fixed to your tripod and using larger lenses, will ensure that the central mass of weight is taken up by the tripod and thus prevent

▶ Fig. 2.4
Working in a controlled environment in low key conditions may invite the use of a tripod or stand to ensure tack sharpness without compromising or losing the moment.

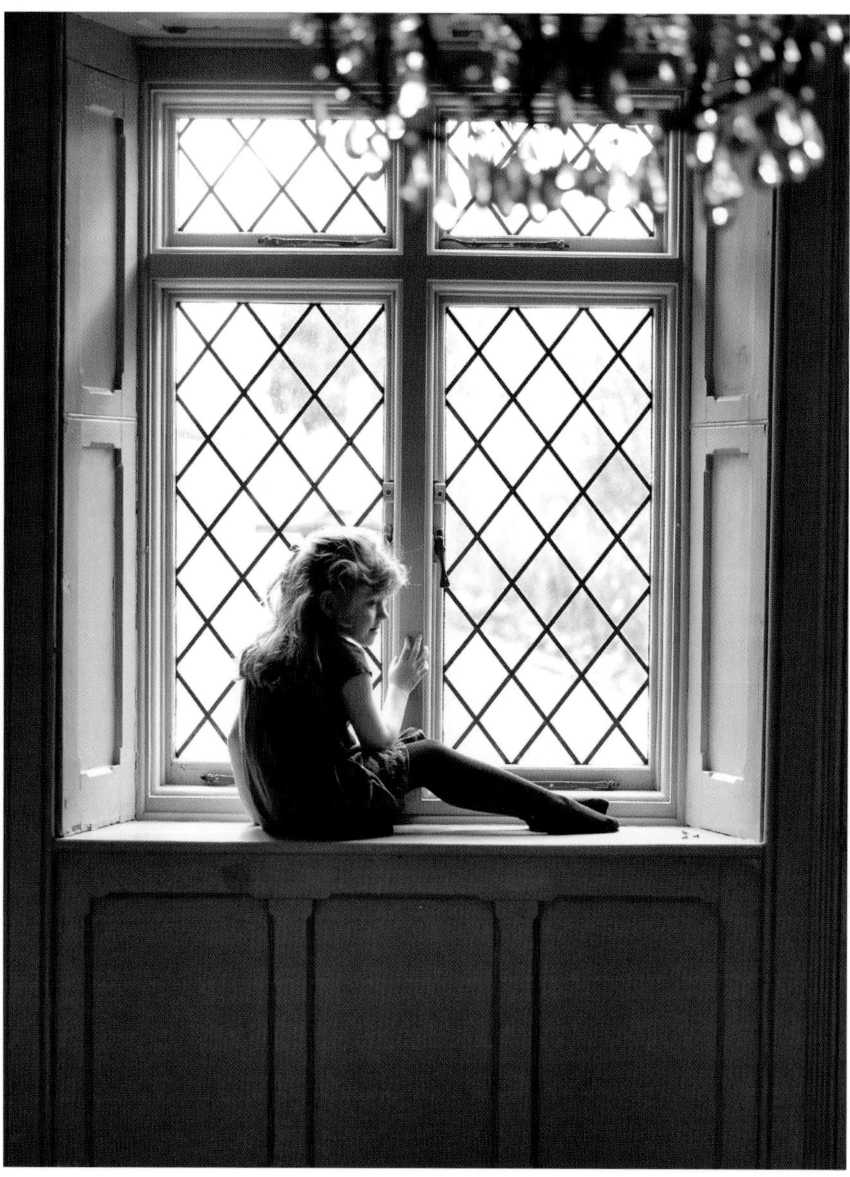

'dipping' and movement; even depressing the shutter can cause critical movement in very low light.

When working with a second camera, ensure that you have the settings in place so that you're ready to grab any opportune moments. You will soon find that the two cameras work in unison and take on their own roles and, in fact, through using different choices of lenses on each, you find you become both photographer and second shooter in one – taking on two different perspectives.

Working on location you will want to minimize the weight of your gear, so take some time to choose the right tripod for you. Carbon fibre tends to be lighter, albeit a little more expensive than its aluminum equivalent. A monopod, which is not static to the ground, gives you more flexibility with regard to moving around, but is not as secure to curb camera shake as a tripod fixed to the ground. You also have to factor the weight of your overall kit. If you feel you are walking long distances throughout

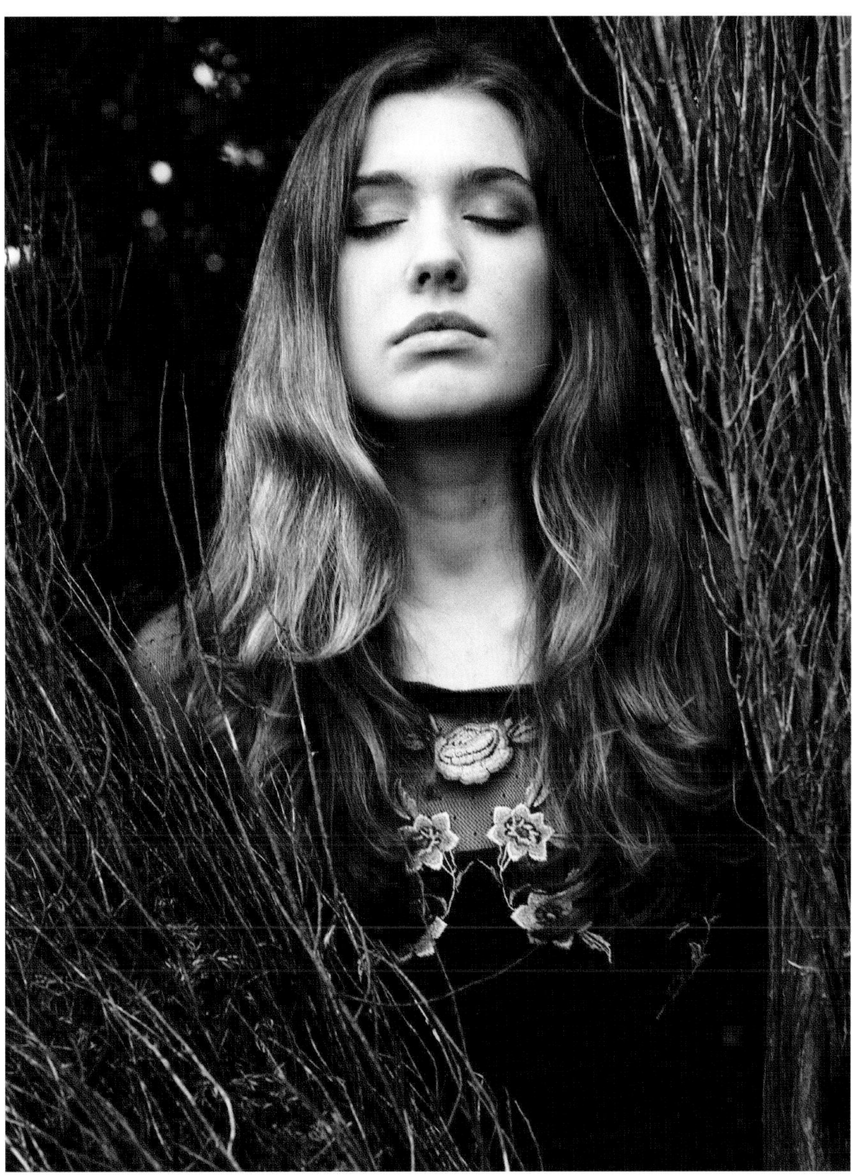

▲ Fig. 2.5
An image that's not quite sharp or with camera shake. Depending on the feel of the image you are hoping to achieve, movement in a portrait needs to demonstrate conviction and meaning. Being 'a little bit out' is out of focus and irretrievable post-capture.

the shoot, ask yourself whether you need to have the tripod. In general you do get what you pay for with regard to sturdiness, but a more lightweight one out on location might be more useful.

To free your camera while keeping it static, ball heads are generally more effective to quickly point the camera freely in any direction before locking it into position. They are typically also a little more compact than equivalent pan-tilt heads. Some ball heads come with a rotation-only ability for just this type of situation.

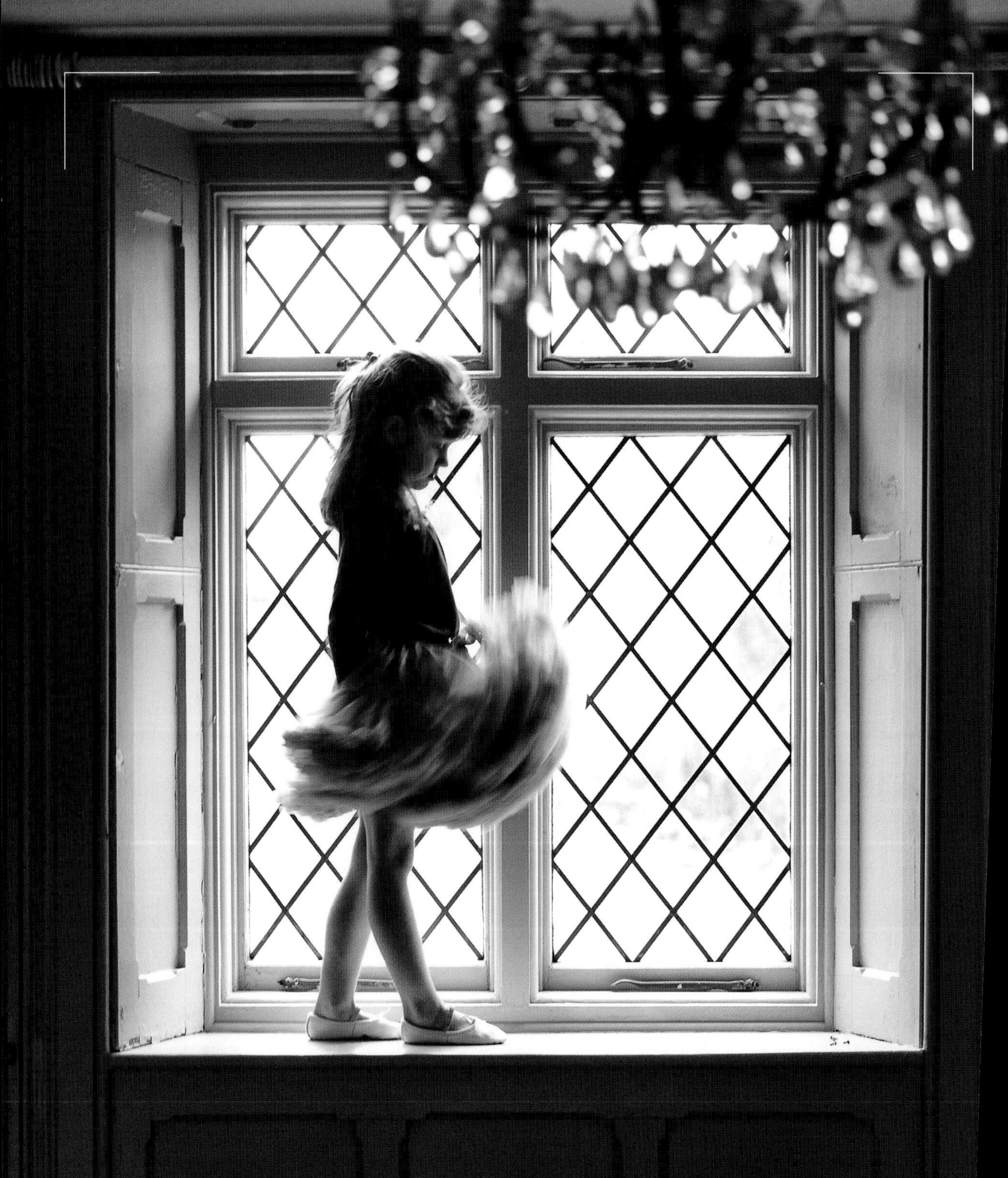

Chapter 3

An Idea, Inspiration and Getting Creative

The value of a portrait is determined by a number of parameters; all the elements must come together to create equilibrium and harmony. We are looking to produce work which is a culmination of style and technique on a level that our clients will understand and appreciate. Your client needs to feel excited, to expect the unexpected.

The parents of the children you are photographing are commissioning you to create something that is beyond the norm, something beyond their own capabilities and expectations. In an age of digital domination where everyone has access to a respectable standard of snapshot, this is not always easy.

Portraits need not be complex in make-up. Simplicity can be very powerful if constructed with the fundamental elements of directional light, tone, emotion and form to create something which not only exudes impact but invites the reader to question a narrative – an image which will hang on the wall for years to evoke discussion, emotion and response.

It's important to think about the feel of an image and the style you wish to portray. You don't necessarily need a firm view, just an inkling – being too specific or fixed on an idea for a certain picture can lead to disappointment given what can be an equivocal method of working. Allow yourself to be open to change and the possibility of goalposts being moved through nature, technical limitations, or just the unpredictable character of children. All the same, an idea of the type of feel of image is

necessary so that you can plan the shoot and emanate confidence to your investing client. Factoring in the ages of the children, the client brief, chosen location, time of year, and so on, can give you plenty of food for thought: a feel of ethereal quality, high fashion, quiet, vocal, classical, contemporary, for example. You can then implement how the image will grow from that and the degree of visual stimulation you wish to demonstrate.

In the competitive marketplace that is the world of social photography, it is vital that the individual photographer creates a reputation for work that is not necessarily unique but at the highest level of his or her ability. Striving to be unique is perhaps an unrealistic ideal; it is almost impossible to be unique in photography (and remember you are targeting the realms of a marketplace), but it *is* possible to be individual and to have your own recognized style and way of working. This involves being a perfectionist in your work and having an individual sense of what you want to portray, from the initial idea through to the final embellishment of a print: being able to build on ideas and discipline yourself to create the ideas and images that are in your head.

If you are not yet confident or bold enough to translate your ideas into practice, try stamping your style firmly on each of your assignments in a more subtle, experimental way, doing something for yourself on each job as well as ticking the boxes of a formula that you know works – playing safe, if you like. A useful method of self-improvement is to take on personal projects in order to test your

◀ Fig. 3.0

A dramatic location need not be the background to your image; what you do within your canvas and being able to build on an idea will set you apart. Flirting with movement, graphic, atmosphere, tonal harmony in a cohesive method will allow you to bring all the elements together.

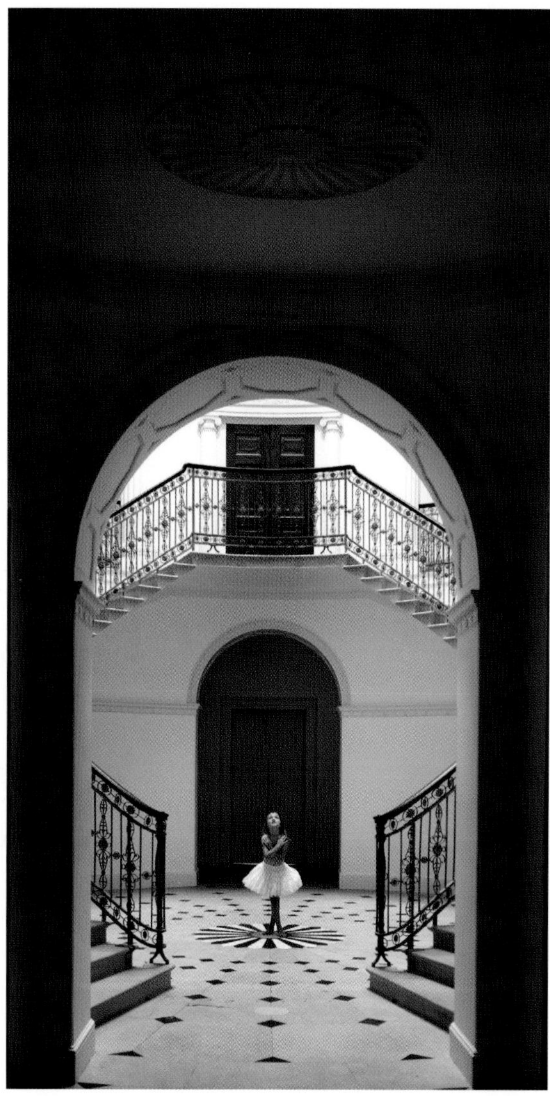

▲ **Fig. 3.1**
The multi-sensor focusing option within a camera has enabled us to use negative space with more ease and to great effect and this style was popular for a while.

When you have a method and style of working, it is natural to become, if not complacent, at least in a safe zone where you don't have to think ahead. However, we need to be looking ahead in order to stay current, to keep ideas and imagery fresh. This shouldn't mean making dramatic changes overnight – more a gentle transition, a step forward in self-improvement.

Despite having something that 'works' and is popular with your clients, keeping yourself inspired, working on personal projects and staying current is essential. Like the fashion and design trades, photography is constantly evolving around trends. If you look at successful fashion labels, they possess a very distinctive style of course to assuage their client base, yet they still have to be seen to be current, to be one step ahead of the market, otherwise their clients move on to the next best thing. Gentle evolving consistency is a powerful tool in the creative world. What works today will have progressed to something new tomorrow – style remains but trends change. It's not advisable to be drawn into trends and fads if you can't sustain a recognized style.

The photographic industry is the same and your clients will expect you to be trend-aware as well as having a solid style running through. Even in portraiture, elements go through styles, often dictated by the current mood. Take composition and the fashion for an increased focus on negative space (*see* Fig. 3.1). Perhaps we will soon see the reinstatement of the subject bang in the middle of the image, bold and direct, making a comeback. Might this coincide with the return to a more classical trend of portraiture?

Over-manipulation, spot colour, toning, vintage styles – these phases have come and gone. 'Reportage' or 'documentary' were adjectives thrown around in the late '80s and throughout the '90s, moving into the era of 'lifestyle' – a more candid way of working. It is natural to follow market demand, but perhaps better only to glance at it and play with it within our work. To go down a wholly definitive

limitations, as well as to join training workshops and courses with reputable professionals whose work you respect.

Maybe you want to work as a professional photographer. You have understood the need to take your photography to a higher level in order to remain competitive so are looking to build on your existing portfolio. It's easy to fall into a comfort zone, especially if you have something in place that works.

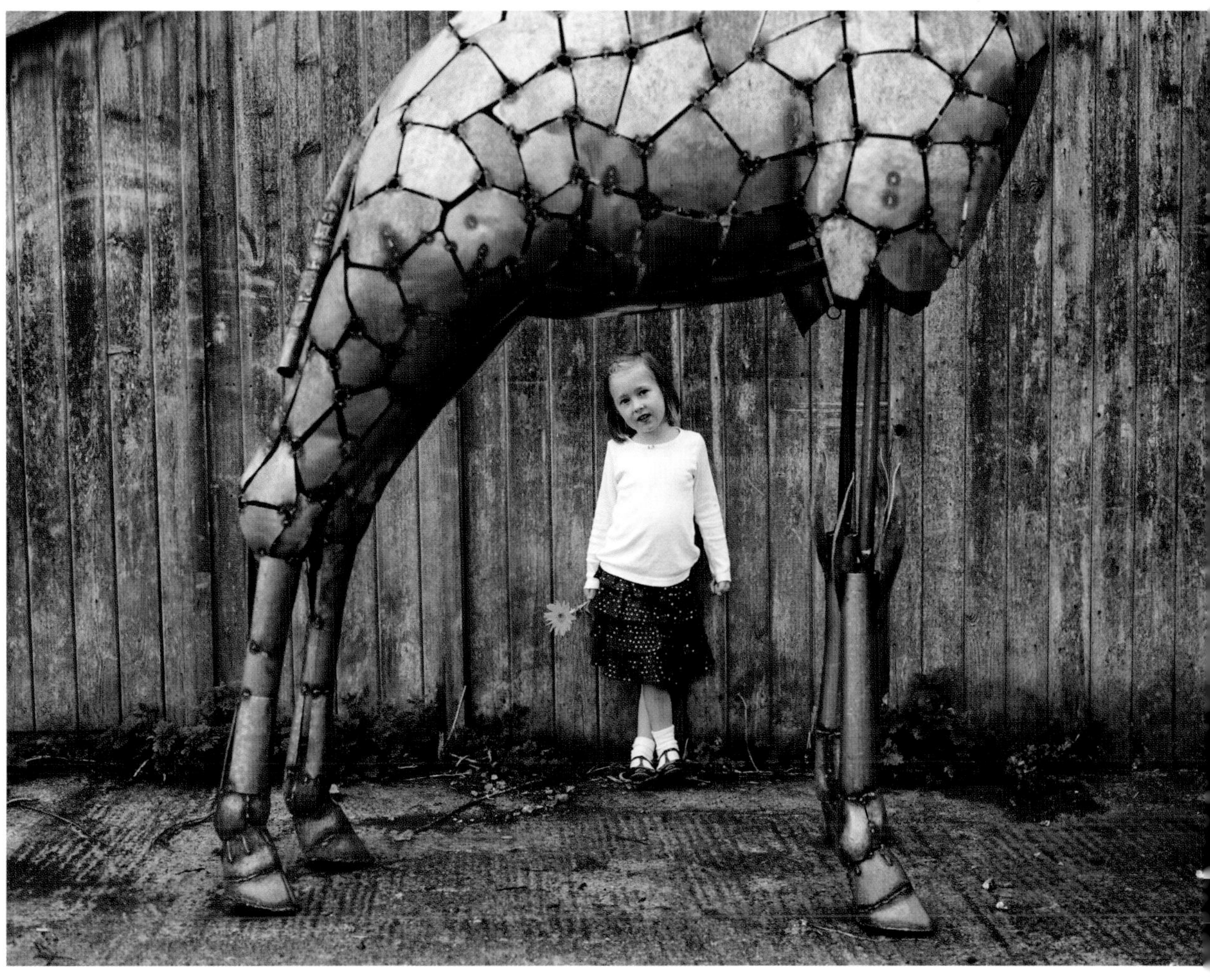

▲ Fig. 3.2
A metal giraffe sculpture is an unusual find, and it makes for an
interesting element to this picture, either in its entirety or cropped as
here. The black and white conversion has very much lifted the grain
and texture in both the wood panelling and the metal structure of
the giraffe. The perfect positioning of the child creates scale and
accentuates the small child in a big world, yet the giraffe is almost
acting as a protective shield around her.

change of style on a whim can be disruptive to
marketing and confusing potential clients. We need
to think ahead to the next trend, or in an ideal world
create our own. We must be honest with ourselves
as to what moves us, and always be one step ahead.

Above all, being consistent is paramount to retaining client confidence. Remember that an image is a
process of creation; it should never be experienced
as a mere product.

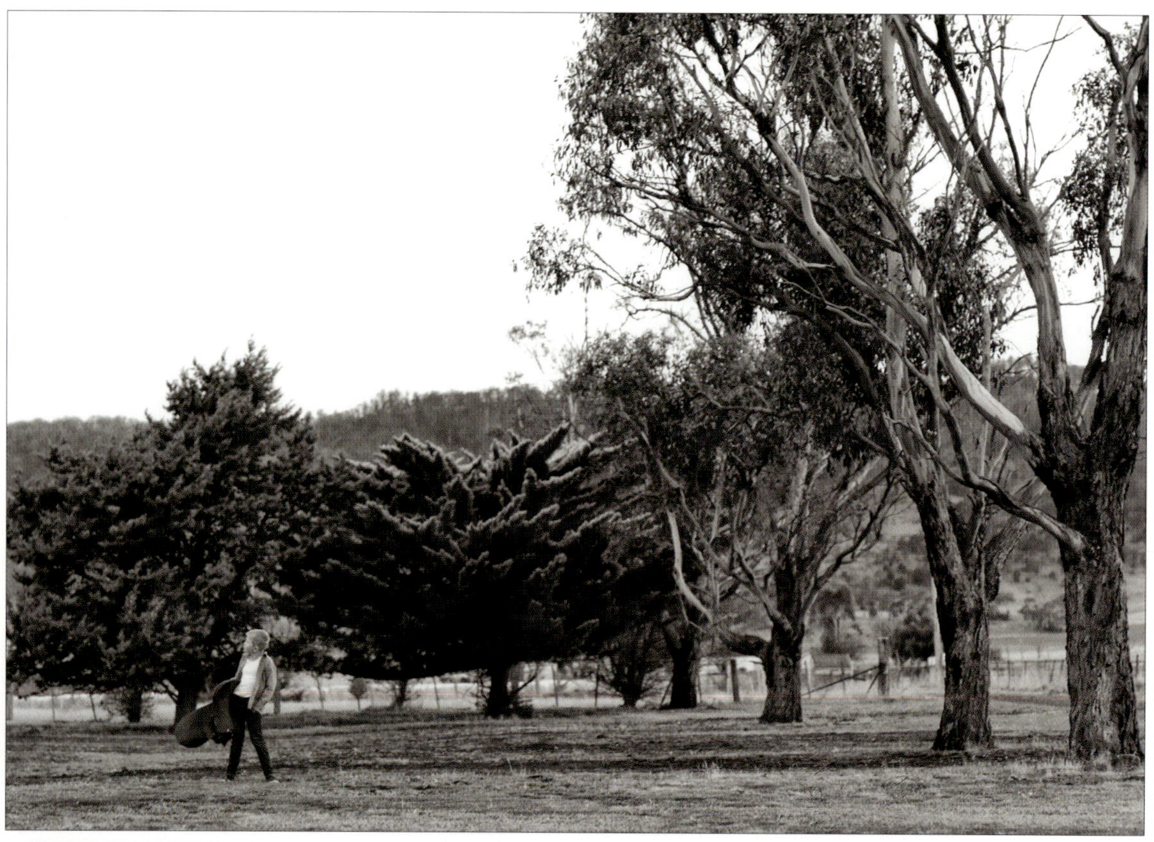

▲ Fig. 3.3
This location offers several options – utilizing the trees to the right or the graphic shapes of the trees behind. Alternatively it works well in its entirety as here.

Natural Light Portraits as a Trend

This style of portraiture interestingly runs along-side the growth of the digital era, having come through the more controlled, classical times of film. Photography became accessible, and the public were starting to understand that they could have their portraits taken fast and candidly, with the cost of producing one image drastically reduced. With that came a new breed of photographer who discovered the power of a long, fast focal length lens to create images on the hoof that would produce a viable, saleable product, wholly accessible to all.

In some ways this had a negative effect on the marketplace of portrait photography, by diluting skill, making it too easy perhaps – which it has to some.

But for the serious photographer, the artist who can marry ideas with skill, who can control light and can relate great ideas onto paper (or a digital chip), it has opened the door. As previously said, ideas for portraits have not changed since Steichen's day. What has moved on is the way we achieve the final results. The saturation of the market has opened the door wider for those who can push themselves to a far higher standard in order to set themselves apart. This takes imagination, vision, skill and a recogni-tion of the importance of developing personal style. These are elements that emanate naturally from us, with the exception of skill, which requires nurturing and educating.

So how do you recognize what your strength is in order to define a style? Well, it doesn't necessarily have to be an area of initial strength – skill can be learnt – but the ideas and ways of working should come naturally to you. When you are inspired by someone's work and are very clear about what kind of imagery moves you, this can be the basis for your seed. It can also go beyond that: what moves you in your day-to-day life can be influential to creativity. In order for you to effectively market yourself, you need to love a style of portraiture – something you would put on your own wall. By doing this, you will find it easier to learn (as with everything, it is easier to learn what you enjoy).

Here are some questions you should ask yourself with regard to where you want to go with your portraits:

1   How saleable is your style or the style you are looking to develop?
2   Does it fit in some way into how you are currently working?
3   Is a competitor working in this way within your commercial area? If so, what can you do to set yourself apart from him or her?
4   Do you love your style – would you hang it on your own walls?

There is a lot to be said for being individual, sometimes a little off the wall, but if you are serious about making a living from portraiture you need to understand what sells, what appeals and who your target audience is. Being outspoken with your style may of course mean a smaller market place, but it does give you the opportunity to be a specialist and perhaps command higher fees. It will take longer to build your reputation and you may need to work harder at marketing yourself; however, an artist who is offering something beyond the norm is very attractive. Clients may like that unpredictable mystique and feel they are receiving something personal and to a very high standard. I do reiterate the importance of being able to keep moving forward with your work in order to offer this bespoke portraiture, and it is crucial that you hold belief in yourself and your ability to translate your style to a viable market.

When we talk about moving forward, it's not a dramatic change in style – it's adding or removing elements of an existing way of working. The likes of Irvin Penn and Cecil Beaton had recognizable styles. How often do we hear ourselves saying 'that's very David Bailey' or 'that's a good take on Rankin' – it's because they have something which we recognize. Importantly, they keep their work consistently fresh and current within their own capsule of style. How they do this is by incorporating new fashion, new locations, perhaps different ways of lighting, but these elements are all a periphery of that seed which is a permanent component – identity.

Look at the fashion designer Vivienne Westwood, an icon of design for over thirty years. She consistently produces pieces that are current, in fact beyond current, always one step ahead but with an intrinsically recognizable element of shock value. Still in demand, she is the epitome of an artist who has a strong style running through her work but who gently adapts it to a current market place. This approach applies to all creatives, not just photographers.

A portrait is created through building blocks and with that you need foundations, which are formed from your initial ideas. Inspiration and where it is sourced is as important perhaps as technical ability; without it you may find it difficult to create the foundations. Where to get ideas can often be the most difficult stage. They can be found in the most unexpected places within your daily life: from a location, life experiences, or just a feeling. This is part of creating an identity, but let's look at what moves you to create your art. A starting point is the world of photography, but there is a wealth of areas to inspire you beyond this and they're not always where you would expect.

Inspiration

From inspiration comes an idea. You may see something in a movie, you may notice the shape of someone's profile or a part of their features, you may be inspired by movement and dance. Creative block is something many artists fear, which is why we need to keep our eyes and minds open. Sometimes the most ordinary of situations can stimulate those creative juices.

Drawing inspiration from our peers and others in our field is natural and can help us decide what moves us and which direction we want to take with our own work. However, there is a fine line between emulating and plagiarism – specifically copying another photographer's work. Making pictures that come from your own head and heart will resonate in your work, and new images will naturally develop from that. By copying someone else's images you will miss out a huge chunk of what is most important in a picture, such as the building process and the natural formation. It is not conducive to the development of your own personal style. Above all, it will not set you apart and you will need to rely wholly on your price rather than your imaging; this in turn cheapens your work and makes it more difficult to separate you from your competition.

Films/Movies

Just as directors often draw inspiration for a scene from photographic stills, being observant to how a film is lit, how it is directed and filmed can fill the imagination with ideas for portraits. You may connect with just a split second in a film but it can be enough to apply to your own work. It may be a fly-on-the-wall approach that moves you, or perhaps something about the fashion and styling that could be brought into your photography.

This isn't considered plagiarism. It's about being observant to what is possible, taking snippets and redeveloping ideas to make a picture of your own: noticing how the camera has composed a scene incorporating areas that were perhaps not the most obvious, or the director's use of scale to create narrative as well as a visual story. How actors communicate with each other and their cohesion with the camera can often give you an insight into the connection the director has with his actors in order to interpret the story effectively. And, of course, there's the lighting set-up, which determines the scene, mood and feel of a set.

In the filming of a movie, the way a scene is lit will influence the response from the viewer. Three or more lights are often used in high-end film-making, so the logistics of the shoot are different from how we are working. But the overall ambience of the scene is what dictates the mood and how it is interpreted. As with shooting natural light stills, movies tend to be lit to look unobtrusive and the lighting is unnoticed until the cinematographer wants to make a statement or dramatize a scene by using it to add to the narrative or drama. By watching each scene in a film closely and imagining it as a frame of a photograph, you will soon understand how the director has used light and placement to create a visual story. Ask yourself where the light source is coming from and, if a particular scene is styled in a way that moves you, how you can use it in your own work. Placement and composition are also fundamental to how you feel about the characters and the unfolding of the story; this can be surreal, which is so often the case in film, or it can hold a mirror up to life. Film teaches us that anything is possible – it's really just our imagination that limits our creativity. Of course, in contrast, an evocative still image or portrait relating to a film can give the viewer an idea of the style and feel of the film before they have watched it, so it works both ways.

Daily Life

There are many great artists/photographers whose personal lives are documented visually – sometimes subconsciously – within their work. This personal element can make for interesting viewing, though be aware that, if you want to create a saleable

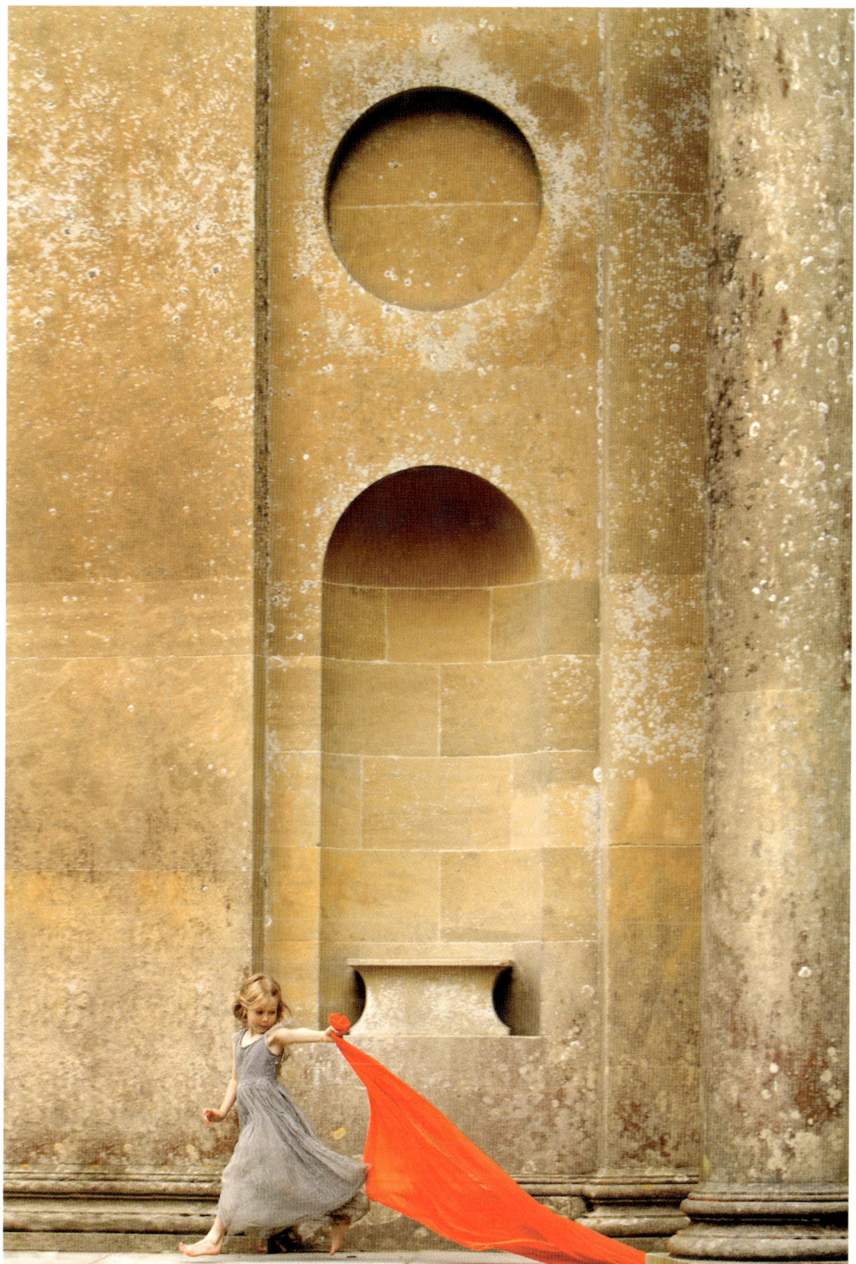

◀ Fig. 3.4
This image was drawn from a moment in a film, using the static grandeur of the building against the animation and colour created by the subject. Notice the child is small in the frame but still the main focus, the location acting as a canvas.

product, it should incorporate a personal style that is recognizably yours but, more so, personal to your client. What is it that makes you laugh out loud, cry, feel relaxed? Make use of anything that stimulates the emotive in you. Location portraiture is very much about stirring the emotions and it can be useful to know what moves people in order to apply this to your own work. Drawing on the ever-evolving adventures of life can often transport you from perhaps a difficult time to somewhere else with your photography. Like designers, photographers have to be open to and aware of their environment and to the things that shape everyday life.

PHOTOGRAPHY AND MUSIC

There is an interesting link between great music and visual art – they both contain similar elements that can stimulate the senses. All these elements contribute to how we feel about an image and are contributing factors in music also:

Dynamic range: this is present in how a piece of music is played and in the composition or make-up of a portrait. In music it means more than just the level of activity or denseness of sound; it can also relate to the drama of a musical element. It's almost about how the music breathes – its growing and waning dynamism, the amount of energy at certain points. So the quietest bit might be the most dramatic, the climax. All of this demands a response from the listener not dissimilar to that of a powerful portrait.

Impact: the sound of a piece of music can transfix the listener in the same way as a photograph can confront the viewer with arresting imagery.

Emotion: being transported back to a time or place through the content of a song, a portrait of a child, a reminder of someone special, or a particular time in life.

Shape: light and tone.

Rhythm

Structure

Density

Scale: using scale within a photograph, especially with children, can create something powerful that emphasizes, not necessarily their vulnerability, but the enormity of the world around them.

Narrative: telling the story. As with music, the story within a portrait can be hugely powerful and often the most interesting image is the one that is left open to interpretation so that viewers are encouraged to create their own story.

Music

There is a certain correlation between the expressive language of music and art (the great Ansel Adams was torn between the piano and the camera) and they can both stimulate the emotions. Both media have the ability to transport the viewer/listener back to a particular time in their lives – perhaps childhood, a first relationship, a friendship, family member, or someone who was significant. Even a time of sadness. Music and pictures can resonate and correspond in so many ways. When we watch films, the music is often integral to how we feel about a scene, whether it's fear, sadness, or whatever.

The camera and a musical instrument have the same power to connect but both require skill. You may hear a great piece of music but you wouldn't know how to start playing it; likewise a great idea for

an image does not bring certain success unless the skillbase is honed and all the elements have been put in place to produce something compelling.

From an inspiration perspective, the feel or lyrics of a piece of music can encourage themes or concepts, just as they can with the creation of a portrait. Making this connection can be very personal but you should not be afraid of applying this to your work – this is a part of creating something individual to you. As an example, the holistic music of Effervescence could encourage something ethereal taken in soft early light or perhaps fog; it could trigger a foundation for your image. You can then build on this idea and apply it within your work by adding the additional segments such as location, attire and pose. Engaging this foundation (music) and the idea born from it allows you to break down the portrait into segments and to consider each element before bringing it together. It's an interesting exercise and may help you with ideas for a concept. Try to take something from the music and apply it to an idea for your next shoot.

Children

If you are a parent, an aunt or uncle, or perhaps just have children close to you, you will understand the value of creating memories – being able to freeze a moment within a child's life when daily they grow and change so fast. A successful photograph is one that stimulates emotion in thirty to forty years' time, when perhaps the children themselves are parents. A portrait that contains the wonderment of a child at a time in their life which will never be repeated stands alone. It's a moment gone, and you cannot put a value on that.

To create something that captures this longevity means you have to respect the value of the child to the parent, grandparents and the future, and be prepared to invest a degree of emotion into those relationships. Understanding the importance of this will give your images soul, depth of emotion and individuality, rather than being 'just another snapshot'.

Art

Look at art – not to mirror it, but to appreciate the components of what makes a painting, landscape, portrait or sculpture. Studying art (not just the classics) can give us ideas on composition, lighting, posing, colour, shape, and so on. Sometimes just a glance can give you the foundation for something individual to you. Art (including photography) is hugely subjective. It can also be beneficial to view work that perhaps doesn't move you; be open minded and try to understand how the author has lit the subject, and the thought process behind the picture. A portrait photographer would not necessarily naturally be a follower of, say, an architectural photographer or a landscape artist, but you will draw inspiration and appreciation from viewing this

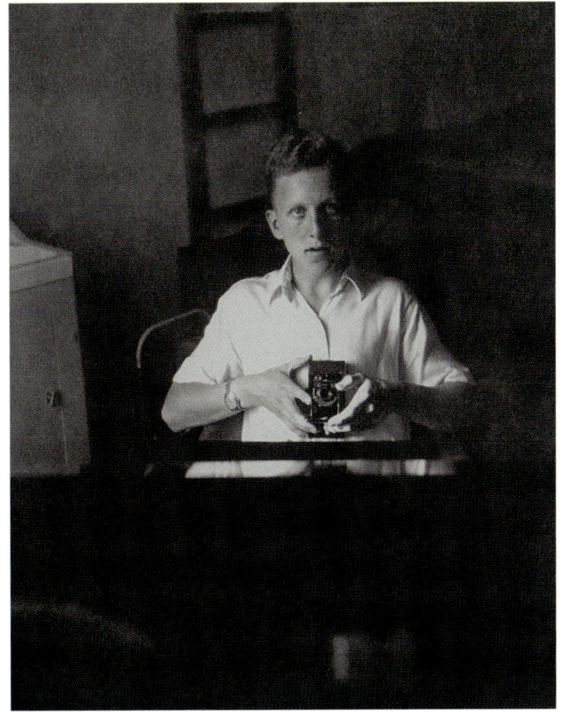

▲ Fig. 3.5
Self-portrait of the author's late father, taken in his teenage years: an important heirloom and part of a family's legacy. The popularity of photography now ensures that everyone has access to a visual history of their lives.

kind of work that you may be able to incorporate into your own. It is perhaps worth factoring these variables into your training, perhaps by attending a landscape workshop; you will be amazed how it helps you with your portrait work, not to mention your patience! Working on location is not just about your subject. It is the bigger picture that's important: it's about recognizing light in a given room, or if symmetry is to play a part then architectural uprights need to be just that, upright without converging where possible. We need to look beyond our own genre to learn and nurture our skill base.

Design

Artists in the form of painters, designers of graphics, textiles, typography, ceramic, photographers, architects and such like continue to define and redefine design, expanding our understanding of it not only

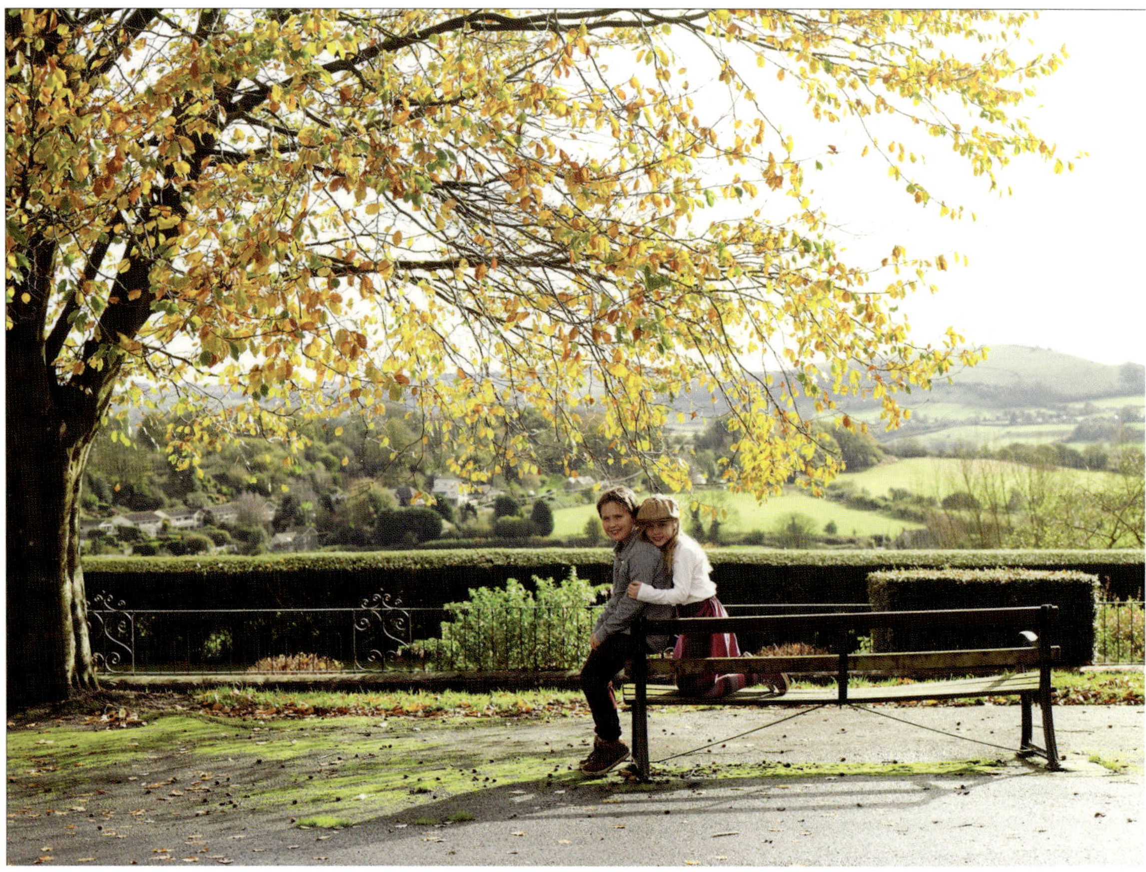

▲ Fig. 3.6
Incorporating the natural landscape into a picture. Much can be learnt from looking outside the portraiture genre, into the work of landscape, architectural and commercial photographers.

as a creative discipline but also as a social translator, a true communicator of stories and lives.

In an age of digital sensors and interfaces, the evolving communication between people and objects is still rooted in our inextricable and increasingly complex relationship with the analogue world. Design is always in a state of constant invention and reinvention. Photography can be very much led by what is current in this area; it can drag its heels a little behind that of design, yet the two work hand in hand.

As well as landscape, looking outside the photographic arena will encourage you to look at things beyond the mainstream to create your own imagery. Design incorporates a vast spectrum of sources and genres from architecture, furniture, fashion, sculpture, lighting, font design, product packaging – in fact, anything that is made or designed. Access to all this through the internet has invited us into a world where anything, even the unimaginable, is imaginable. Branding design is now an intrinsic part of the photographer's identity with regard to creating an image for the world to see – your shop window. Having an understanding of and keeping current with changes within the world of web design is key to keeping your style running through, yet making it a visually stimulating experience for the viewer. With this in mind, keeping our style of branding parallel with our photography allows the flow of style to run through.

Magazines, blogs and websites such as *The World of Interiors*, *Dezeen*, *Tank*, *inspirationhut.net* and

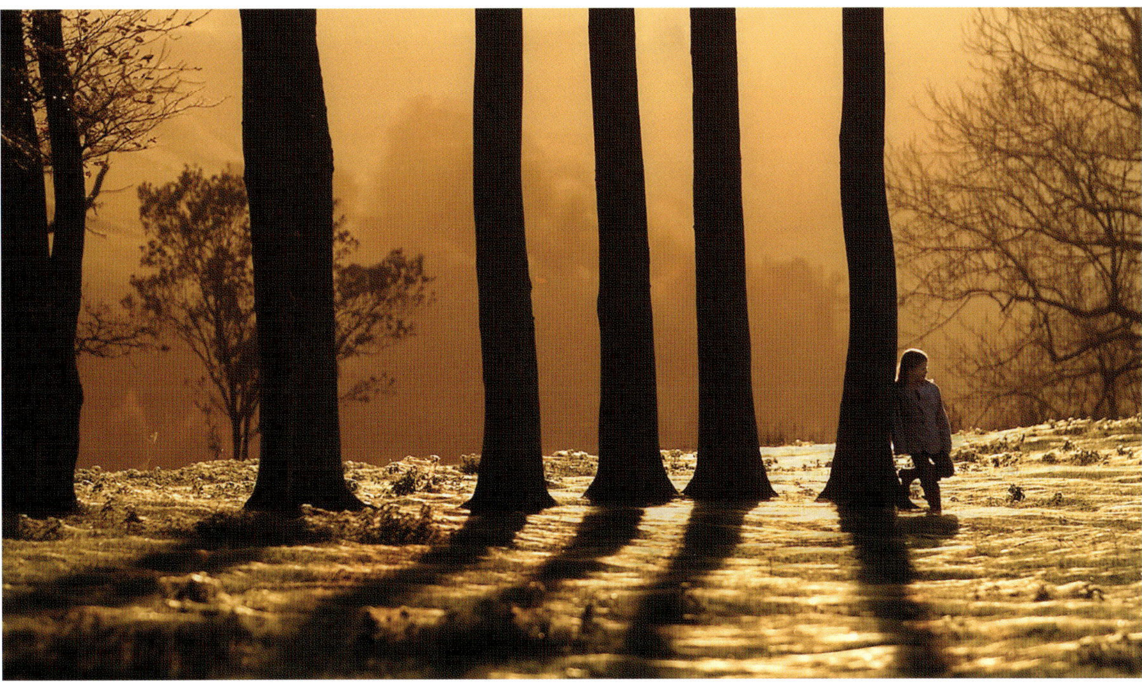

▲ Fig. 3.7

Being out on location and using natural light is not far removed from landscape photography, timing being essential in order to create the ambience. The only difference is that you are introducing another element, a child. This image was taken at 4pm in early April. Because of the shadows created by a low sun and because the shot was backlit, a reflector was added to the right to lift the detail in the face. The shadows were strong; some burning down of the trees (post-production) in the foreground has emphasized this effectively without being detrimental to the final image.

Wallpaper are visual aids that can stimulate and help us recognize what moves us and what we desire within our own work. If you are not from an artistic background but are searching for a specific style that will help you move forward then these are excellent resources. More importantly they perhaps tell us what *doesn't* move us.

Online adventures such as *The Library of Nineteenth-Century Photography* is a wonderful, humorous look at where photography really began to become part of people lives and when the power of the still image was recognized. Some of the imagery here would sit well in today's marketplace. As previously discussed, ideas are not unique, it's just the way the image is taken that has changed. We are not better photographers for the birth of digital, we just have access to a wealth of teaching and inspiration. And everything is immediate. What you will understand is that design, like photography, does not need to be complex to be powerful, but simplistic and classical in content with a strong message of quality which keeps the work current.

This ethos can be applied to portraiture: for example, a beautiful portrait taken in natural light often needs very little other than a key element such as directional light. 'Less is more' is a phrase that is often bandied about, but it's hugely relevant in the world of children's portraiture and sometimes to strengthen an image we need to remove elements rather than add to it and over complicating what is already a beautiful portrait. As with design, if we feel we need to add more for effect, it can appear to the viewer that we perhaps lack confidence in our product, our imagery. Some of the finest advertising campaigns are bold, minimalistic and very effectively to the point. The Apple brand is an excellent example of an effective simple showcase.

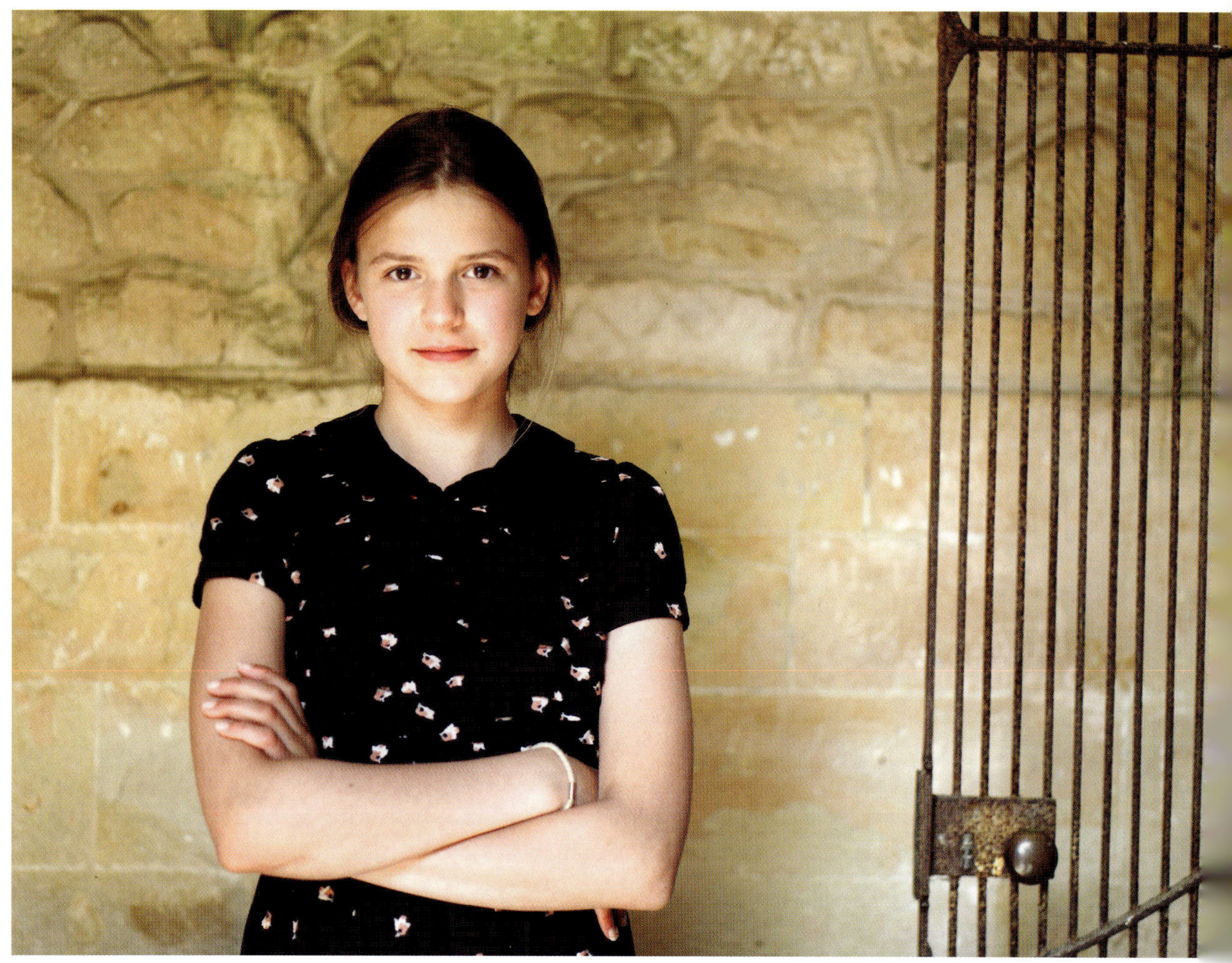

▲ Fig. 3.8
Strength in simplicity. Beautiful light with an accent of graphic
interest, which in no way detracts from the child.

Personal Work

Despite all the inspiration we can draw from outside
the immediate world of photography, implementing
changes in our way of working or our visual style
needs to be done with some subtlety. Moving your
work forward and keeping things fresh is important
but your current way of working is perhaps recognized by your market, so making dramatic changes
can have a negative effect with regard to clients'
expectations. Gently introducing new ways of
working and building on your current style in order
to strengthen rather than to make knee jerk changes
will slowly take your pictures in new directions
without damaging your current client relationships.
Playing with different compositions, using colour
or black and white more or less, experimenting with
movement, working with reflectors and different
natural light scenarios can give your work this new
direction. Having personal projects is elementary
to your creative growth. It can take you out of your
comfort zone without the pressure of conforming to
your current way of working.

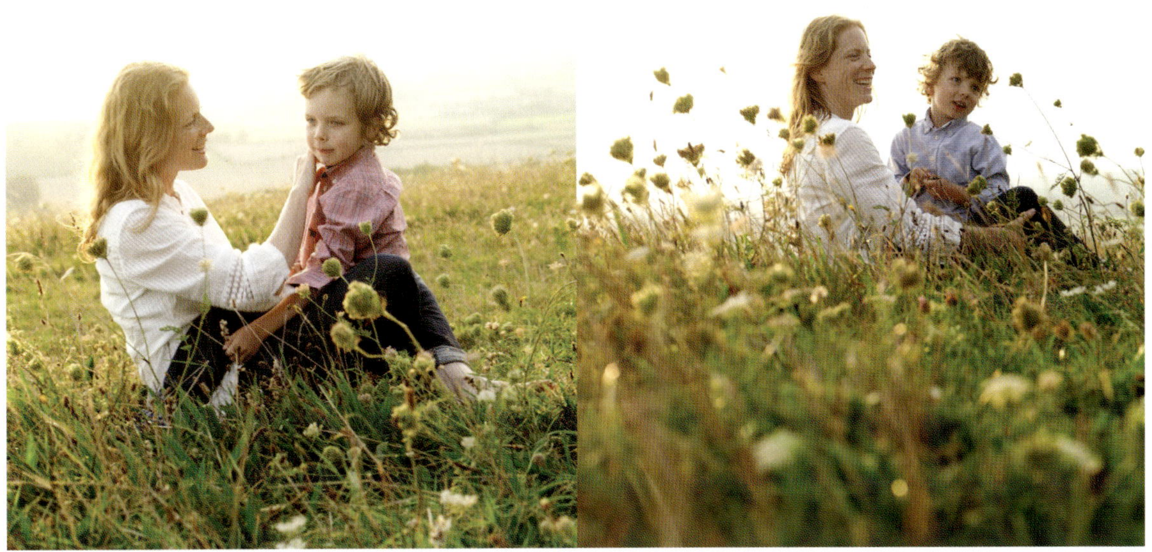

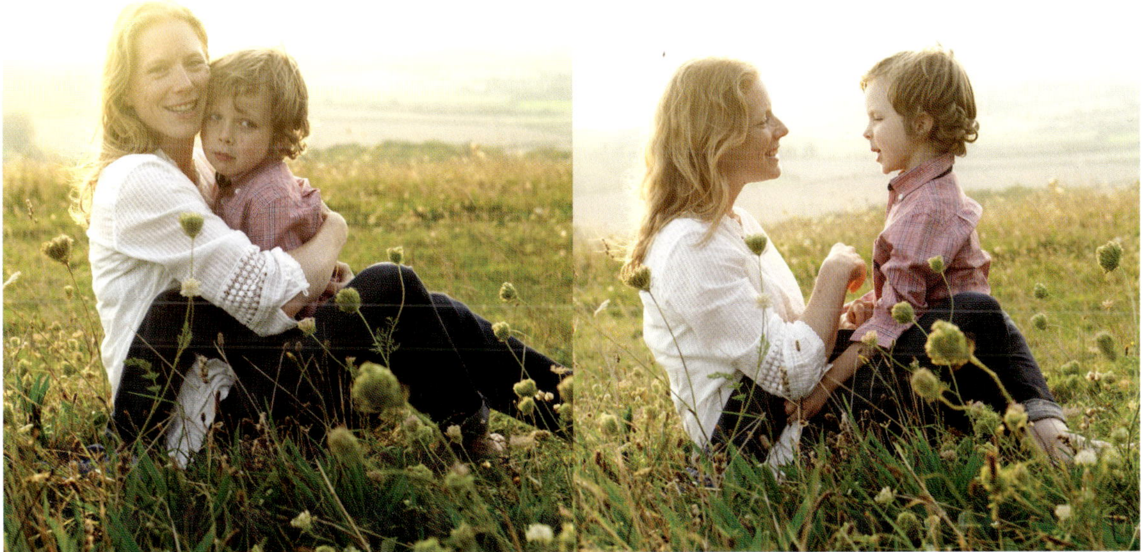

▲ Fig. 3.9
Watch, observe, and let the images take their natural course.

Travelling, working with different cultures and adapting your methods of communicating will take you out of your safe arena. Collaborating with artists, clothing designers, street artists, for example, and building on ideas where you can all benefit is a way for you to test yourself and to create something.

The elements of your creation can then be transferred into your own day-to-day work at your own pace. Above all, removing yourself from your usual environment and testing skills in new areas is an active progression method; if it doesn't work for you, try other avenues.

The Art of Observation

Children are unpredictable; they have a wonderful way of being naturally capricious in their mannerisms. What they say and how they carry themselves is what makes up that wonderful aura of sincerity and innocence that photographers hope to capture as a fleeting moment in those children's lives. This isn't always about being overly creative, artistic or complex – it's very much about a moment. But it must go beyond a snapshot moment, and it's important that we still factor all the elements into our candid work as we would do for something more contrived. This is what will set us apart. There's not such a fine line between what is a snapshot and what is considered a professional image, however it is taken. A snapshot can be taken in any light, any format, although perhaps with quality issues. Yet sometimes a snapshot can be the most incredibly moving image, with a diaristic power, a 'one chance' picture that's special to someone. We all have those somewhere – something about the moment caught moves us or holds a special nostalgia.

Being observant and knowing when to take control and when to leave things to develop is part of our discipline. There is nothing better than watching a child laughing uncontrollably and not interfering so that you can capture the emotion at its best. Beyond that, reacting to reactions from others is a way of crystallizing the spirit of a family and the enchantment that children bring to people around them. Part of your personal project could be to work in a more documentary style, relying on being reactive to responses and being aware of how people behave in different situations. For example, if you watch two people deep in conversation, invariably this will end in a smile – it's a natural reaction to the closure of a conversation. So without the need to engage yourself with people, by watching and waiting, you will reap the rewards of a reaction. It just takes a little patience. This quiet observant approach, still using the quality of light, lends itself to natural and sensitive imagery – an emotional attachment between parent and child, siblings and families as a whole that perhaps is less likely if contrived.

Listening is another skill that can open up photographic opportunities – children scheming, playing, arguing and unaware of you knowing their next move. Perhaps there are siblings or other family members who are not in the immediate portrait but who are interacting together: having a longer focal length lens to hand will give you the chance to photograph them unawares, in a natural scenario. A large part of being a portrait photographer is not just the taking of pictures, it's your methods of working and your ability to anticipate a reaction or change of mood, and to be there to react to it. This comes with experience – you will become adept at reading situations. One tip when photographing one member of a family is to ask the remaining family to be placed in a position which is backlit or in acceptable light while they wait. While photographing the one child, you can then keep an ear and an eye on the family, and if special moments are naturally formed you have them in place to grab some lovely moments.

The Client Brief

Do we shoot for ourselves or for our clients? Perhaps we should do both. You have been commissioned because of your style and your way of working, but it is essential in your planning to communicate with your client, the family of the child/children, to determine the look and feel. There still needs to be an empathetic appeal to your client – you have to be sure they will love the image as well as it moving you. There has to be emotional depth which goes beyond your own creative needs. Ask some questions. Which of your portraits have they seen in your portfolio that move them with regard to the overall feel? Do they have strong feelings about a particular location? Should there be a creation of a concept or subtle theme running through? Do they foresee the final product to be colour or black and white? Consider all this so that you can implement the other elements into the shoot. Remember that you are

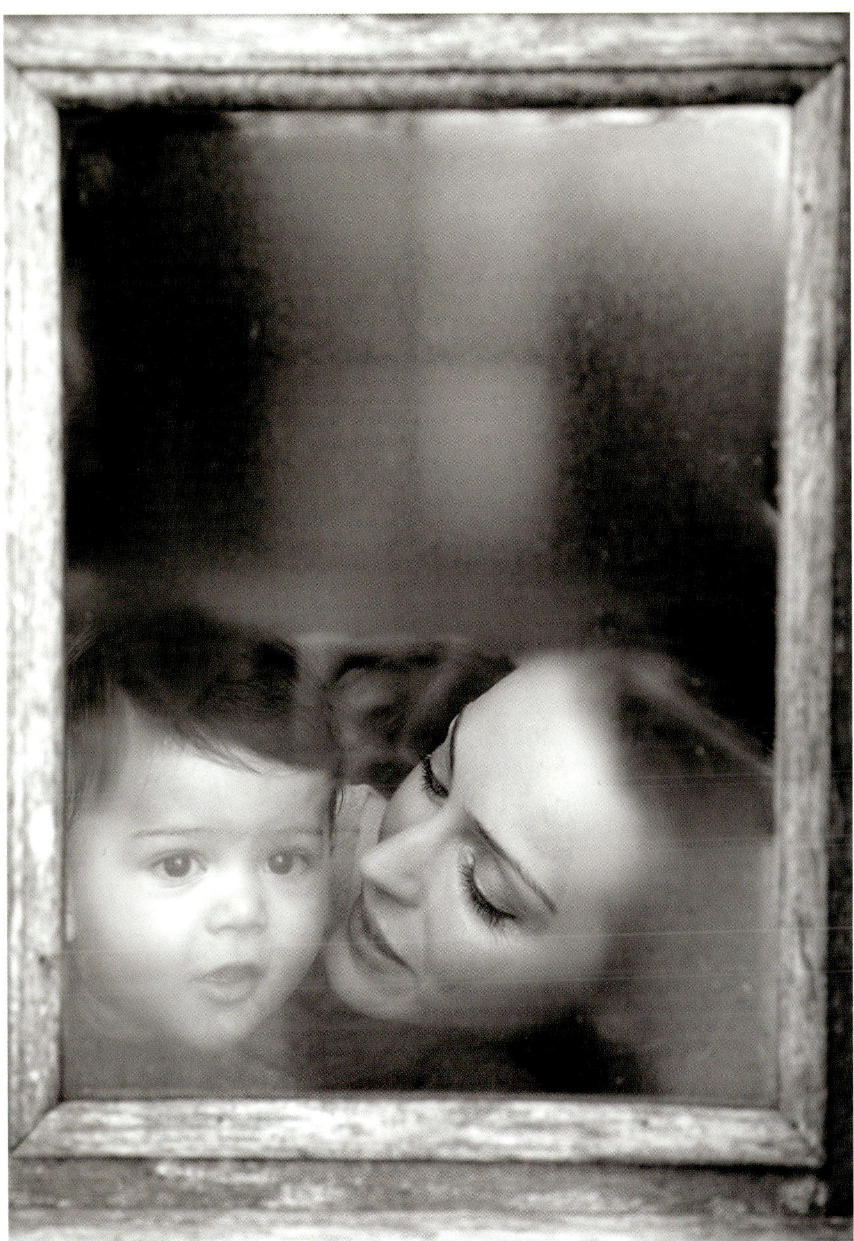

Fig. 3.10
Allowing mother and child space to interact in a natural fashion leads to sensitive, honest portraits. Don't feel you need to interact to gain a response – quietly observing and allowing a closeness to develop in front of you can be as, if not more, powerful.

the artist and, although it is important to work with your clients, they are often happy to be led by you. You may find that the client doesn't know what they want and will give you complete creative licence. You will need to discuss timing, clothing, location and so on with them. Bear in mind that children often like to choose their own clothes (first lesson in photographing children: don't question a ten-year-old's fashion ideas!). As much as possible, try to keep the look and feel in keeping with the location choice and overall aesthetic of the final portrait. If there is a particular symbolism that is to be introduced into the final images, incorporate relevant clothing or, to a degree, props in order to fit in with this.

From a commercial point of view, when photographing a family unit, factor the requirements of the extended family into your shoot too. Offer the family a fairly broad spectrum of choice. For example, if you are photographing two children and a mother and father, mix up the combinations, i.e. children together, parents individually with each of the children, and so on.

Remember, you are the professional, you are being paid to create something very special for your client, so you need to take control and use your ideas and knowledge to implement something wholly bespoke and to the best of your ability, with your style firmly stamped on it – your client will expect this.

Clothing to Fit the Feel

Whether you are flirting with a theme, looking to implement uniformity or just want some cohesion in your portraits, some thought needs to be put into the clothing of the subject.

But be aware: children can be very particular about what they wear, at all ages, so encourage their involvement. If you are looking for a particular feel, you will want to have some input into what is worn in order to fit this.

The child's parents may also have certain ideas, so encourage them to join in the process. Be wary of anything too heavily themed in order to avoid it being a cliché (or having too strong a sense of era). A subtle theme running through will invite viewers to read their own story into the picture as opposed to it being very visually obvious. Allowing this 'tease' encourages viewers to create their own interpretation of the work, and that is what makes portrait photography interesting.

In Fig. 3.11, the girl's clothing and the location work together to create an organic feel. There is graffiti to the right – if she had been wearing perhaps jeans or something more contemporary then the pose and the overall effect would have been completely different (the photographer might

have chosen to use this in colour and approached the pose, placement and composition in order to sit with the narrative of the symbolism of the graffiti). As it is, the photographer has incorporated the lichen and texture of the wall as the canvas, the tunic and styling giving the location great depth. In this case the choice of clothing and the location have collaborated and given the image a timeless, inherent nature.

Encouraging your client to be led by you is not a luxury we all have. As commercial photographers, we don't always have the control to specify our particular ideas and dictate what the children should wear. This makes your development as a specialist all the more important – building a portfolio of images which defines you and your work as individual, thus enabling you to lead your clients towards imagery which is bespoke and within the range of your style, thus giving you control.

Slowing Down

A culmination of the elements of lighting, posing, great location, and most importantly your observation skills will in time give you the ability to anticipate when a great image is about to happen. Disciplining yourself to wait for it to occur will give you the satisfaction that you have created one beautiful image rather than ten mediocre.

The digital medium has enabled us to experiment and push our creativity in a way we perhaps couldn't do with film because of reasons of cost, although it has perhaps gone too far the other way and we sometimes take less care. The greatest satisfaction one has as a photographer is knowing that something special has been created by you and your subject, that you've made a connection. The camera is almost irrelevant with regard to the process – a middle man if you like, or simply data storage.

▶ Fig. 3.11
There is an organic feel to the location and the child's choice of clothing that is relevant to the overall aesthetic of this final image.

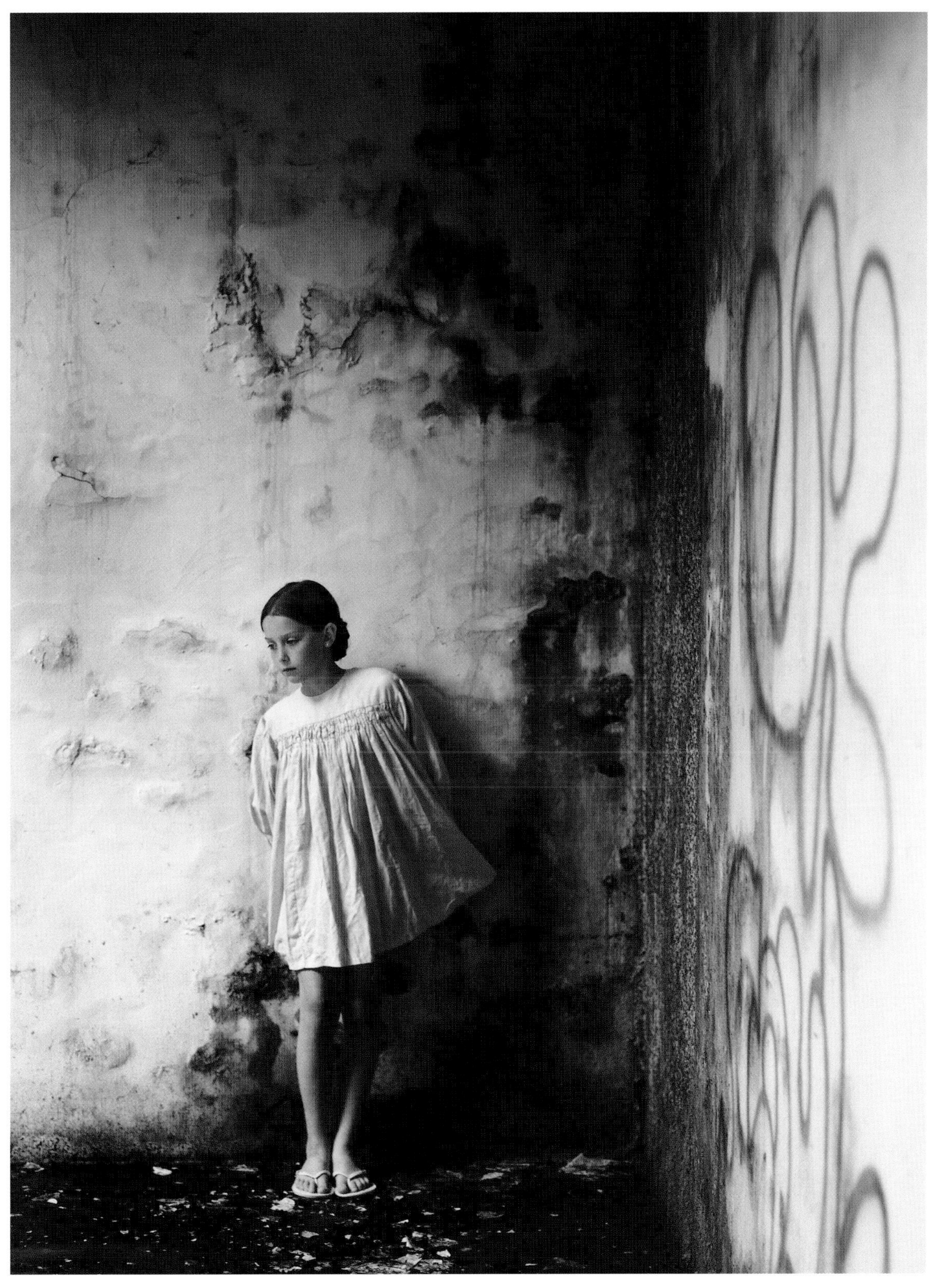

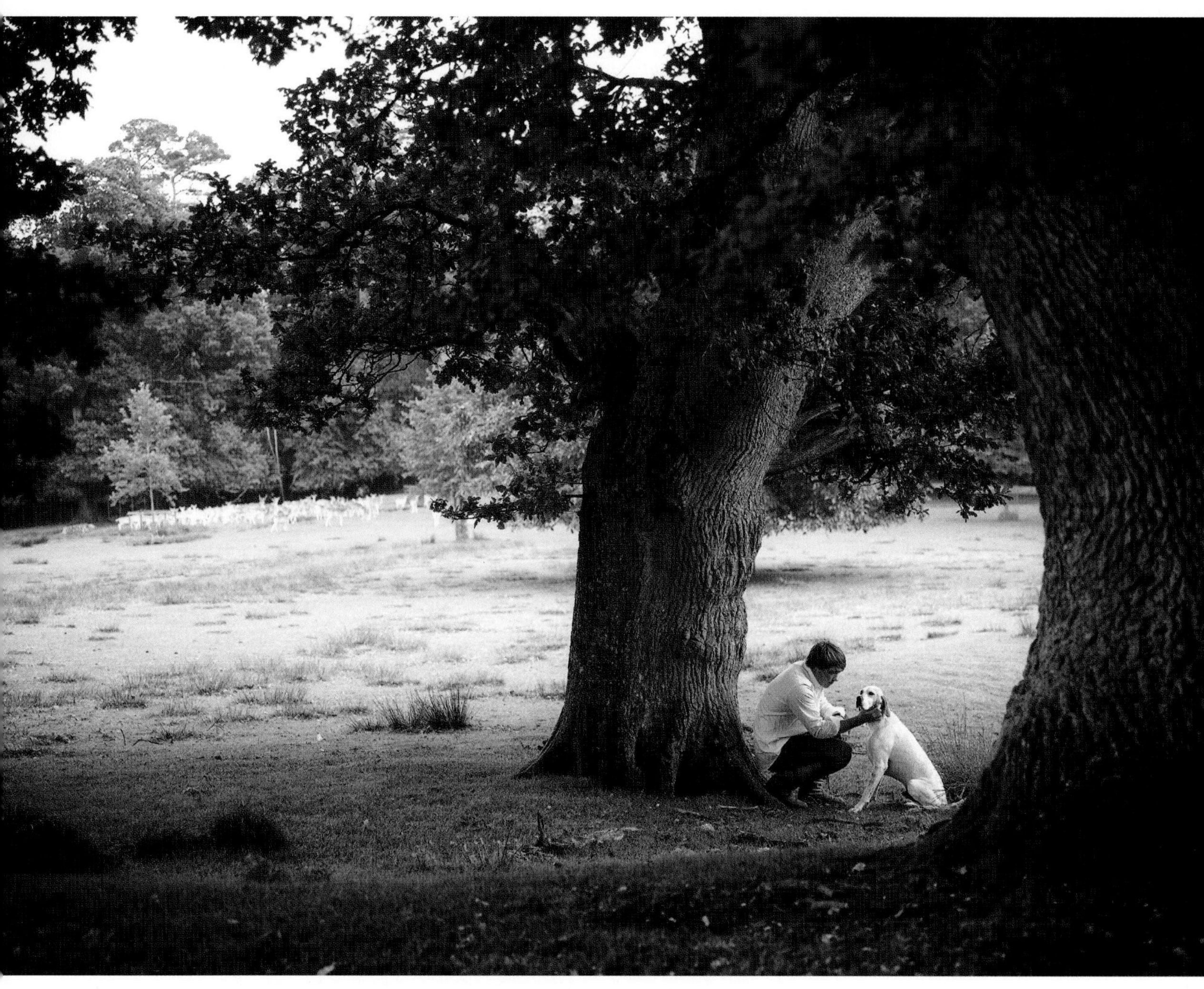

▲ Fig. 3.12
This young man and his dog were perfectly placed in a pocket of light with wonderful natural framing. He was then encouraged to spend time with the dog while the photographer moved away, this disconnection keeping the communication between the dog and his owner natural. Taking an almost voyeuristic approach, the photographer then developed the composition around them. Everything else was set and the photographer did not see a need to communicate further while the boy and dog were engaging.

Relying on automatic exposure is not always the most effective method of metering. Yes, it's quicker and you don't have to think, but the camera has no imagination or understanding of the type of portrait you are hoping to achieve so, as with any computer, we have to program it. We will talk about the building process of a portrait later in the book, but allowing ourselves to take some time leaves room for creative stimulation, to think and build rather than take multiple images.

This may take you out of your comfort zone, yet applying the rudimentary components of natural classical lighting on location, attending to the finer details of positioning and placement, and then pushing for something more that very much comes from you, takes time and consideration. By taking this time, you become a more efficient photographer, have a stronger connection with your subject, and have the chance to set your scene then sit back and decide where you would like to take it

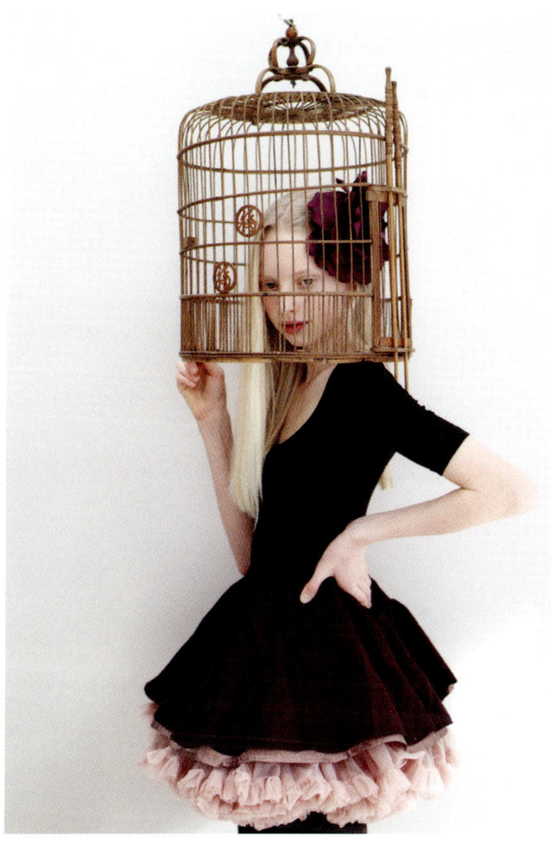

▲ Fig. 3.13
A statement piece, taking a portrait from something fairly ordinary, and retaining simplicity, to a dramatic portrait.

next. With small children, you often don't get that time, so having an idea in your head of where you would like to go with your portrait will mean you can work more effectively within their small period of concentration.

Waiting for that moment to come to you once you are positioned for the light, composing and recomposing, not taking your eye off your subject yet retaining an awareness of what is around you – all these things enable you to be more concentrated in your picture-taking, even if you are working in a more documentary style,

As part of a project, buy a film camera and a couple of rolls of film (film cameras can be picked up very cheaply on eBay). Shoot a personal project on film. If you don't have access to a film camera, cover

the rear monitor of your digital camera so that you're thinking more about what is happening inside the camera before you make your picture.

Concentrate on your metering, over- or under-compensating where necessary and bracketing for effect, and keep a note of your settings. This all sounds very old school but it is about slowing everything down and *you* doing the thinking rather than the camera. If you are using digital, check your settings when you download. It's a personal project, not a paid commission, so making mistakes is part of learning and understanding your camera. Without the crutch of being able to check the back of the camera, you will find that you concentrate more on your composition before you take your image.

Movement and Anonymity

Anonymity can be used as symbolism, to create discussion, or just to accentuate quiet contemplation.

To take a child's portrait to a comprehensive level, to stimulate emotional attachment, needs little more than imagination as well as a degree of boldness and conviction in your ideas. Possessing the fundamentals of good portraiture will give you the 'seed' to develop and spread creative wings.

Taking your work from being a perfectly acceptable and saleable portrait to a fine art piece requires you to look deeper into the emotive value of a picture. This can be enhanced by way of creating atmosphere through use of movement, yet retaining the cohesion (and graphic stability) of location, subject and light. There has to be conviction in the way you use movement – on a commercial level, an image which is just ' a little soft' or out of focus is just that. Out of focus. Unacceptable. Movement needs to be definitive and contribute something to the image, such as animation, graphic, storytelling and a strong sense of atmosphere. This can be done through following a moving child (panning) or with subtle movements introduced to add just a tease of movement.

▶ **Fig. 3.14**
A portrait's power if not just through the subject's eyes. Using anonymity can invite the viewer to create their own story – combined with strong composition, this can be very powerful.

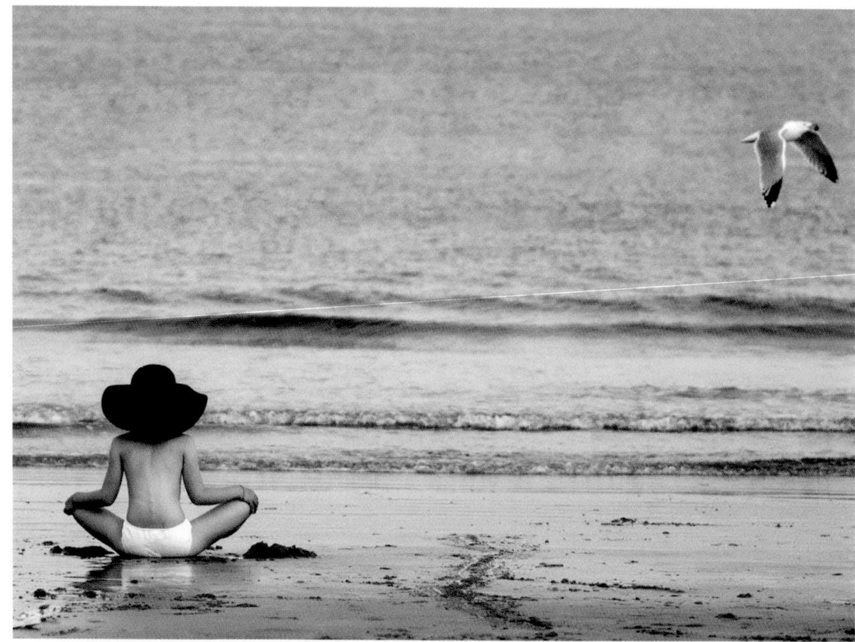

▶ **Fig. 3.15**
Movement is also a powerful accessory to lift an image in order to add feeling, curiosity or just to animate a portrait. In this image, the movement works cohesively with the written message to give a feeling of freedom and the carefree world of a child.

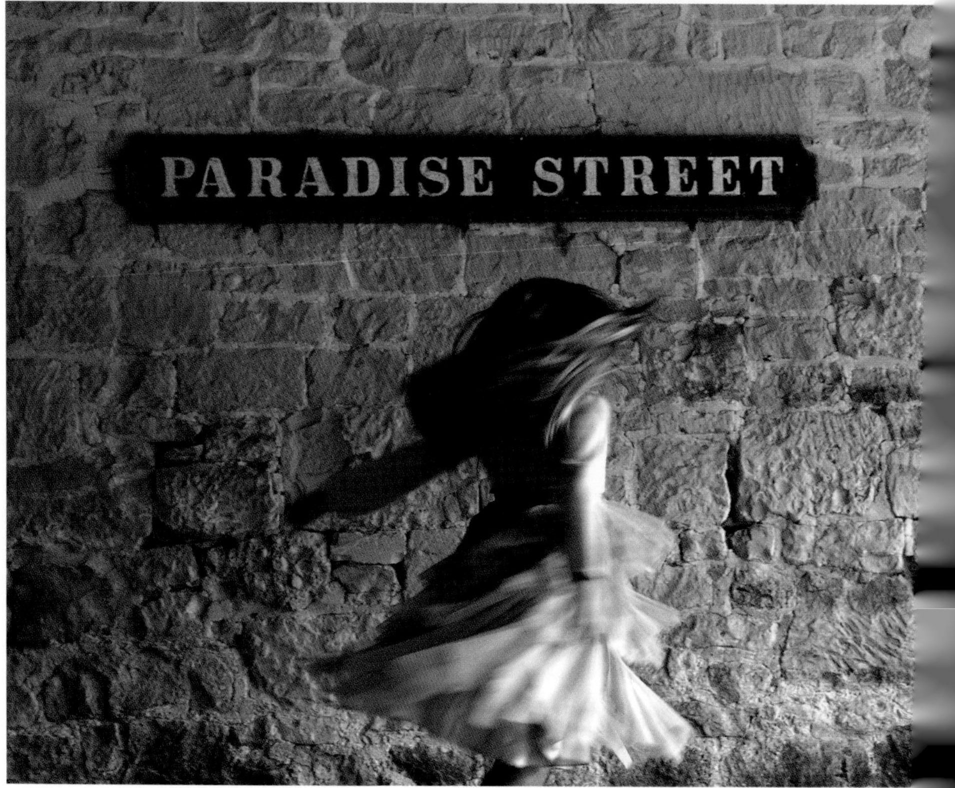

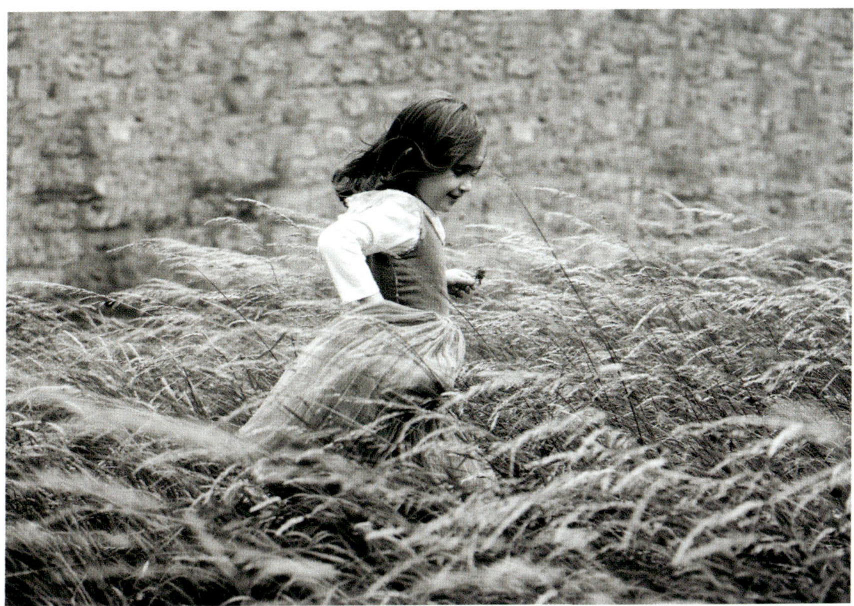

SUBTLE MOVEMENT

The natural framing of the background arch could have been utilized for the placement here, but that would risk a clash between the two main elements of the architecture – the arch and the leading line of the pillars to the left. In order to keep the focus on the child the placement is off-centre so the eye goes from the subject to the lines leading out. The shallow depth of field has diffused the arch so, although it adds an aesthetic contribution, it's neither dominant nor distracting. The pillars, sharp in the foreground, fall off, leading the eye to the arch. The first thing you see is the child: she is the most important part of the image and then the story around her. This is a typical scenario where an element has to be removed, in this case the dominance of the arch.

Once the scene is set we can then think about lifting the image with subtle movement. We could afford to use extreme movement, but in this case it's more gentle, focusing on the face but asking her to move the dress a little. If she had wanted to move, dance or be more animated that would have been fine; because she is within a lovely pocket of light, anything goes, as does the opportunity for creative interpretation.

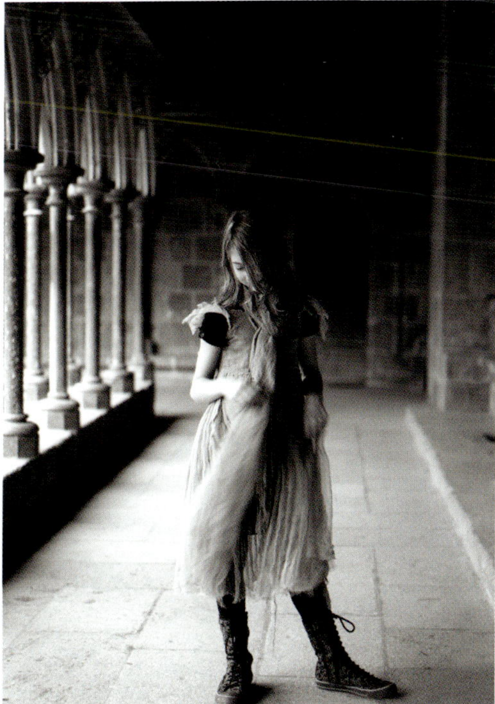

▲ Fig. 3.17

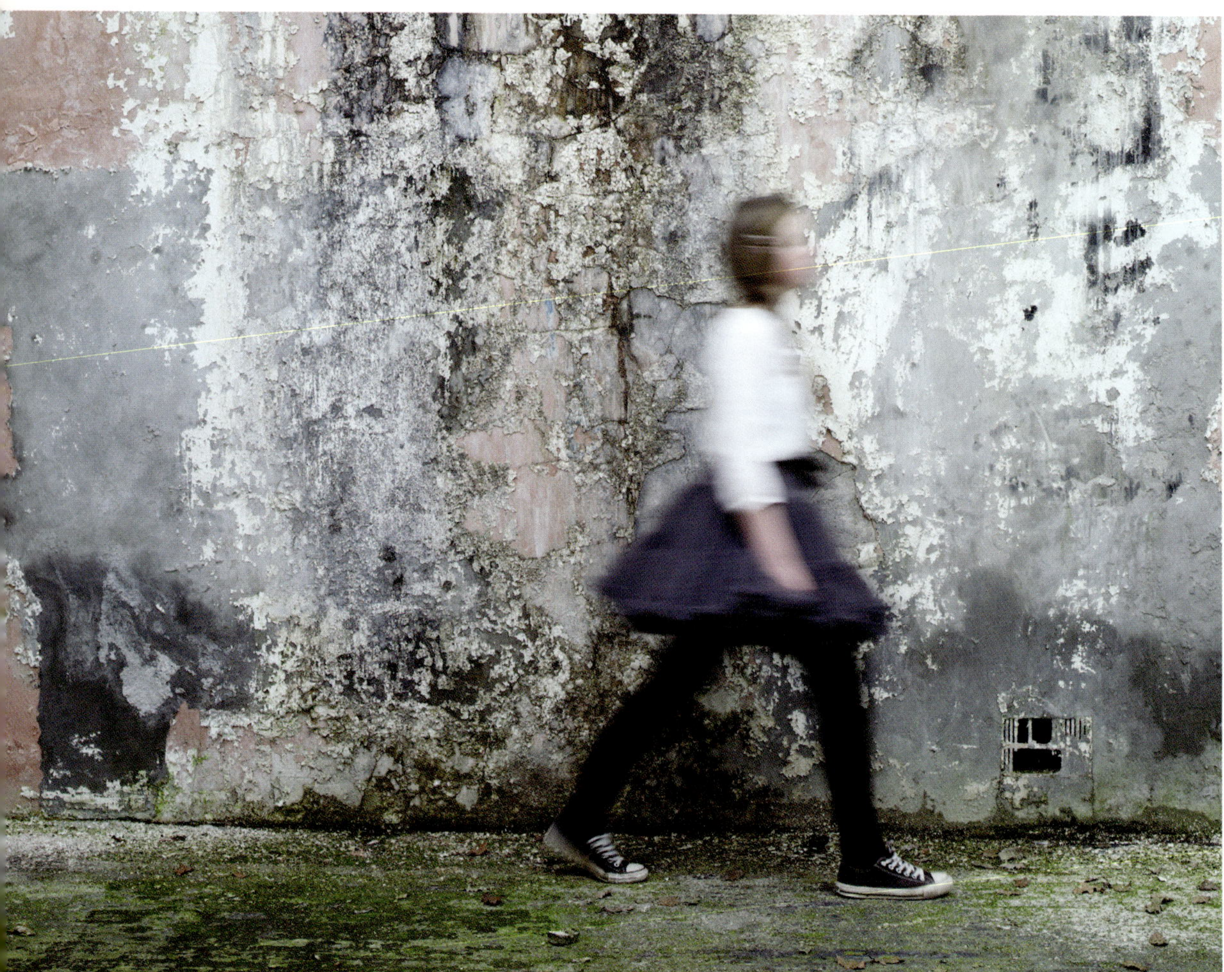

▲ Fig. 3.18
Creating harmony between the colours of the distressed wall,
the clothing and the skin tones of the model. Being aware of the
colour palette available gives you options to incorporate your
subject with the background. In this case the photographer has
kept the texture sharp and vibrant while keeping the colour theme
simple, then added contrast through the use of movement. It would
be a perfectly acceptable image had the model been sharp, but
adding movement has given this portrait a strong aura. In fact the
movement could be further accentuated, but the colour will always
blend with the background. That gives the image anonymity.

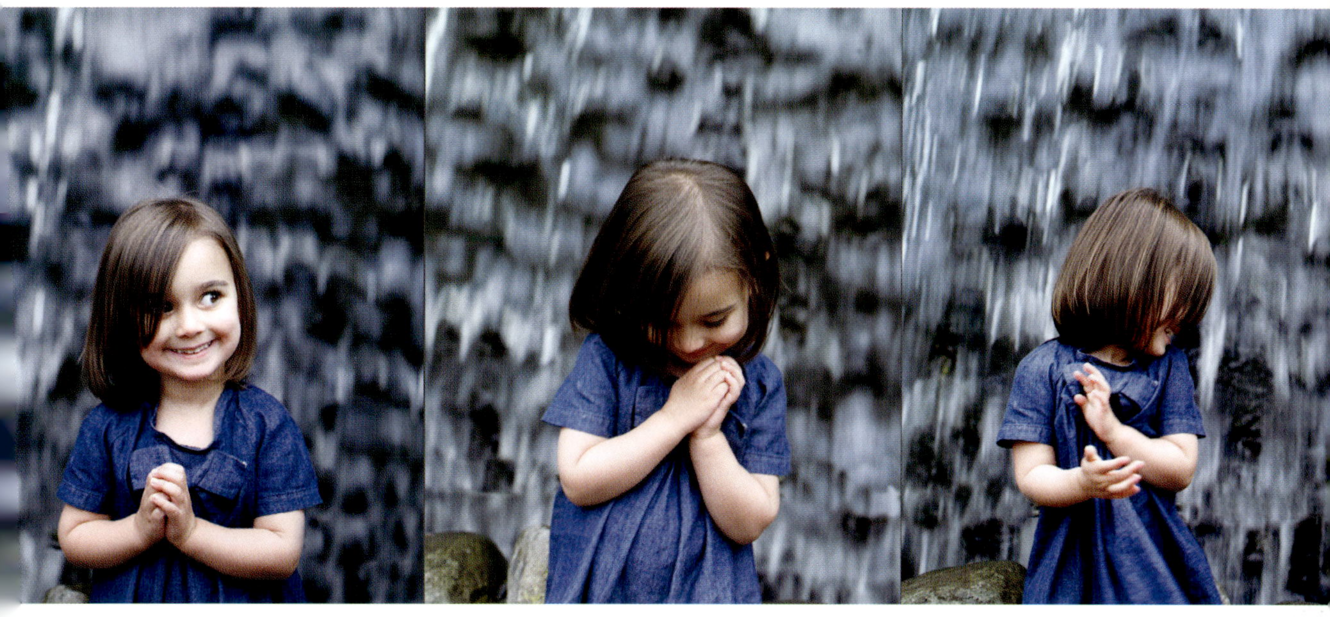

▲ Fig. 3.19
The emphasis here on the little girl, but movement from the waterfall behind her is incorporated: a shutter speed of 1/40sec, but remaining sharp on the face.

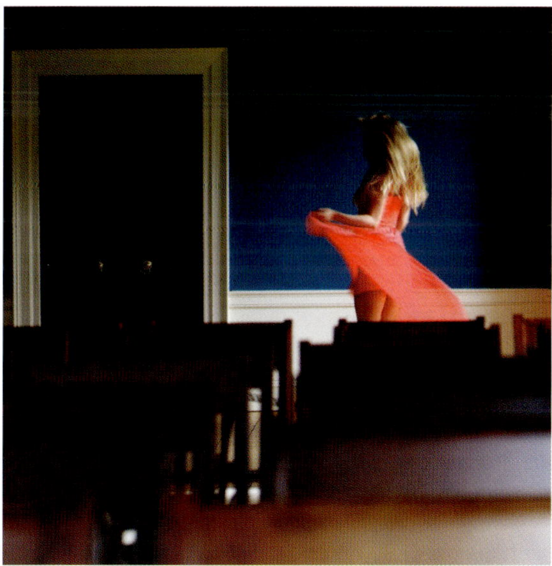

▲ Fig. 3.20
This picture takes a less obvious approach. The factors that make up this image are fundamental to its impact; the final process is the purposeful placing of the face in the shadows.

In Fig. 3.20, the obvious placement would be to use the pool of light by the blue wall, which would give a perfectly acceptable portrait, classic by design. This quality of light is your seed. What you do around this is allow the image to grow branches. So, first of all, the photographer has moved away from the subject and looked at alternative compositions, using the chairs as the leading line into that light. A shallow depth of field (f4) has not made the chairs dominant but acts as an accent to the main part of the image, similar to natural framing. The photographer could have taken this at f11, creating more detail in the chairs and a stronger line rather than a soft framing, but perhaps didn't want the chairs to be dominant. Perhaps the photographer did both (and this is where digital comes into its own: experimentation). These are the choices we can make when working on the hoof. A photographer should always be using his or her observation skills to pinpoint colour and allow it to work in harmony with the location and bring cohesion. The primary colours here work well, as does the richness in the wood. So compositionally this works. The photographer has then pushed for movement in the colour, bringing the elements together.

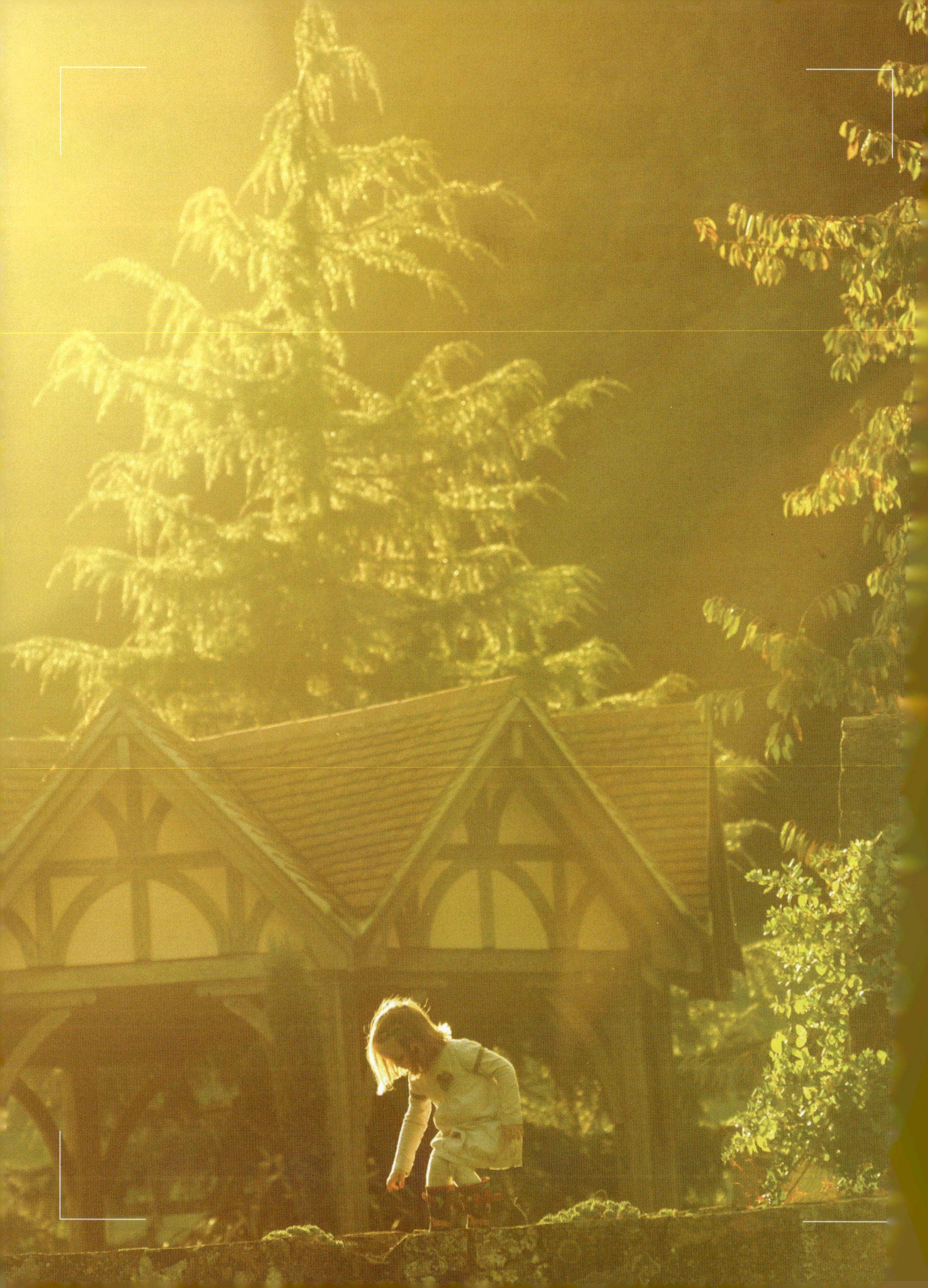

Location

A great location is a canvas to build on. It can be a significant factor in determining the overall feel of the final collection of images: a dominant feature in your portrait or a subtle accent to quietly embellish.

We mentioned observation skills earlier with regard to finding inspiration – this applies to watching for potential locations. Look for areas in everyday life which perhaps aren't the most obvious. For example, a stately home such as a National Trust property offers wonderful opportunities for incorporating great architecture, sculpture and landscape. Sometimes, however, the most wonderful images are taken in the most ordinary places. Working in small areas of a client's home can be testing, with perhaps not the most aesthetically pleasing of backdrops, so being able to source locations for the best light is important, as is being observant to the possibilities of an area.

Portraits shot in the natural environment are taken around the world, in the form of editorial or documentary photography, fashion shoots or even holiday snaps. Don't just stick to what is considered a suitably obvious location or deemed as the norm. If you have an understanding of light and how it can lift a location, you will find opportunities for artistry all around you. Sometimes it's useful to look beyond the immediate area as a wide open space; target perhaps a wall, look at the way grain and texture appears on some sleepers, or choose a plain wall if the way the directional light falls on it is attractive. The location needs to fit the feel of the image you have in mind – or indeed, it can decide this for you.

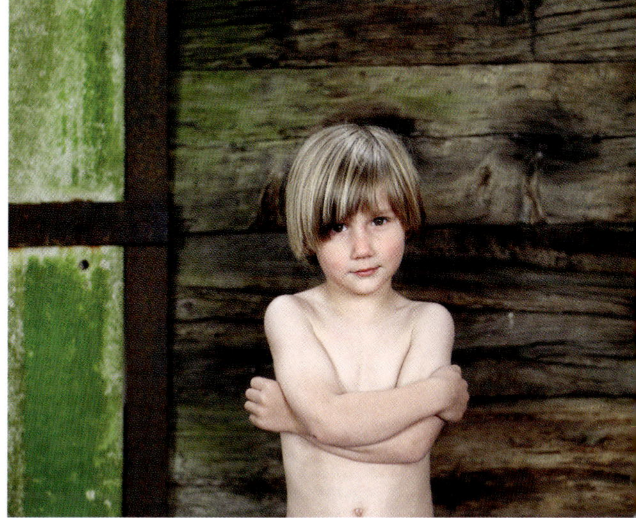

▲ Fig. 4.1
A great location doesn't have to be opulent or visually impressive. It is made strong through the way that you interpret it.

Utilize texture, colour/tonal range, how the light falls on an area, graphic, natural framing. If you like the look of a location, revisit it at different times of day. If it's outside and south-facing, the light may well be too strong at midday but quite beautiful late afternoon. In contrast, an interior window which is south-facing may need that strength of light coming in in order to illuminate the room as you wish. When viewing locations, walk around the area to see the various angles that could be shot, not just the most obvious. Could you shoot through doors or foliage into the room or area to give a stronger dimension to the image? Could you incorporate colour and does this give you ideas about clothing?

Your clients may have particular ideas as to where they would like the shoot to be done: maybe at

◀ Fig. 4.0
A location is only as good as the light within it.

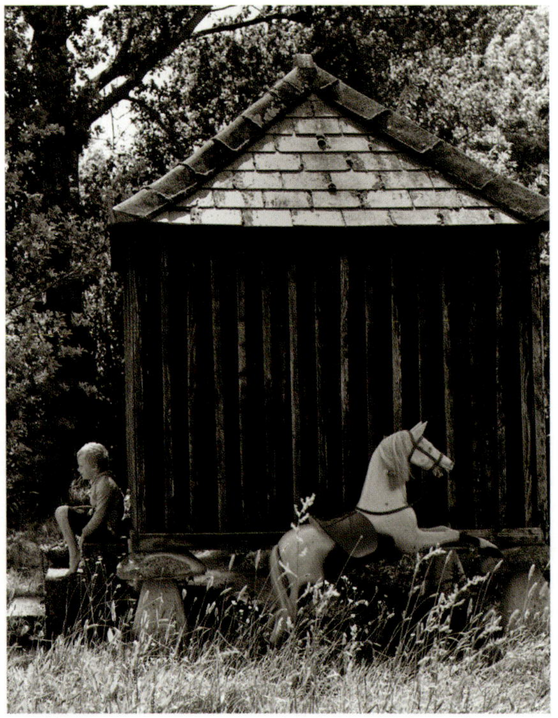

▲ Fig. 4.2
Consider the ages of the children when selecting locations and advise your client accordingly – a teenage boy may not want to be photographed in field of cow parsley!

You may, however, be given free rein to choose the location yourself. Take into consideration the age and gender of the children. For example, a thirteen-year-old girl may be happy to be photographed in a soft, backlit poppy field, but a thirteen-year-old boy may prefer somewhere more edgy or industrial; choose somewhere with a strong graphic element rather than flowers! If working with a teenage brothers and sisters, you may want to select a more 'universal' location to suit all ages and tastes, such as the beach.

There really is no excuse for not finding the ideal location, wherever you find yourself in the world. Whether it's in an inner city, a housing estate, a rural area, there is always light and there will always an area that can be interpreted into something special. It just takes a little imagination, keen observation and sometimes the ability to focus on a small section rather than a large area.

The Client's Home

There are times when you will struggle to find the space, suitable light, and a clutter-free zone. Be led by the light and if you need to move furniture then don't be afraid to ask. You may need to be creative with composition and placement, but occasionally we have to put creativity to one side and concentrate on getting a pleasing, safe portrait. If you are in a location which you are finding challenging, ensure you find an area which has a little space for your subject to move position, for example some window light.

Clients often request that their children's portraits are taken in the family home and garden. Your ability to adapt and see things which are not aesthetically obvious is key.

The Beach

If you are fortunate to live near a beach, you will understand the wonderful organic essence that it can bring to an image, in all seasons. You may find you have to battle with crowds in the height of summer

home, or perhaps in a place that is special to them as a family. If you are not confident or want to plan in more detail, carry out a recce of the home so that you can plan your shoot around where the light is at a given time of day. It will also encourage you to think about how you can compose the images, and give you a little time to consider the best options. Having this in mind is a guide, but remember that goalposts get moved constantly and you must be prepared to adapt. The light changes, small children can have their own agendas, and you need to be open to new ideas. Another matter to consider when arranging times with your clients is that they may have very small children who still need to nap in the day. Plan the shoot around when they are at their most alert and responsive – and not hungry!

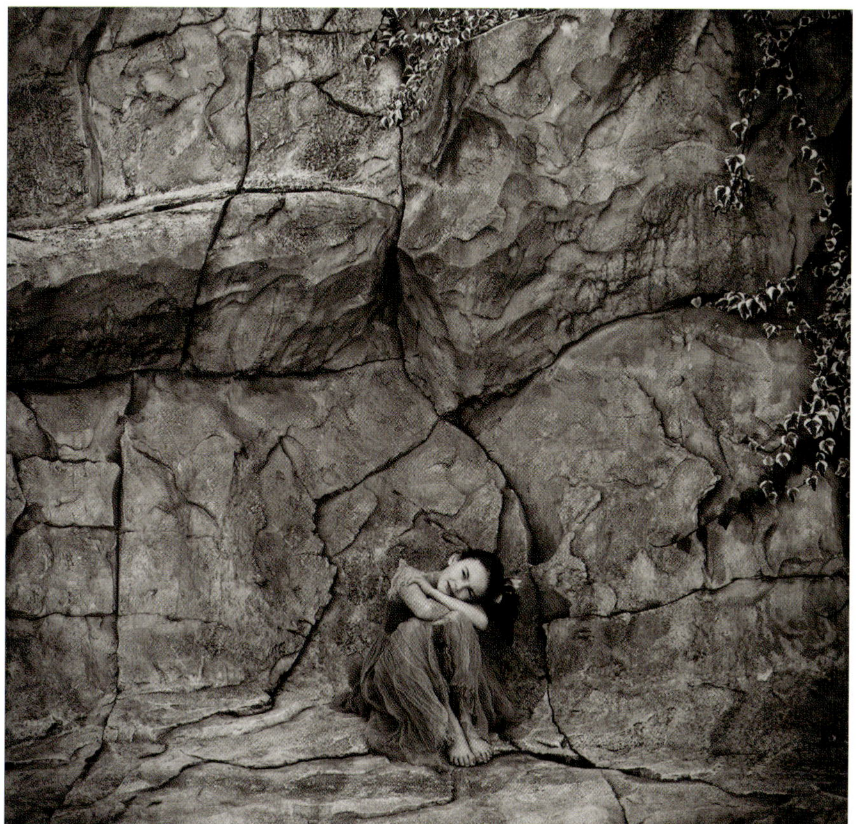

◀ Fig. 4.3
Use the natural forms
available to you on a beach
along with wide open spaces
to encourage children to
be completely relaxed.
The result will be carefree,
nostalgic images.

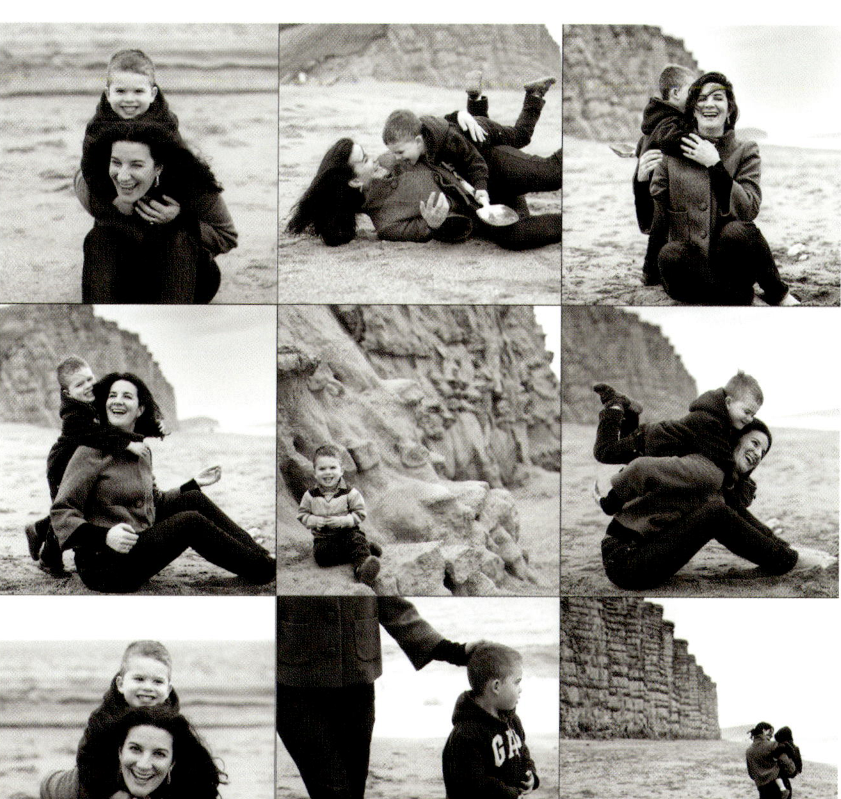

◀ Fig. 4.4
Taking advantage of a
deserted beach in winter.

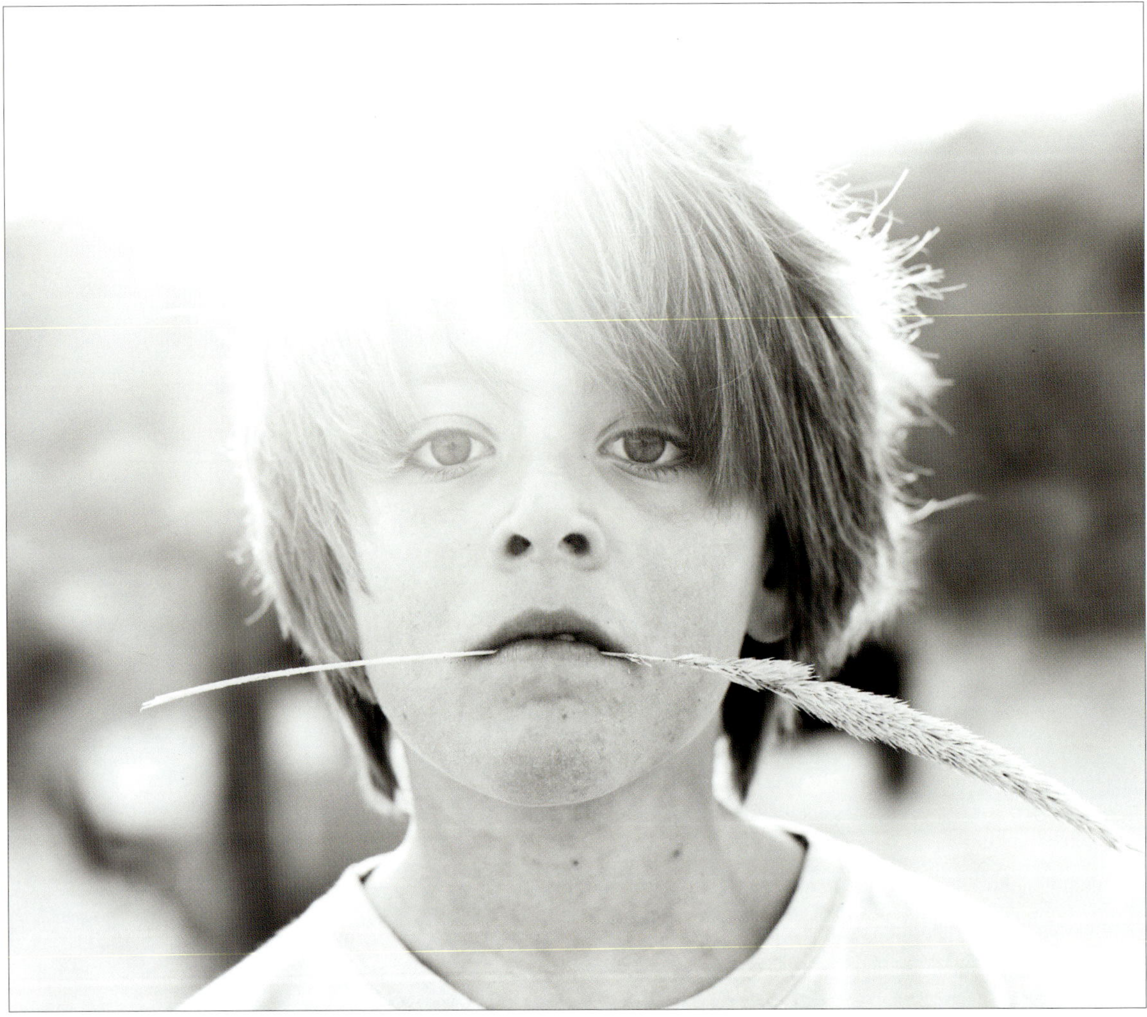

▲ Fig. 4.5
Soft evening light on the beach.

– all the more reason to arrange an early morning or evening session. However, in winter the beach really comes into its own, with soft muted tones offering endless opportunities for images that are wholly natural in their aesthetics but, more importantly, where children seem to find their wild side.

Gaining Permission

Using private property without permission is not only rude, but it can cause embarrassment between you and your client if you are asked to leave (not to mention potential health and safety risks). It is also unprofessional – imagine someone entering your own property without your knowledge. You will find most people generous in allowing you to use their land or buildings if you ask; do offer payment or perhaps a portrait in return. Some parks, the beach, woodland and common land are easily accessible, but if you want to use, for example, a National Trust property, it is advisable to ask and to perhaps make a

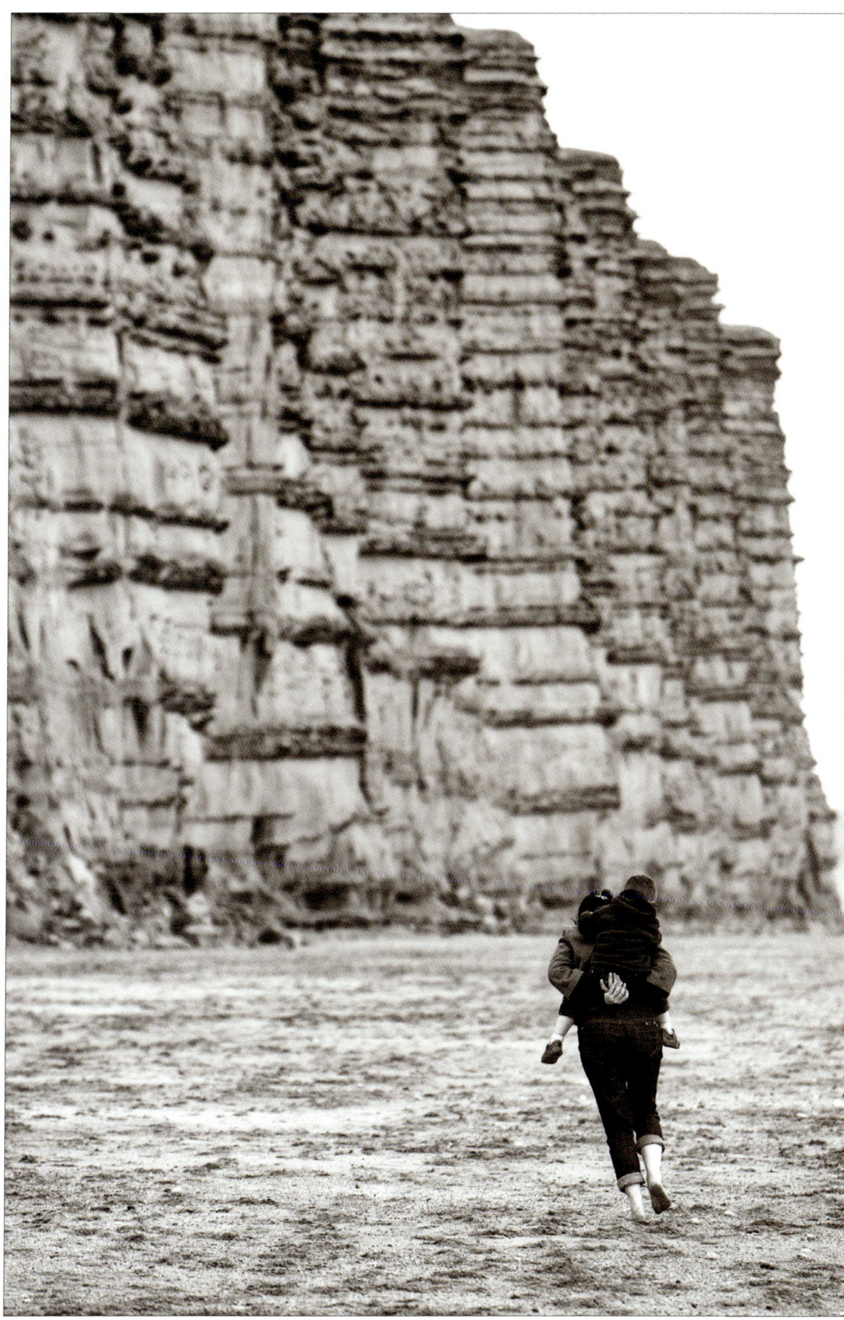

donation. Landowners are far more amenable if you approach them rather than assume you can enter their land for your own benefit!

You may not want to change where you shoot too regularly. If you find somewhere that works for you at a certain time of year, make it a regular site. It will save you time and you will become familiar with its creative possibilities and limitations.

SUITABLE BACKDROPS AND LOCATIONS

▼ Figs 4.7a–e

You will find locations all around you. Take some time to walk around your home town; look at specific small areas rather than 'a big picture'. Examples here include a fairly nondescript building with some wonderful foliage texture, part of a children's play area, and the lockers in an entrance to a Post Office.

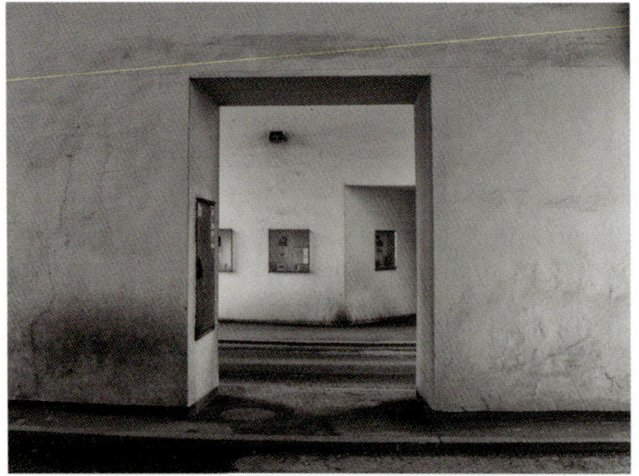

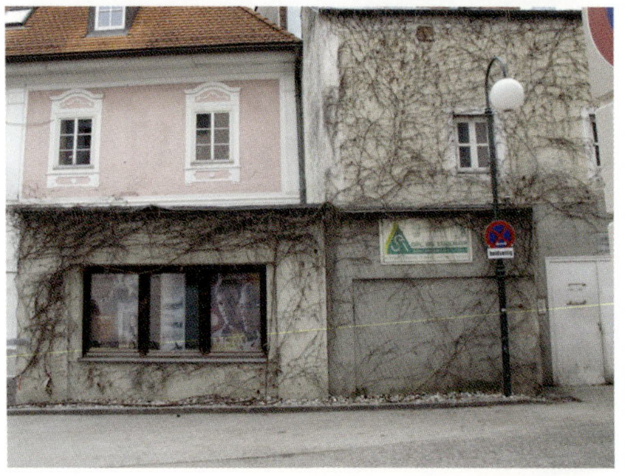

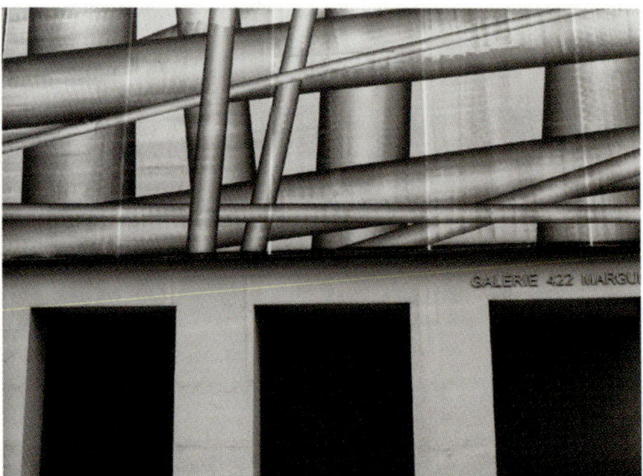

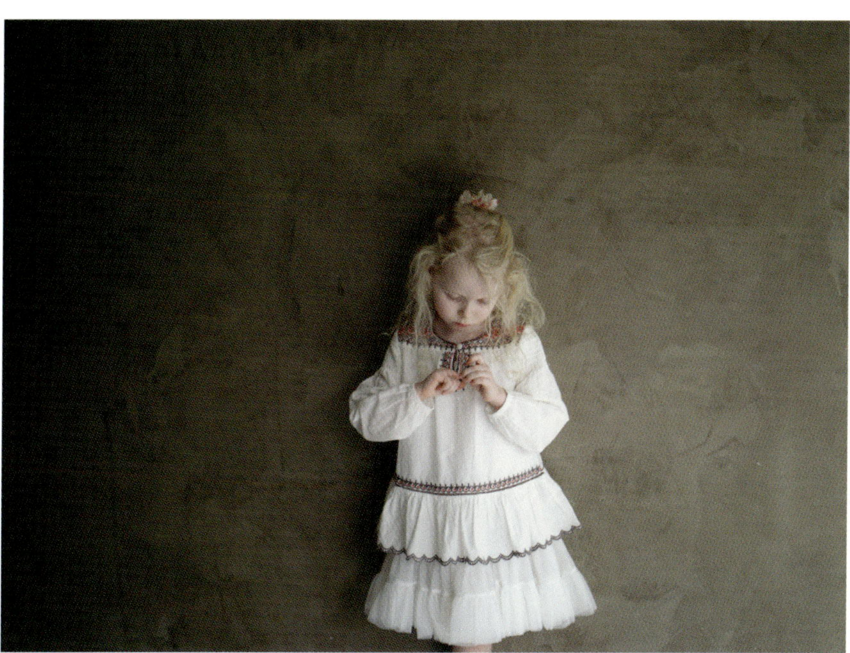

Fig. 4.8
A fairly insignificant wall, soft window light and a child embroiled in her own world. Note the colours and tones of the child's clothing and how they fit with that of the location. If she had been wearing bright clothing, this may not have worked so well.

Fig. 4.9
Given the quality of the light and tones, this image lends itself well to black and white with perhaps a tone. Notice how the texture of the wallpaper has been naturally enhanced in the black and white conversion.

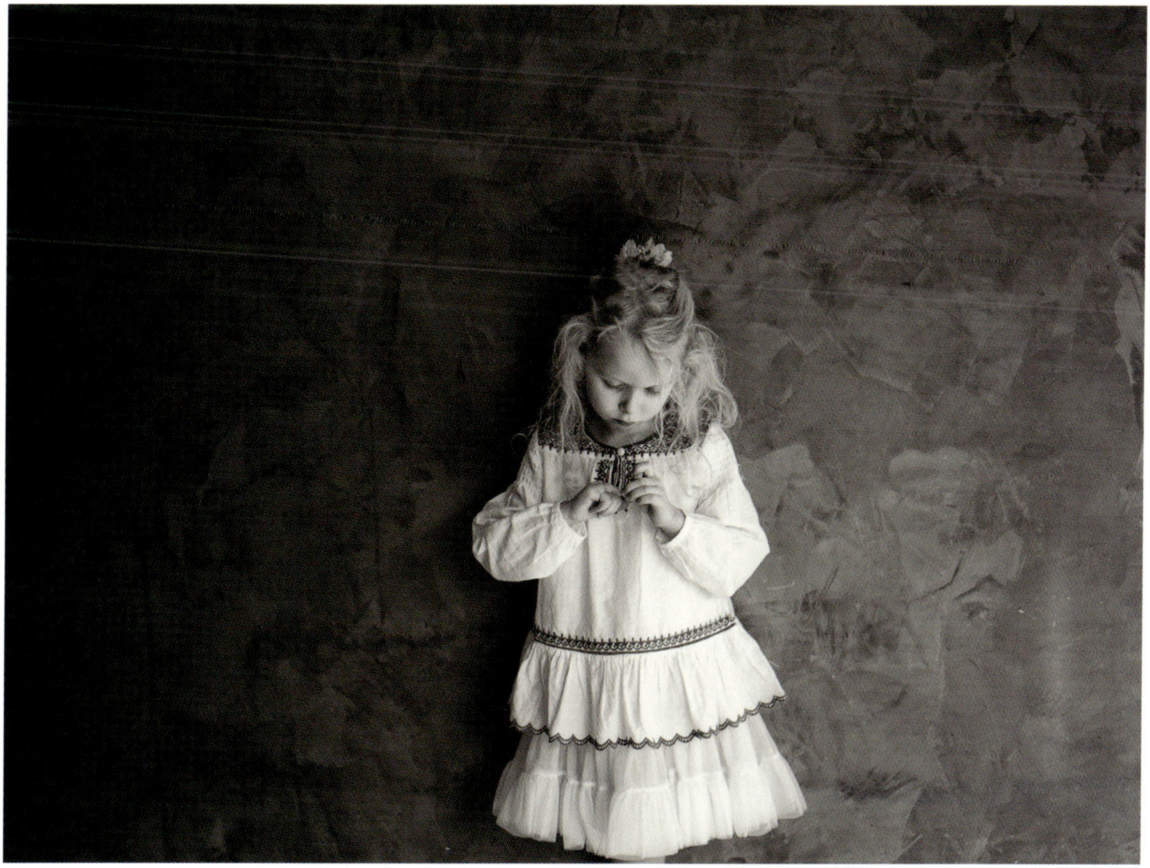

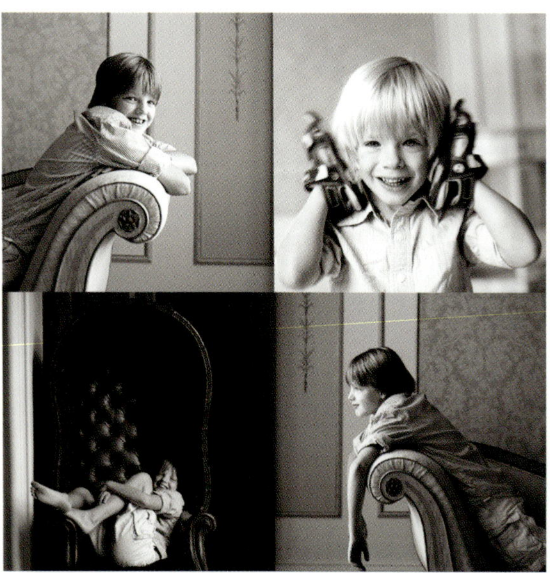

▲ Fig. 4.10
Portraits in the client's home offer familiar surroundings for children.

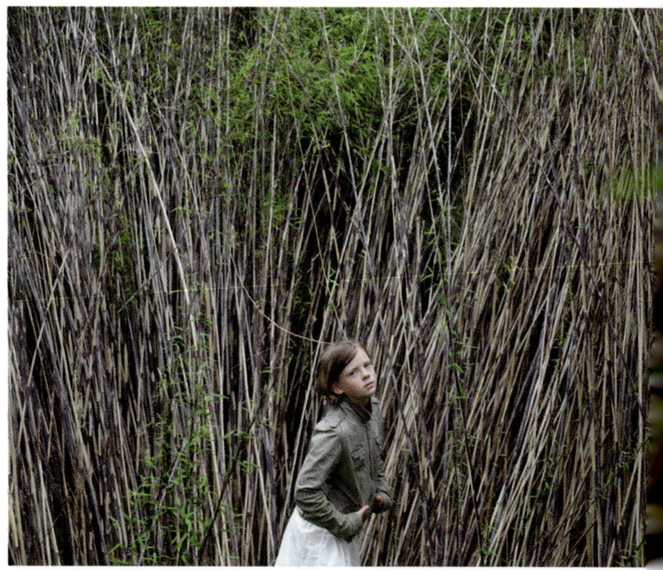

▲ Fig. 4.11a

Figs 4.11a–b
Using common land or having permission to use open fields is an invitation for children to enjoy the natural environment. Remember that in open spaces there may be no shelter or shade; here some bamboo has been leant against a hedge. The composition – placing the child in the bottom third – has given what could be quite an ordinary background some impact. Learn to visualize a graphic quality, i.e. this image location. It is fairly insignificant in colour, but a black and white conversion creates a dynamic, graphic portrait.

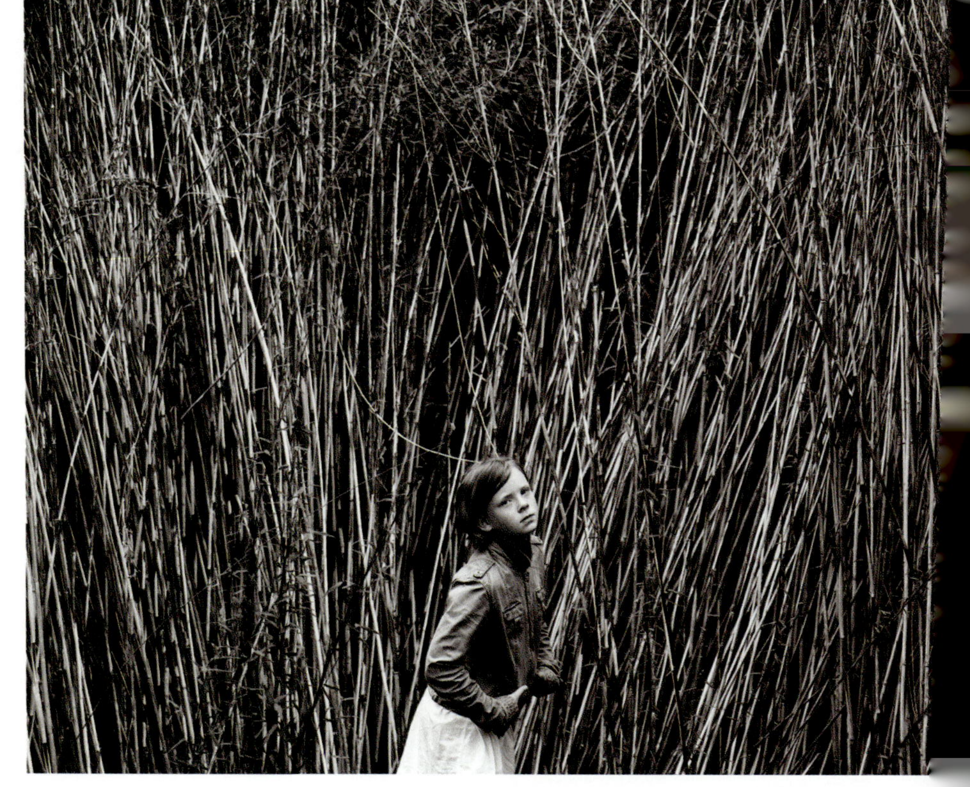

▲ Fig. 4.11b

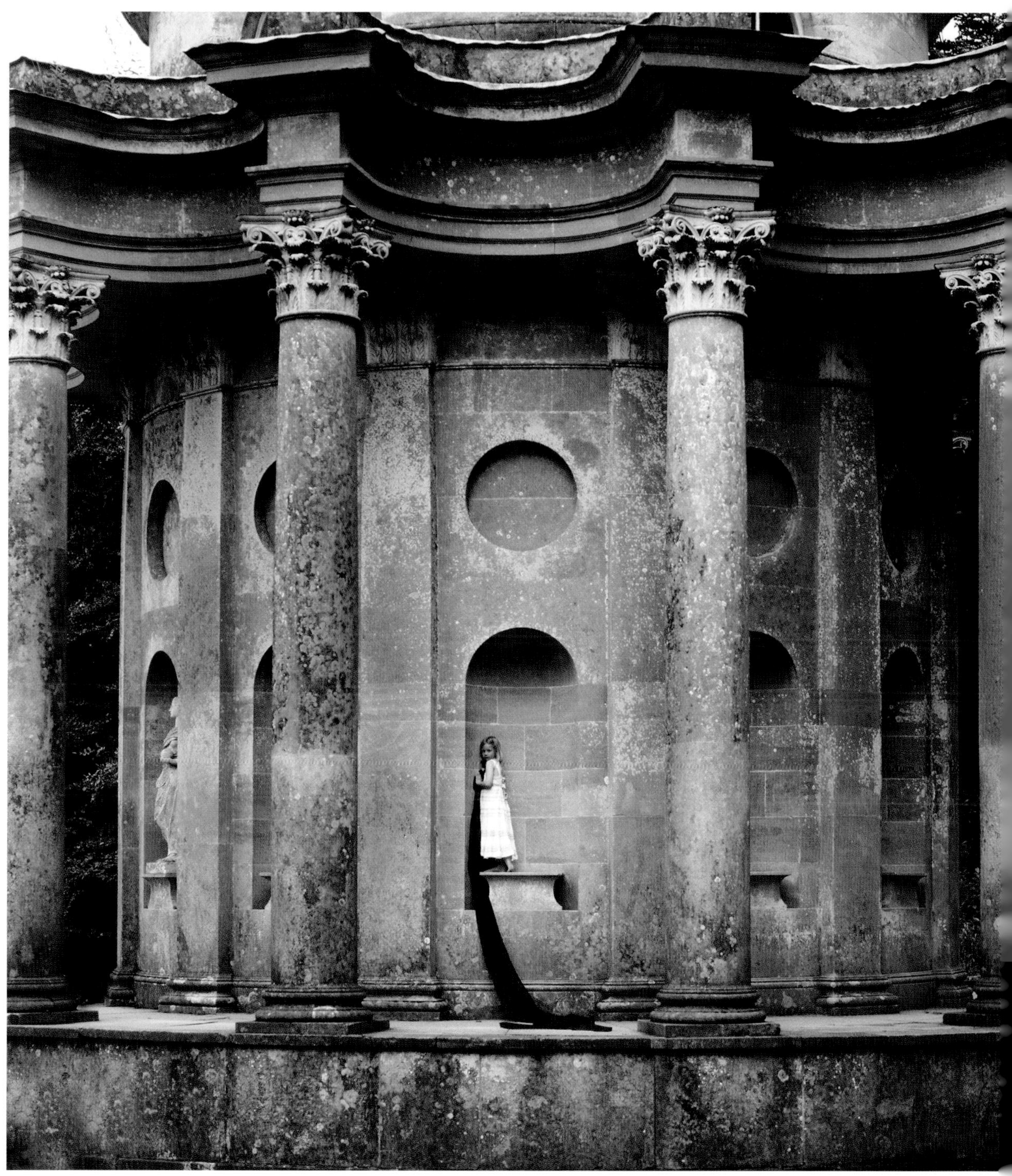

▲ Fig. 4.12
Permission was gained for this image to be taken in the beautiful
grounds of Stourhead, the National Trust property in Wiltshire.

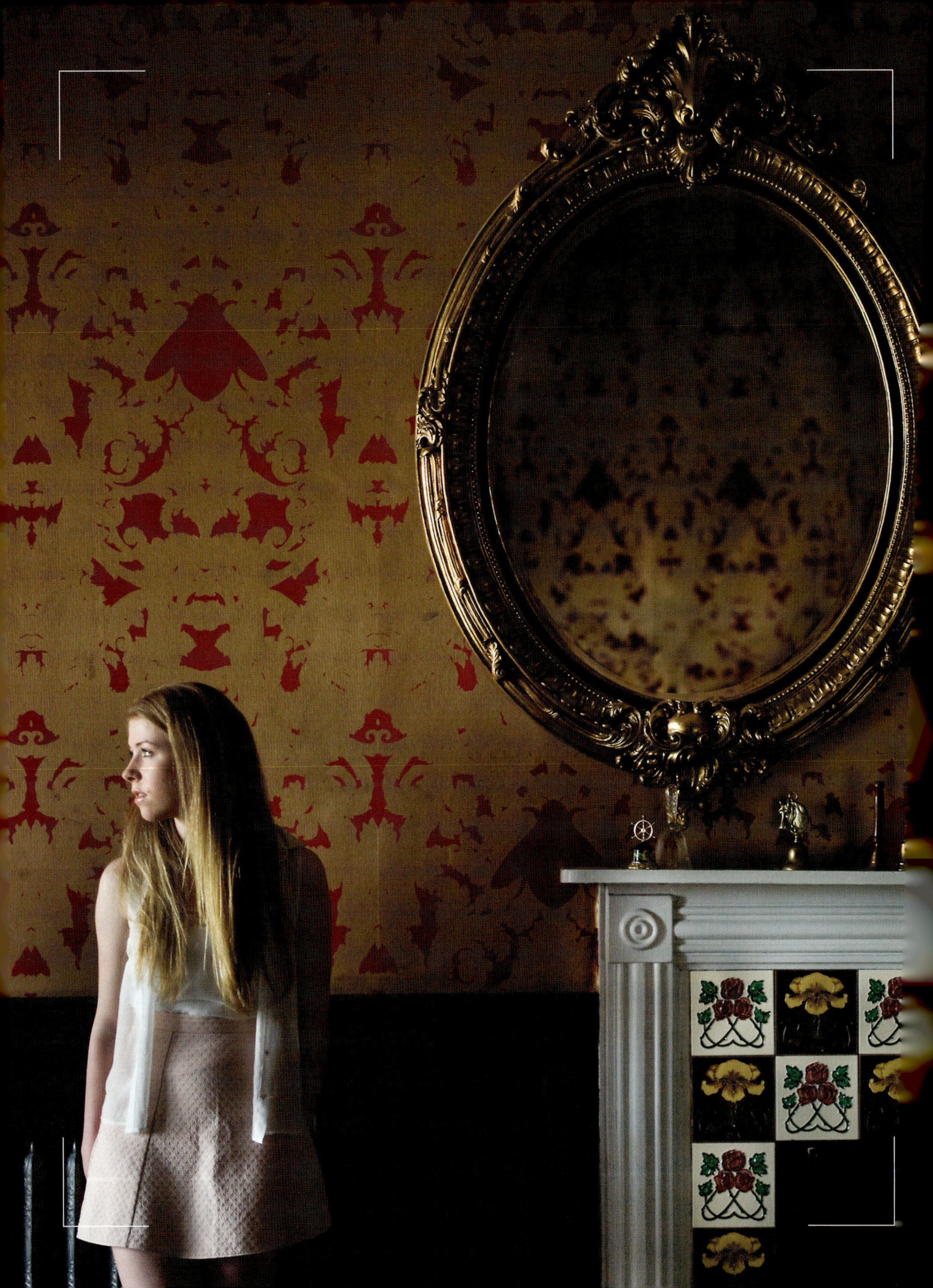

Timing and Natural Light Conditions

A portrait made wholly in natural light only becomes powerful through the quality of the light, as opposed to the brightness or quantity of it. Having a great backdrop is only as good as the time of day and the quality of that light. The given light needs to be used and controlled effectively in order to create atmosphere, graphic, ambience, emotion and energy – all the seeds of what makes great imagery. The time of day and the time of year (in the UK at least) should be major considerations in the planning of your shoot.

With our unpredictable climate, we can never totally be sure of getting the light or weather we planned for, and sometimes a change of tack or location, a moving of goalposts or perhaps playing safe are needed. Alternatively, it might be preferable to reschedule the shoot if the weather is bad. However, unpredictable weather can of course produce nuggets of wonderment, such as dramatic skies, incredible sunrises, frosty mornings, long low shadows – all of which we should embrace as natural additions to our work.

You may feel that the dark winter months are the most difficult to work in due to poor weather and darker days. On the contrary, winter brings with it some beautiful low light, low cloud, frosty mornings and snow, and can open the door to something very special and atmospheric throughout the day, in contrast to the harsh midday sun of summer.

But wherever in the world you are shooting portraits, the location and light will take on their own character as well as that of the individual photographer and that of the subject. Remember, light does not discriminate over location, so do not dismiss a location until you have seen what the light can do to it in the early morning, early evening, at midday, and so on.

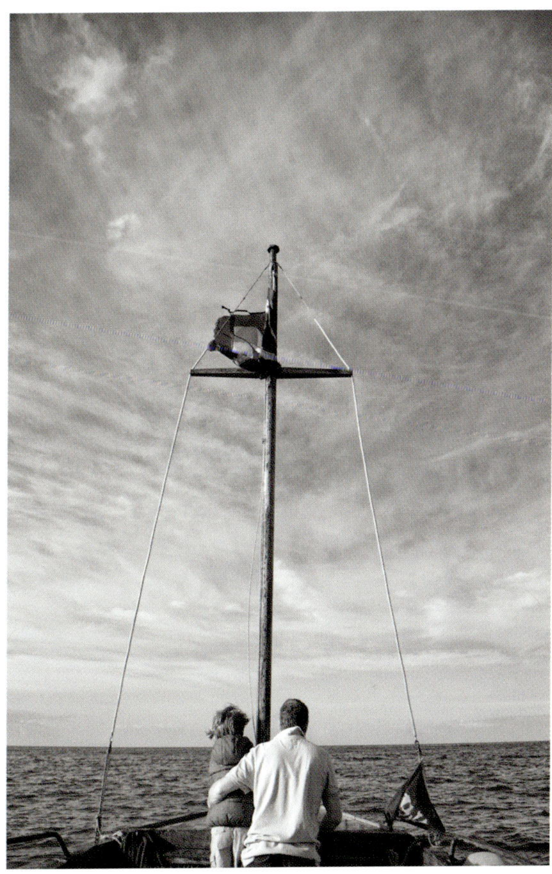

▲ Fig. 5.1
An early morning fishing trip – an unusual and fun adventure for a father and son – avoids the harsh midday sunlight.

◄ Fig. 5.0
Late evening, summer light. Window light may be more effective at certain times of day, coupled with considered placement.

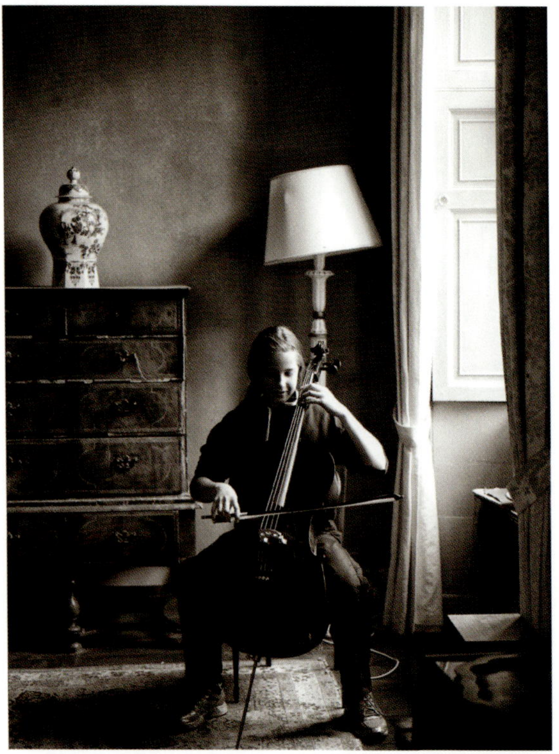

▲ Fig. 5.2a

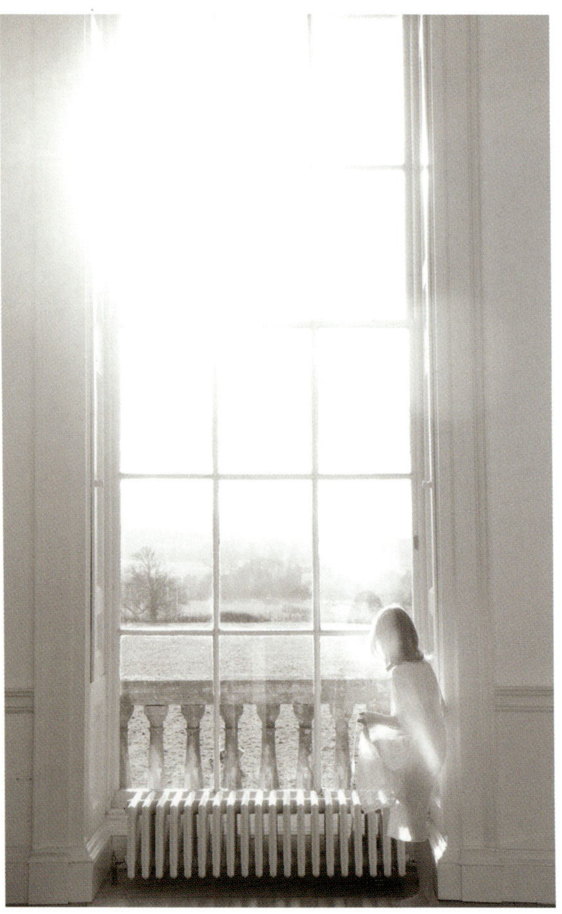

▲ Fig. 5.2b

Figs 5.2a–c
Fig. 5.2a is shot in beautiful soft window light, or you may choose to use flare as demonstrated in Fig. 5.2b, where the sun is low in the sky, enabling the photographer to enhance the atmosphere within the camera. This overexposure needs to look purposeful and not like a technical mistake. Fig. 5.2c, on the other hand, is more controlled, with the use of a reflector to lift the shadow detail. The background is purposefully overexposed somewhat to define the shape and detail of the child and so as not to detract from the subject; alternatively you could select to silhouette.

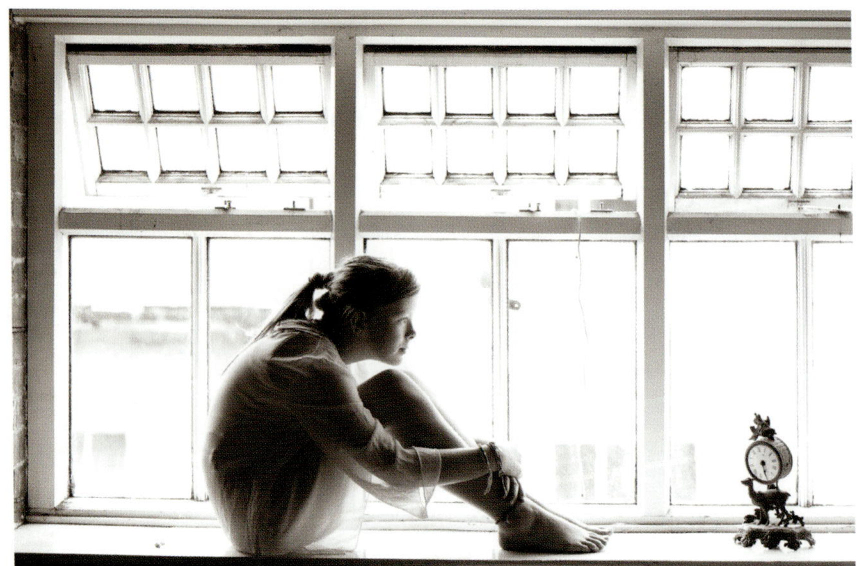

▲ Fig. 5.2c

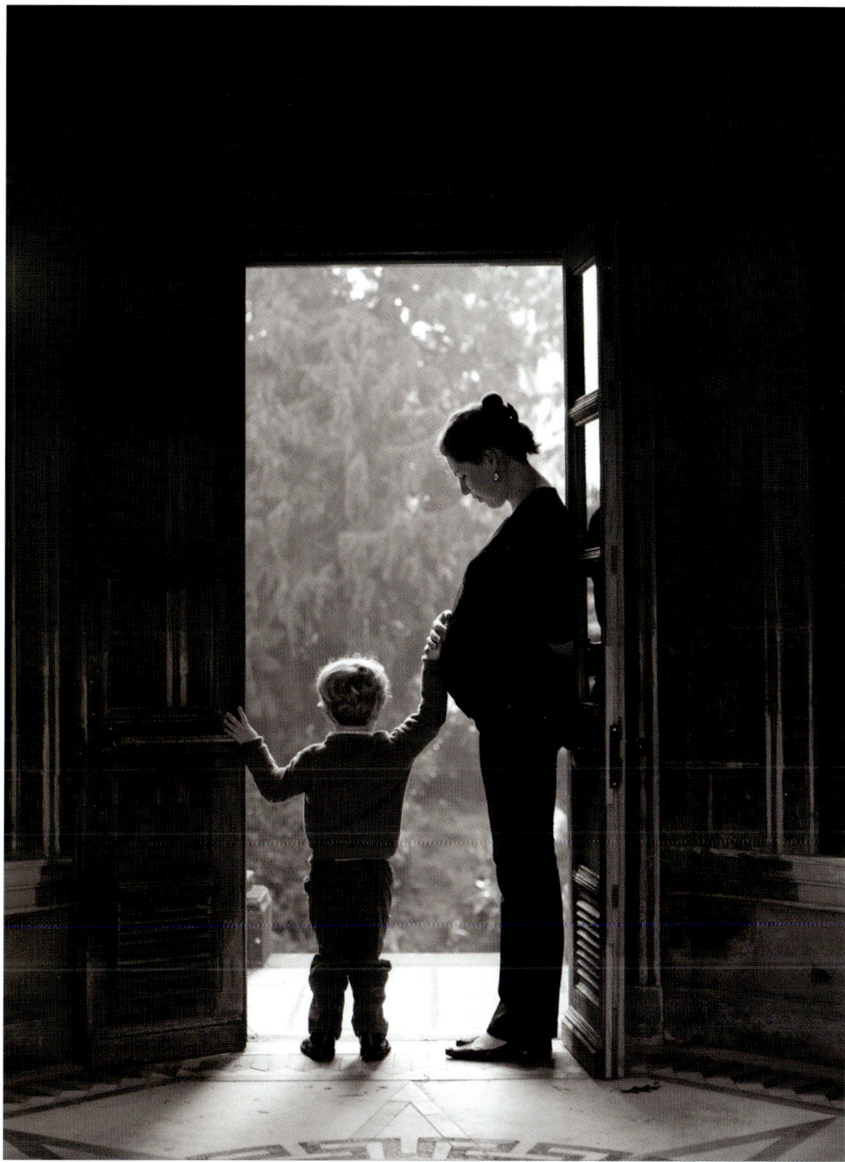

Fig. 5.3
The background is balanced with the inside through the use of a reflector light being thrown into the building from outside, as well as added bonus light being bounced from a white marble floor. Placement of the subject is also significant here, ensuring a flattering rim light around the subjects and retaining detail in the hair.

Window Light

Working in a client's home can often be restrictive if you're trying to find the perfect aesthetic backdrop *and* great light. Using a capsule of window light can often save the day. Despite whatever chaos is surrounding the area, recognizing small areas or pockets of light will ensure you can take a beautiful portrait almost anywhere in someone's house. In this scenario, watch the sun as it shines into the room through the window you are hoping to use. If it is too strong, use a Lastolite diffuser to dampen the harshness. Remember, as with any light source, the further away from the window you place your subject, the softer the light – ideally you are looking for that lovely softness that skims across the subject. And taking the shot from various angles will give you the opportunity to use the light effectively and with variation within one location. When there is

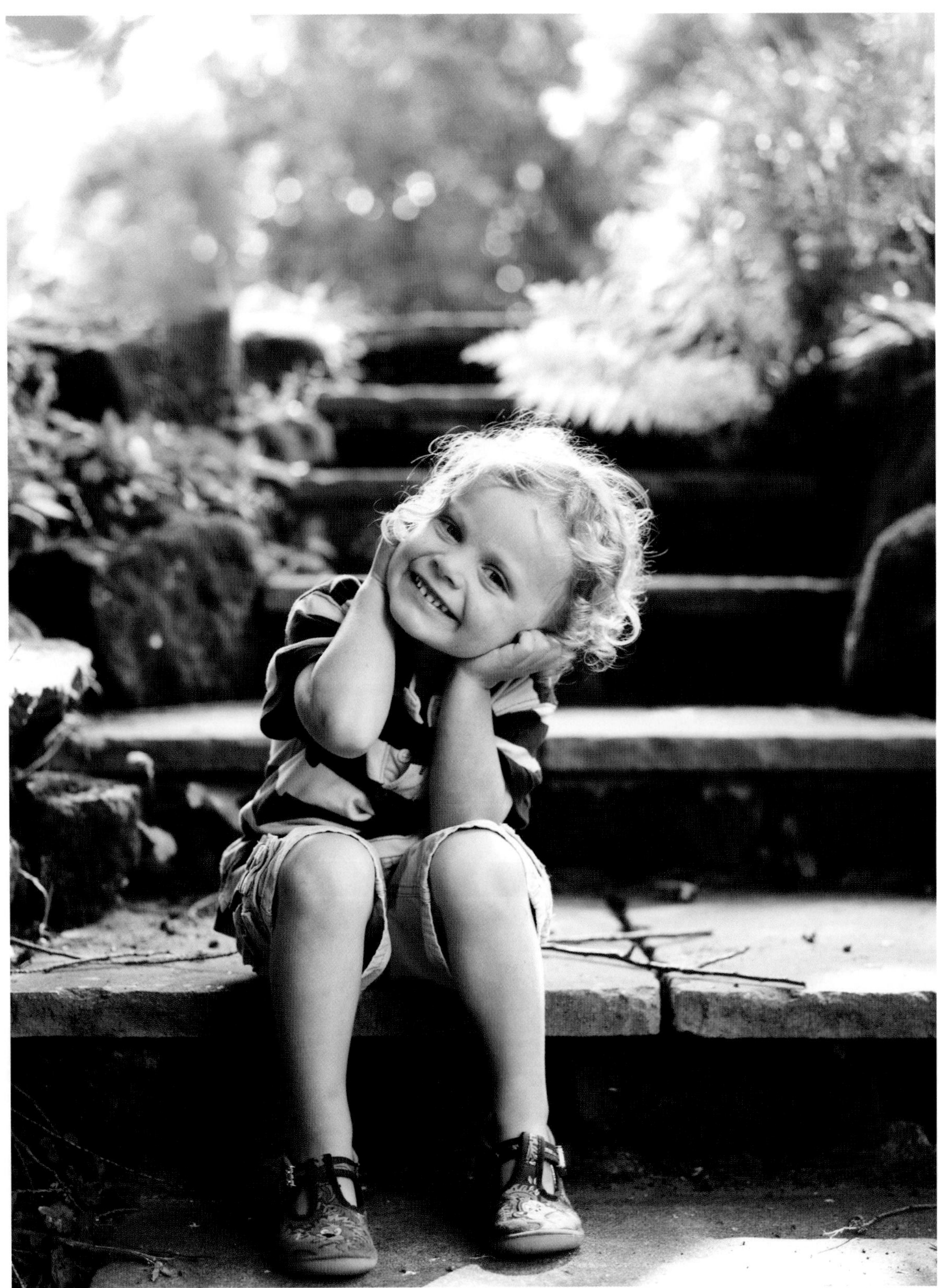

strong light filling the room and you are hoping to frame the subject with the window, using reflectors is essential to bring out the detail in the face and clothing, otherwise you will have a very flat subject.

The Elements

When working in natural light, we should not solely rely on the quantity or brightness of the light. We also need to make use of the elements (rain, snow, fog), cloud cover, the seasons, the time of day, and so on. Looking beyond the fixed view that natural light portraits should only be taken on sunny days opens the door to the possibility of producing something that is unrepeatable and thus wholly bespoke – a one-off. This applies to photographers anywhere in the world. In the UK we have four very definite seasons, which enables us to plan our shoots, brief our clients and, to a degree, preempt the weather and the quality of the light at any given time of year. But there are different obstacles that need to be factored in when you are planning a shoot. When up against the elements, it is vital that you shoot your 'safe' shots first. This is not the time for experimentation – if you have time and you are happy you have got the images the client wants, then by all means push the envelope afterwards.

The same location can look very different at various times of the year, which can work to your advantage as long as you are selective about your timing. The downside, to a degree, of relying on natural light is the unpredictable weather, especially somewhere such as the UK. So all the plans you had of having a beautiful backlit image can sometimes go out of the window, and a 'Plan B' is needed or the shoot has to be rescheduled. If you are after a

particular feel to an image, you may wish to allow some time in order to get it just right. A little like being a landscape or wildlife photographer, it's worth being patient and getting that perfect light. In the UK, our weather is hugely changeable and unpredictable, but the photographer can try to use this to his or her advantage. An understanding of the position of the sun both rising and setting should be a part of your bank of knowledge when planning shoots at particular times of year. There may be a viewpoint where you enjoy shooting which may be prone to low hanging cloud in the early morning, or you may have to contend with those cold February mornings where the frost and ice sticks to cornfields and trees. You may not have the confidence to work in the rain, cold and wind, but the weather can be a great inspiration and you can use it to create something individual.

Shooting on location in available light is a year-round profession and having ideas as well as back-up plans for wet weather is essential. When you are next out on an icy morning, give some thought to how you could use this in your work. Keep your camera with you and just take some images during the 'golden hour', sometimes called the 'magic hour' – roughly the first hour of light after sunrise and the last hour of light before sunset (the exact duration varying between seasons). During these times the sun is low in the sky, producing a soft, diffused light which is much more flattering than the harsh mid-day sun that we have to deal with in the summer. During this short time, the light changes remarkably quickly, and your scene can look vastly different after just a few minutes. It's worth waiting around to see how the light adjusts your scene. Stay for the hour and capture the full range of effects.

◄ Fig. 5.4
This photo was taken at midday, with the sun high in the sky. The photographer has positioned the child in a shaded area yet incorporated the beautiful backlight that is hitting the background. Using shallow depth of field has softened the background, giving a nostalgic, timeless feel.

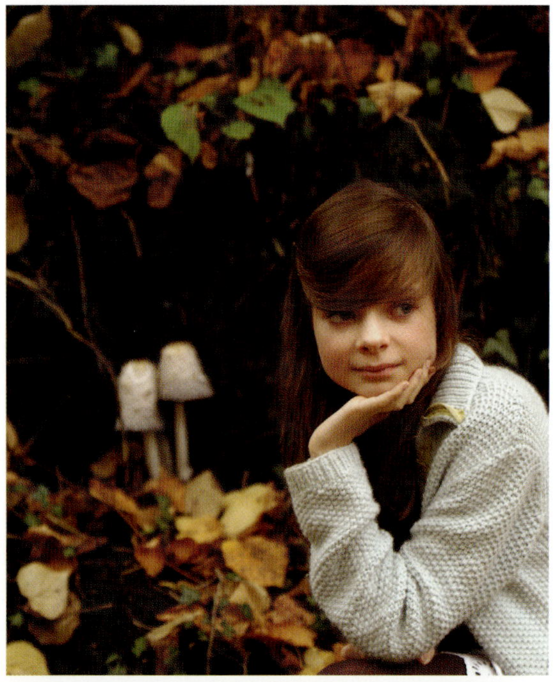

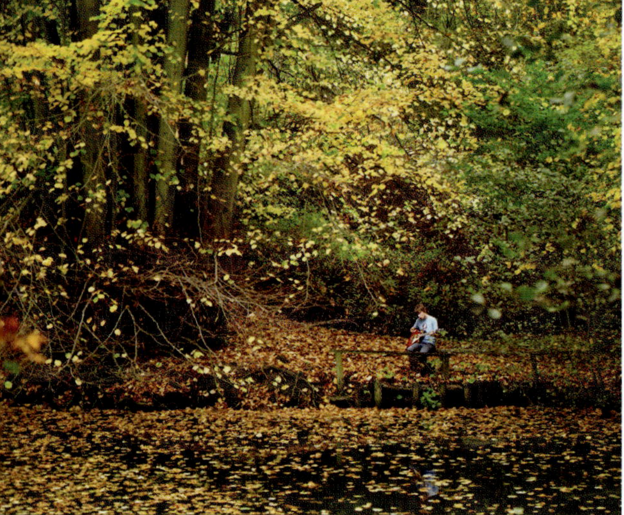

▲ Figs 5.5a–b
The oranges and yellows of the autumn foliage make a glorious backdrop to location shots.

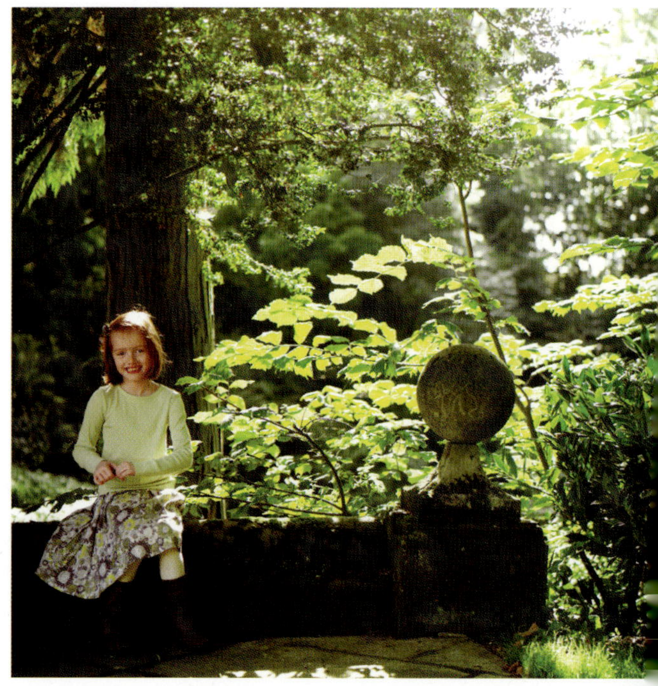

▲ Fig. 5.6
Take advantage of the low sun in autumn. Long shadows can be used to advantage or contained with the use of a reflector.

The Seasons

Autumn

In mid-autumn there is still some foliage in its full glory of colour, and it's a wonderful time for location portraits, offering you endless opportunities to incorporate this into your work. The sun is fairly low in the sky, producing long shadows and warm, natural tones.

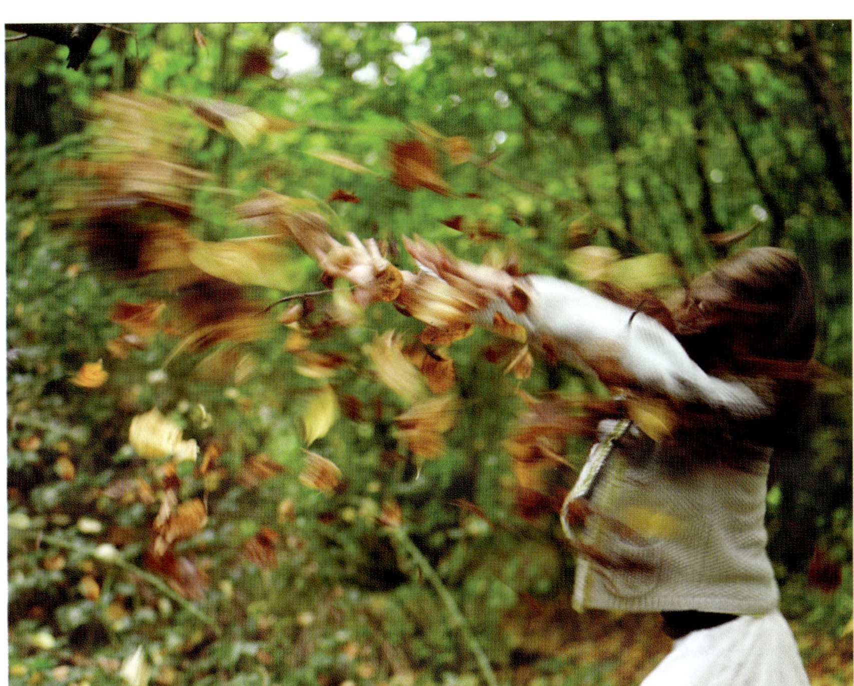

Fig. 5.7
And of course, autumn brings fallen leaves and with that comes a leaf fight...

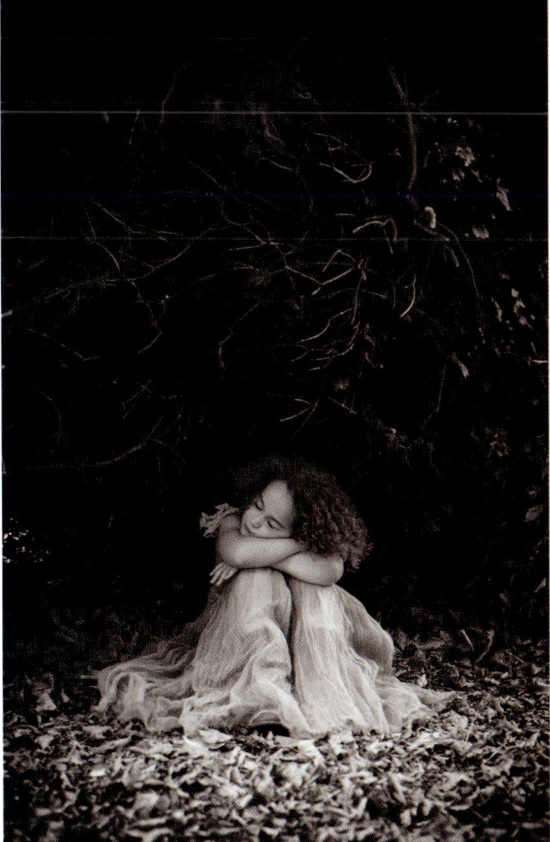

Fig. 5.8
Late autumn, and we are on the cusp of winter harshness, with bare branches and fallen leaves. The leaves, since their lush deep reds have faded, look better in black and white. The graphic of the branches works well as a natural frame, an organic protection for the child.

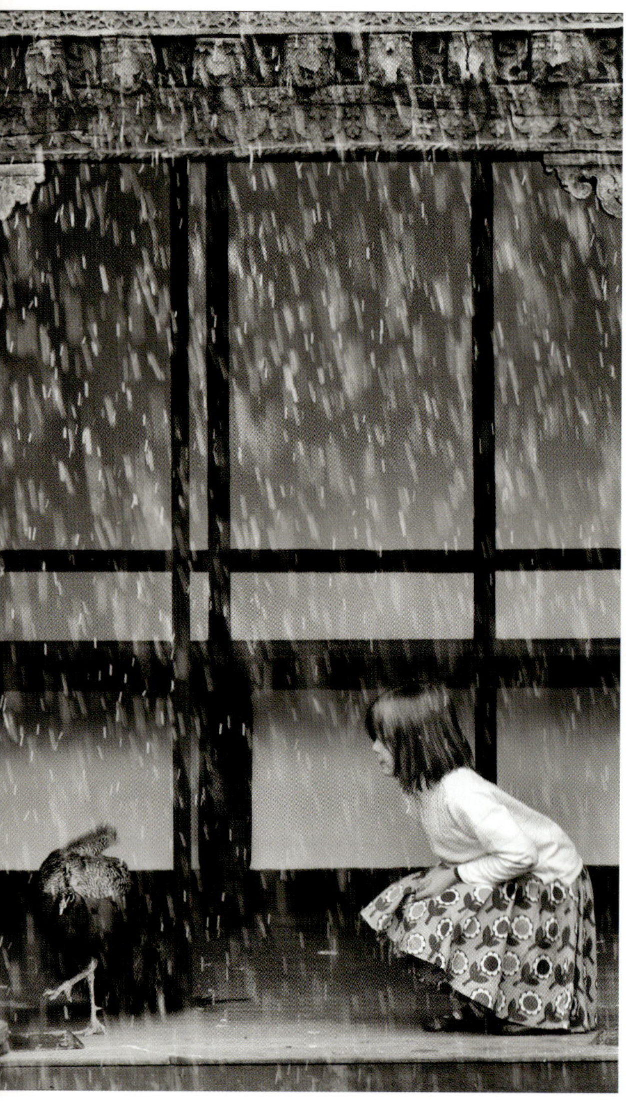

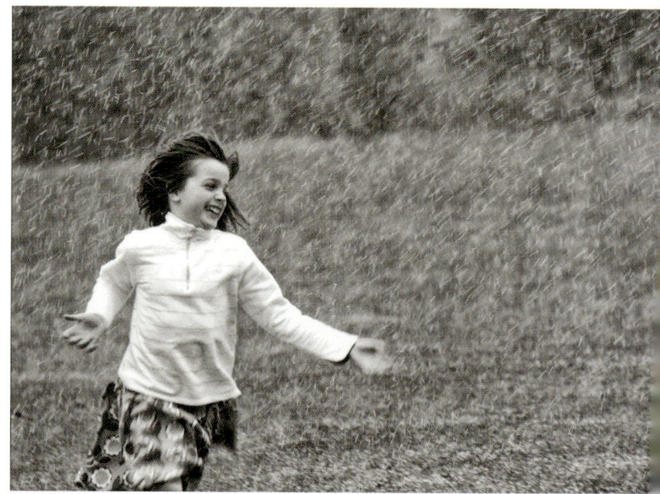

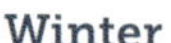 Figs 5.9a–b
The photographer has taken advantage of the falling rain and incorporated it into these two shots.

uncomfortable and ill at ease, almost as if they are just passing and have stopped for a snapshot. If you can, time the shoot so that you can remove coats and replace them with thick jumpers, and keep the subject (and yourself) moving. Embrace the harsh conditions to your advantage and welcome them into your work.

Spring

In spring and with a new, warmer light, a more predictable planning schedule for portraits on location is possible. There may still be a frost underfoot, but fresh colour is coming through which can offer a change of tack. Forest areas and woodland are often at their finest at this time of year, with an abundance of natural colour flora in the form of wild garlic and bluebells – often a popular choice for the portrait photographer. But there are a couple of obstacles to overcome. Firstly, dappled light can cause hot spots on the face. Although this can be used to effect, if we are looking for those all-important 'safe' shots, find a clearing which perhaps has colour surrounding it and place your subject in a clear area to avoid dappling. If you feel you are not incorporating colour

Winter

In addition to bringing together everything such as lighting, location and weather, in winter you also have the added concern of keeping children comfortable and warm. Being organized and knowing where you will be shooting means you can concentrate solely on the child and work quickly and effectively in a short time. Bulky coats look ungainly, have a tendency to lose hands up the sleeves and give an overall feeling of the subject being

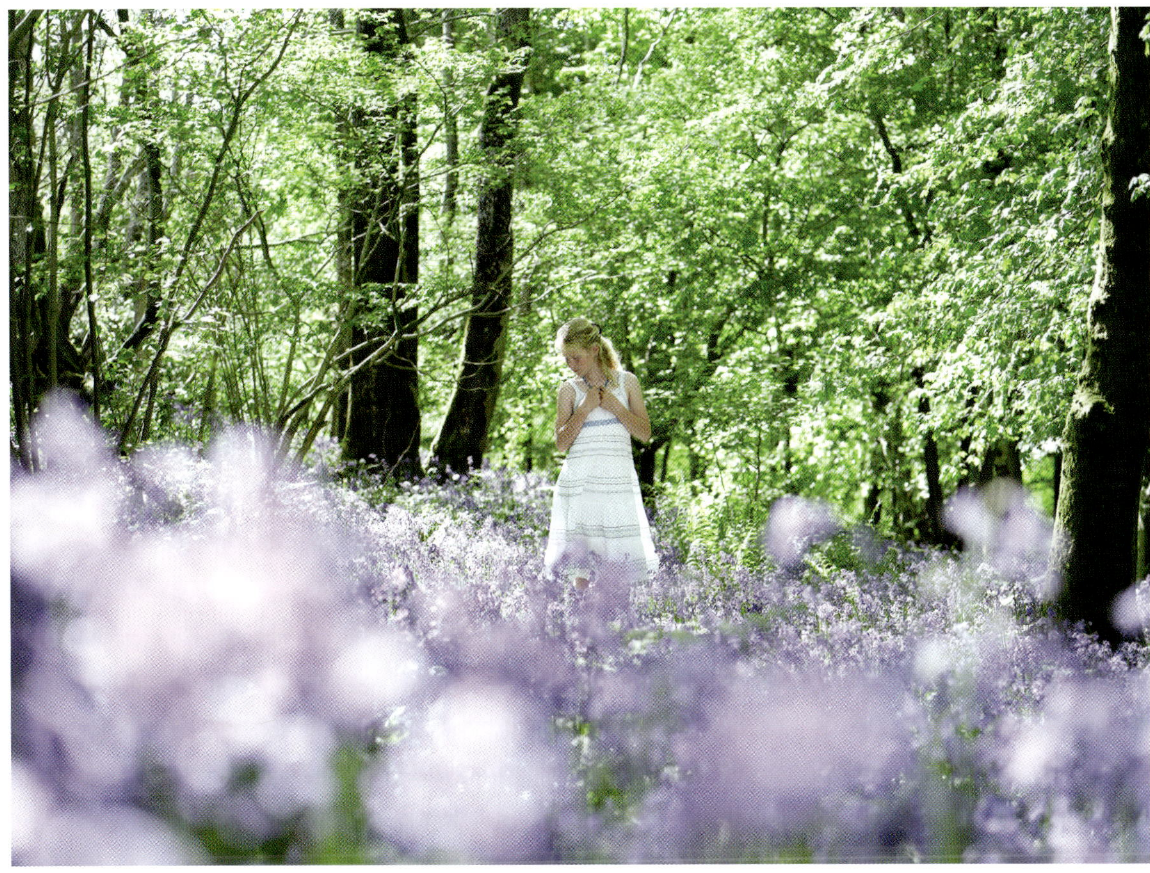

▲ Fig. 5.10

Bluebell woods typify an English country scene. This portrait was taken around 11am on a sunny spring morning. The sun is fairly high in the sky, causing both dappling as well as colour issues. Carefully placing the subject in a more open area can avoid dappling; in addition to this, the child is standing on or near a silver or white reflector, giving a cleaner light on the face and thus overcoming to a degree the issues of dark exposure and colour bias.

sufficiently because of this, try shooting through the colour towards your subject in the clearing. Be bold in any decisions you make to move the location slightly if you feel the light is going to change and affect the way it falls on your subject (shadows, hotspots, and so on), and be confident in your decision to move your subject. You are in control of the shoot and your client is relying on your expertise and experience to make decisions. Much of this is anticipating the light changing in your portrait.

The second problem is coloured light, which can be given off onto skin tones by the strong hues of bluebells and lush fresh green. While the colour of the surrounding area may be wonderful, the colour on the skin can take on a purple hue that is unflattering and flat. To rectify this, use a colour checker to set your WB, provided you are shooting in RAW format; the white side of a reflector will also help in this instance.

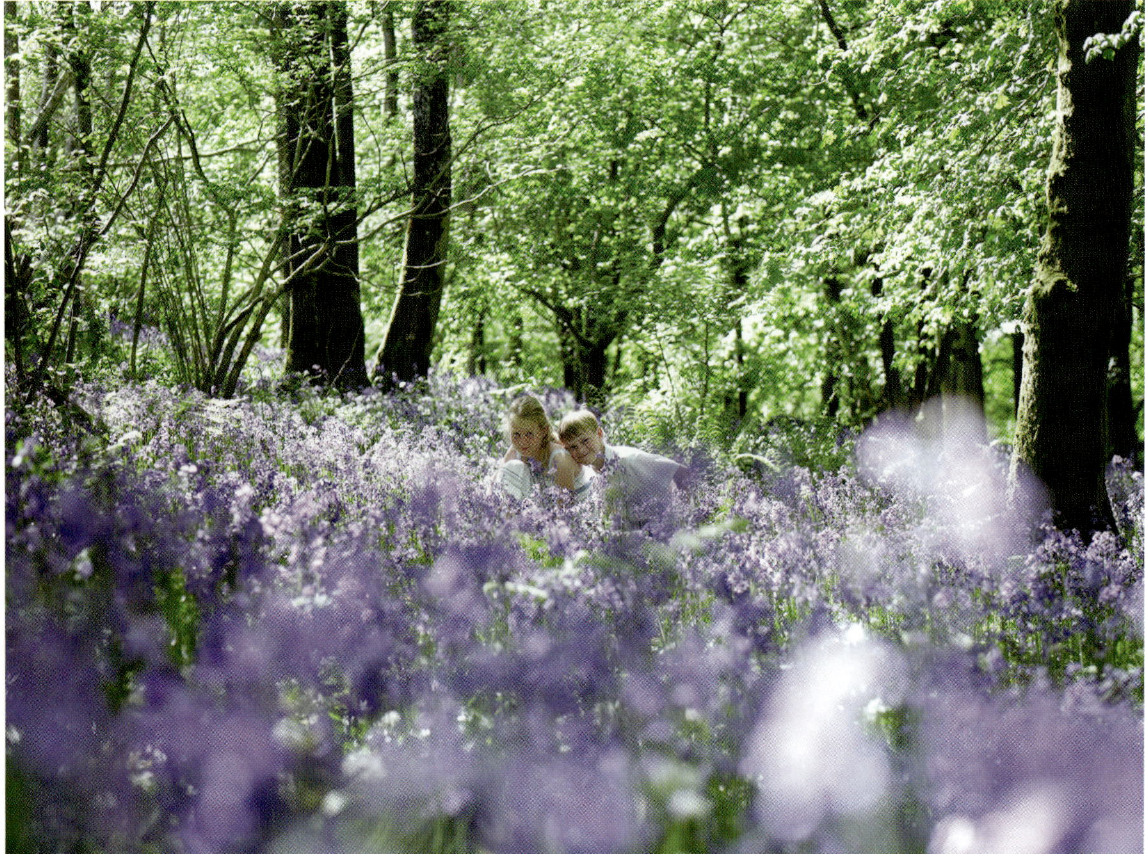

▲ Fig. 5.11
The lovely rim light around this brother and sister is balanced on the faces by a large 6ft Lastolite reflector, which is not visible to the camera. The sun is high and the lovely clean light is bounced back onto their faces to eliminate dark shadows, dappling and colour bias. Taking this from a standard, albeit acceptable portrait to something a little more vibrant, the photographer has chosen to shoot through a sea of colour with a fairly shallow depth of field (*f*4), thus not detracting from the subject, but enhancing the shot with a natural frame of purple and green.

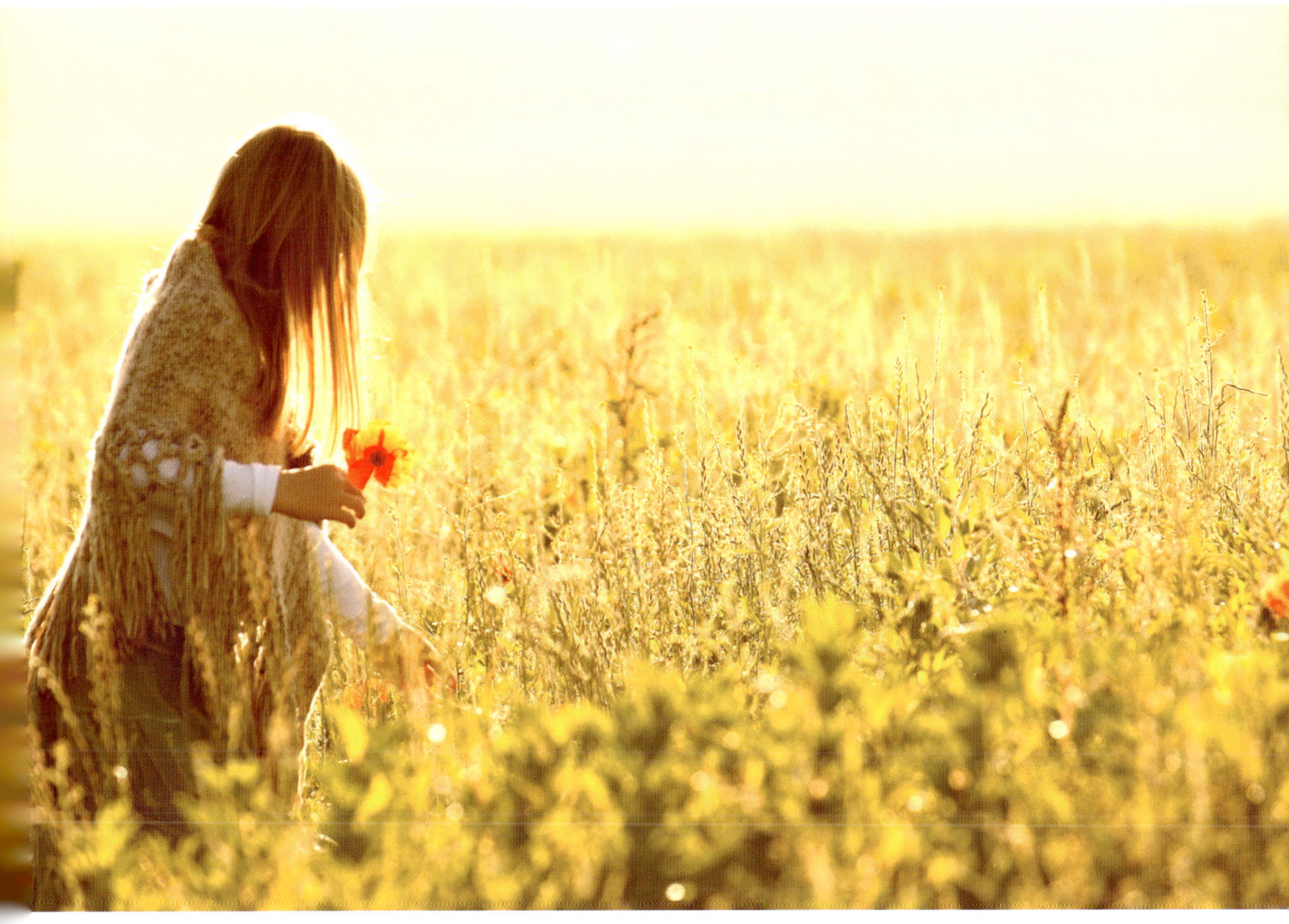

▲ Fig. 5.12
This image was taken around 6.30am at the height of summer
– a small window of opportunity as within minutes the light had
become far stronger, losing its wonderful atmospheric aura.

Summer

The harshness of the midday summer sun can be used to effect rather than be shied away from. You may want a strong contrasting effect in your work. Used effectively, this light can create striking graphic shadows, particularly against buildings and strong architecture, and can lend itself to imagery which has a strong graphic element, while allowing for creative freedom within your compositions. Ideally, book your shoots in the early morning before 10am or after 6pm, when you can take advantage of those wonderful balmy summer evenings.

The role of a portrait photographer is to create portraits that are flattering and show our clients in their best light. Even if a client has a great camera, what sets the professional apart from the amateur is the understanding of the camera and how to program it with the correct information. So, if we find ourselves in a situation where we have no choice but to shoot in midday sun, how do we deal with this if there is no natural shade? The next few examples (Figs 5.13 – 5.18) will show how unflattering harsh light can be, and how we can overcome it with the use of reflectors.

REFLECTORS

Remember, when using reflectors you are not reflecting light from the subject but from the sun, so placement need not be directly underneath the subject. You can bounce it from a good few metres from the subject. The same applies if you are working inside and need to light an area – try taking the reflector outside and bouncing the light in through a door or window rather than struggling to find interior source.

Choose between silver, gold or white reflectors, depending on the aesthetic of the final image. A gold reflector will give a warm, somewhat synthetic feel, whereas silver is clean and perhaps more natural. Working on location, photographers should carry these in situations where they have the time to set things up and keep light under control. Once you have contained that wayward light, you will find it easier to add to it.

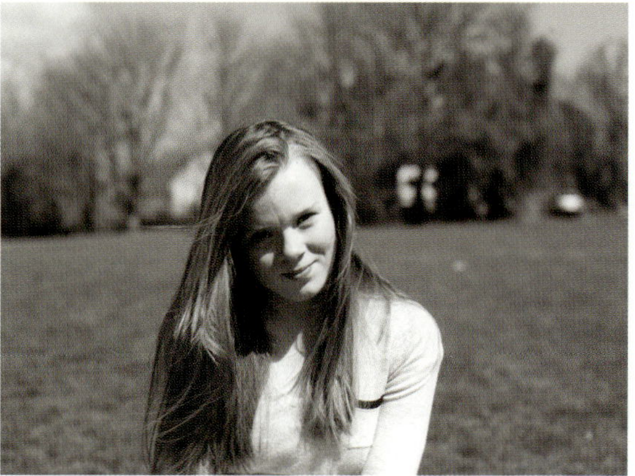

▲ Fig. 5.13
Recognize what doesn't work as a professional or indeed saleable portrait. Harsh midday sunlight causes a bleached out effect on the skin, dark shadows under the eyes and encourages the child to squint. This is a snapshot, with no control of how the light falls on the girl's face.

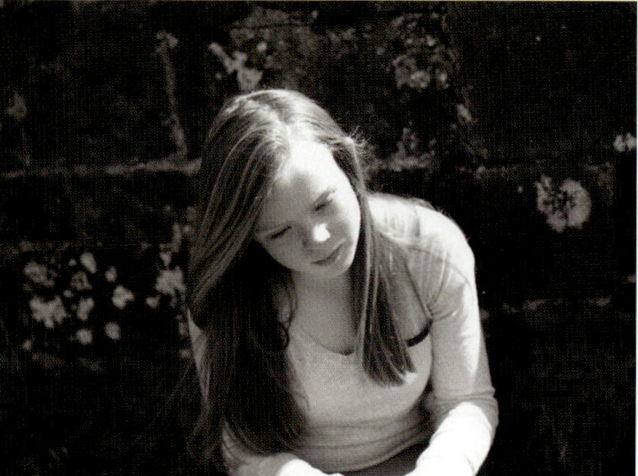

▲ Fig. 5.14
The girl has been moved to a more shaded area. The stonework from the wall presents a more aesthetically interesting backdrop. However, the light is still harsh to the side of the face and hands. The skin tones are burnt out to 254 on the histogram, thus containing no information and therefore irretrievable without some serious Photoshop cloning.

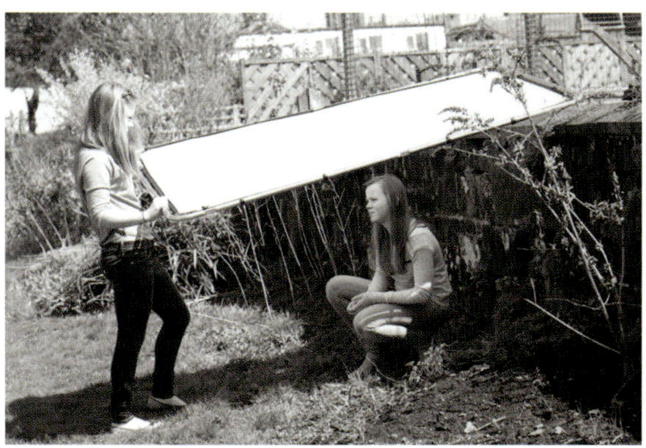

▲ Fig. 5.15
The photographer introduces some top shade using a Lastolite diffuser above and to the side. The light is now consistent, not as directional as perhaps we would want in an ideal environment, but certainly more flattering. It allows the child to look at the camera without squinting.

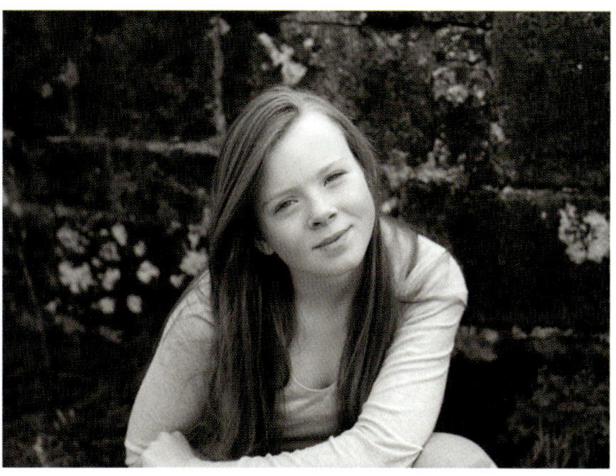

▲ Fig. 5.16
In contrast to where we started, the portrait now has even light across the subject, albeit a little flat in the eyes. We have the light under control, so we can begin to add a kiss of light just to lift the eyes by introducing a Lastolite reflector.

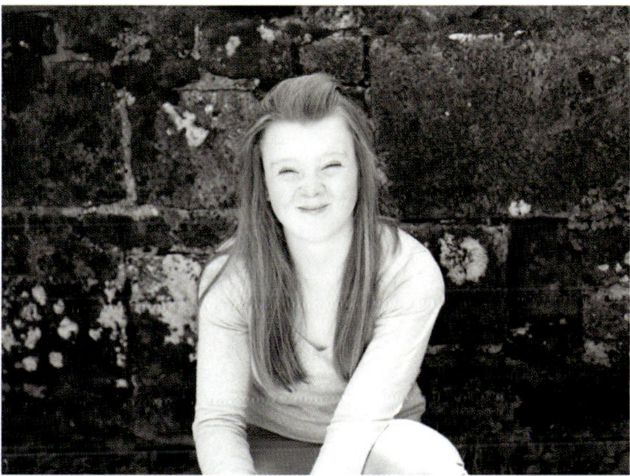

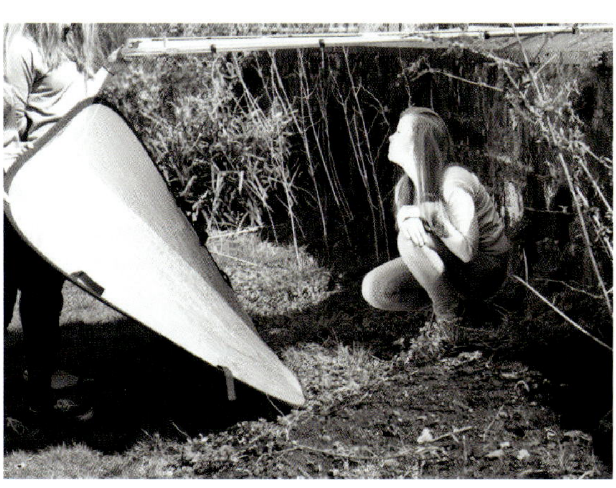

▲ Figs 5.17a–b
The subject is overlit with the reflector. Reflectors are powerful; you only need a subtle hint to make a difference and retain the natural feel of the portrait, rather than it looking as if flash has been used.

▲ Fig. 5.18
A perfect balance of natural light with an accent of reflector to add a flattering catch of light to the eye.

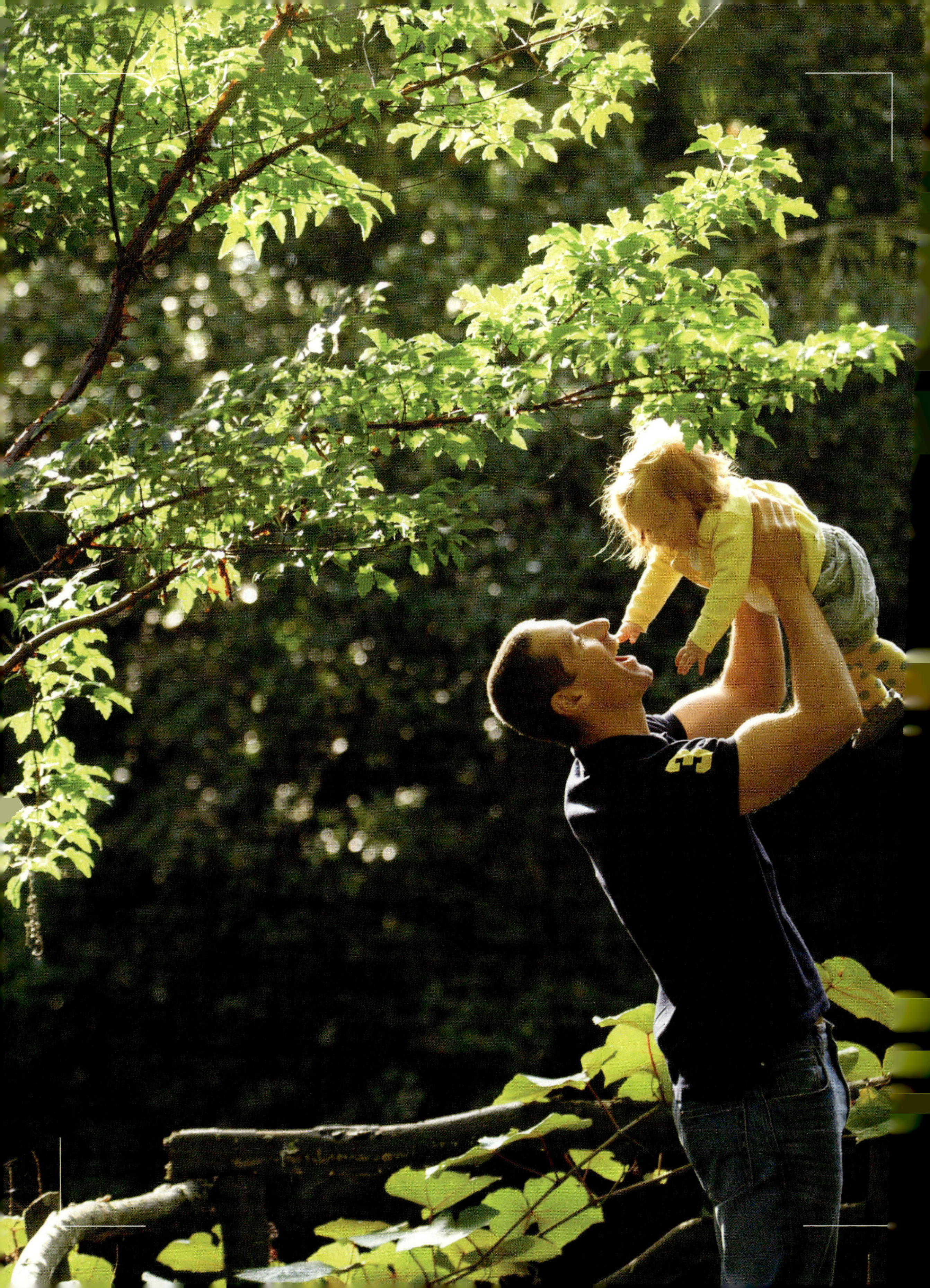

Posing, Placement, Communication

Posing and Placement

Portraiture is about realism; how and where we position and place a child, how that child is dressed, is relevant to a particular time in their life. It places into context the relationship between them and their surroundings, inviting us to question what they are thinking. How and where a child is placed in a location creates a bond and collaboration between the subject and the photographer.

Having a principal point of focus within a portrait is fundamental. There may be many factors contributing to the power of the image but that one area, essentially the subject in most cases, is what holds the picture together. Composition, of course, is different from placement. In a nutshell, composition is the image in its entirety, your take on how you feel the overall image should be viewed and the impact it will have on the viewer. Placement, however, is part of the construction of that composition – the heart of it. The subject needs to be placed in context with the background and illuminated sufficiently in order to retain it as the main focal point. The placement can indeed often dictate the composition, and vice versa.

In Fig. 6.1, the placement of the child central to the frame almost makes the location appear superfluous. In fact it isn't – taken in the fog, there is little detail to be had but the leading lines go out behind the boy towards the light at the end of the

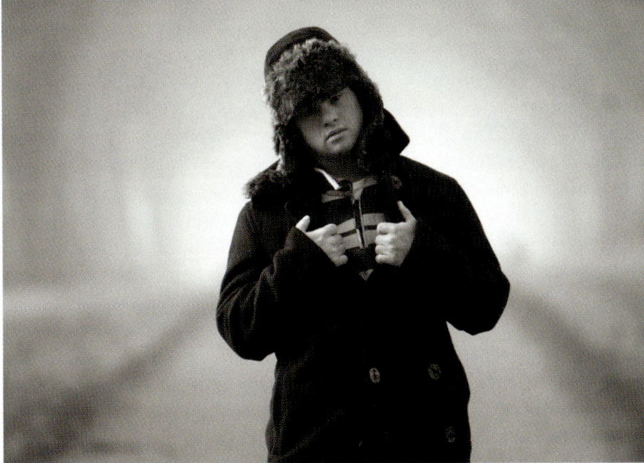

▲ Fig. 6.1
The child's central position provides an element of symmetry within the softness of the location. The pose is immediate and holds conviction and definite eye contact with the camera – the tilt of the head softens the image somewhat in keeping with the location, but whimsical it isn't.

drive behind him creating a halo around his body. There is a subtle natural framing from the trees, but on the whole the background is diffused in contrast with the strong tones of the subject. The trees offer a natural tone and frame, graduating into a lighter area at the end of the road. Figs 6.2 and 6.3 illustrate other placements.

Careful placement can help children relax. Having a tree, wall or building to lean against can offer a feeling of security; it may stop them feeling exposed and give them confidence to move away once the shoot progresses.

Posing a child should be very different from that of an adult. There needs to be a sense of innocence, perhaps vulnerability, honesty, sensitivity and freshness that resonates from the picture. If in doubt, keep it simple. In fact, simplicity is often more powerful than making it appear too forced and

◀ Fig. 6.0
You may be working with all ages of children, including ones who aren't yet walking, which can be challenging when working on location.

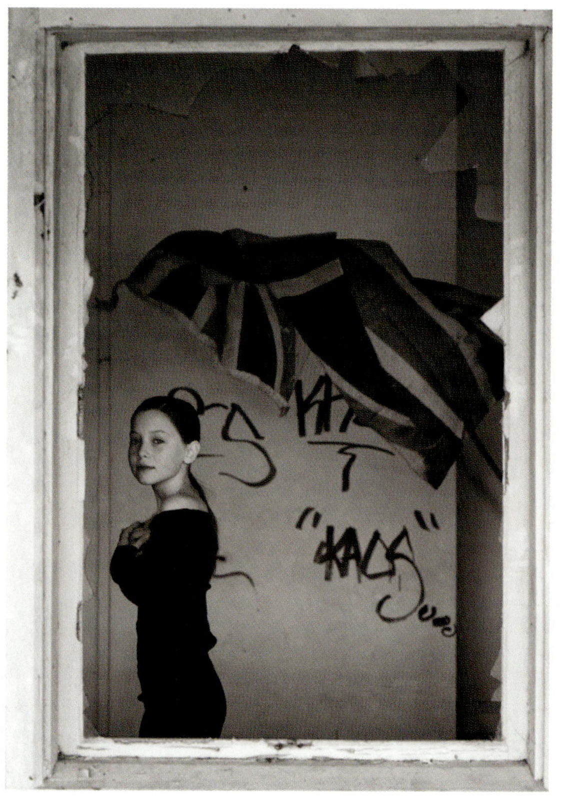

▲ Fig. 6.2
The child is placed to the left of the frame. The addition of the flag to add movement would not have proved so powerful if she had been central; instead it has allowed the image to flow. It would be more of a distraction and less easy to read had she been placed centrally in the window.

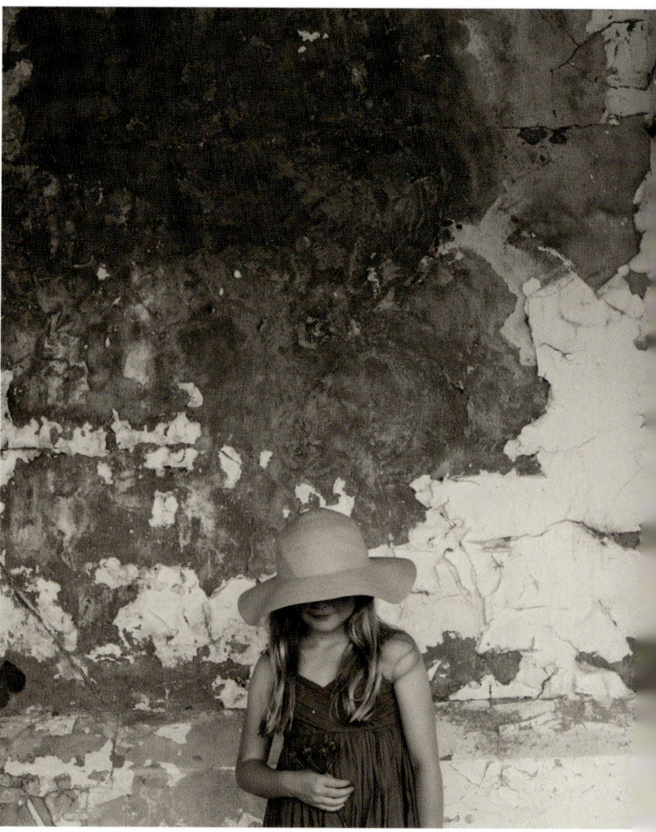

▲ Fig. 6.3
Simplicity reigns in the contrast between backdrop and child.

contrived. There is a skill in developing a picture which, despite being set up, gives a diaristic appeal that looks wholly naturally formed.

The precise placement and pose in Fig. 6.5 is critical to balance the graphics. An alternative could have been to bring the arms down but this would have changed the streamlined quality of the pose. In Fig. 6.6 the pose has merged with the background, giving a sense of freedom and fun, yet the composition of the bench to the left and the tree to the right holds it together.

It's not always necessary to strategically position or pose your subject. By observing how children act, carry themselves and by watching their body language, you can sometimes just let it develop naturally. The less we interfere, the more natural and effective the image. Keep your camera close and remain observant with one eye on your subject – visualize every movement, hesitation, look, and see it as a still frame. Imagine that split second – a questioning look or an arresting expression – as hung, beautifully framed, on a wall for the next fifty years.

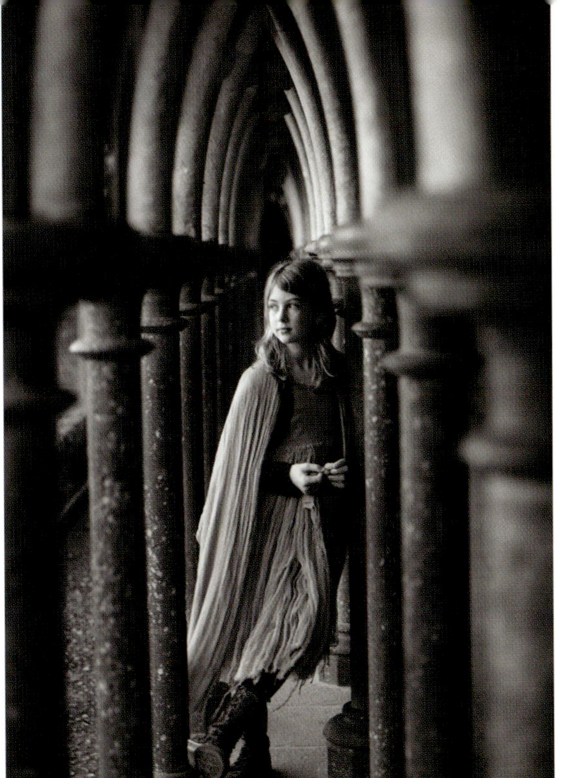

The photographer wishes to contrast the strong uprights of the cloisters with a softer pose from the child in order to retain a natural balance. Positioning her to one side but taking her feet across the diagonal ensures that she fills the area while removing any static feeling through the softness of the pose and keeping the overall feel casual yet framed with uniformity and grandeur. The light is treated as window light, with the child's head turned towards the source.

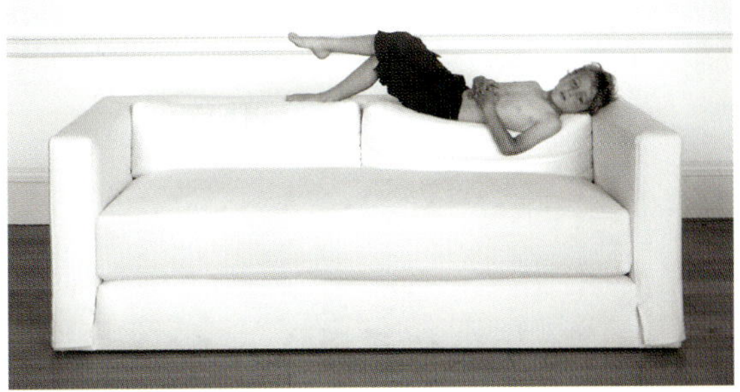

The boy looks relaxed yet the positioning of his leg is running parallel with the dado rail, probably the result of tweaking by the photographer. His placement to the right of the chair gives the image a feeling of space. Notice the right leg over the left, presenting a lovely figure of eight between the legs and his left arm. He may well have been asked to stretch his toes out to run horizontal with the railing. If the child was finding it difficult to follow instructions, the photographer could move up or down in order to have the leg parallel visually – however, photographer perspective here is critical to the symmetrical value of the picture.

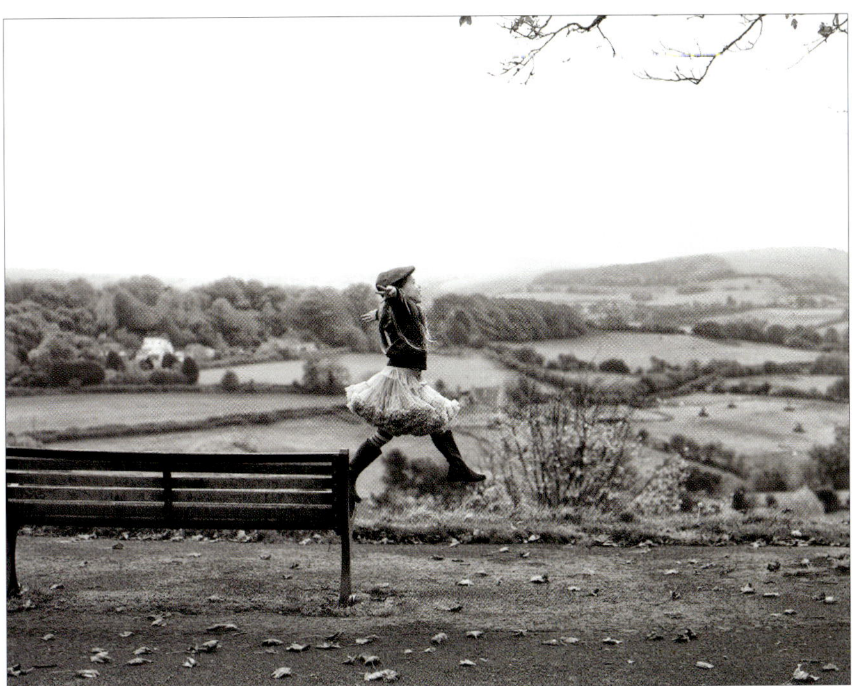

This kind of picture may take some practice and you may need to demonstrate to the child first. The child just jumping off would not have worked so well; there needed to be more conviction, with the child taking on 'world domination', making that leap into the world beyond. Not only do you need to concentrate on timing, ensuring you have the expression and feeling in the pose, but also your composition. Do you want movement in the image or should you shoot this at fast shutter and have it pin sharp? That's your call. These are all questions you need to ask yourself before the shoot so your camera settings are set and you have subconsciously composed the image – this will free you up to communicate with the child.

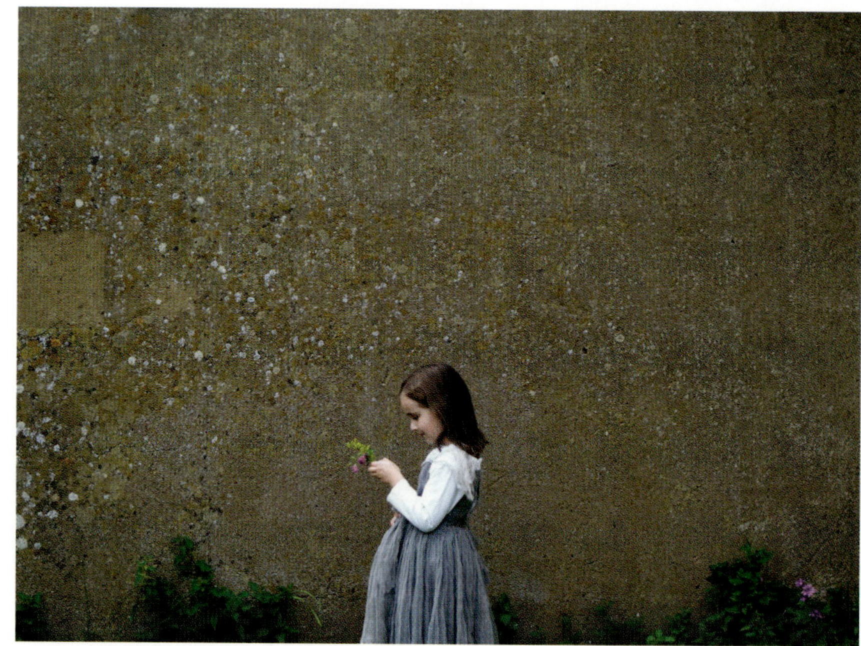

▶ Fig. 6.7
The photographer here has picked up on colour, making use of a fairly ordinary background wall and allowing the image to flirt with cohesive colours throughout. There is a gentle interaction between photographer and child that doesn't rely on forced expression or animation in order to treat the viewer to a quiet, contemplative moment, which is embellished with colour and negative space.

Communication

Communication in some form, if nothing else but to build a rapport with the child, is crucial, especially if you are a stranger to that child. A degree of trust and camaraderie is key to successful communication between photographer and child. You don't need to be unnaturally overexcited, but use your personality and skills to communicate your ideas to your subject. You may be a extroverted, chatty, highly communicative and verbally stimulating character – this will translate into your photography. The way you react and how your subjects react to you can be very visible in your work.

Your ideas for images will often be taken from your own tastes and sourced from inspiration that moves you as both a human and a photographer. This makes it all the more important to be honest with your style and follow what makes you tick, rather than looking to other photographers for ideas.

One exercise you might want to try, once you have built a rapport with the child, is being almost completely silent during the shoot. When you have that connection and the child is engaged with you, try small adjustments to a pose and watch how the child mirrors your own actions: gently tilting your head, adjusting feet, adjusting arms and hands. Take the child's gaze to a different angle by gently lifting your hand to the side in the direction you want the eyes. All movements should be slow and subtle. It can be quite fascinating to watch how this works and to see the responsive reaction. This is only possible once the child has formed a connection with you, so the time you spend developing this is vital; also, your confidence in your own directional skills needs to be visible to them.

When children are asked to move verbally they often move their entire bodies, which is why this subtle, quiet approach, keeping everything calm and slow, can be so effective. There will be occasions when you have everything in place, placement is perfect, light is great but maybe, for example, the head is too far round and possibly the child can't see you in order to copy you. If you were to say to the child (or any model, child or adult): 'OK, can you just...' the immediate response would be for the subject to turn and look at you – move his or her entire body. You've now lost the perfect placement and posing you had in place, but you only wanted

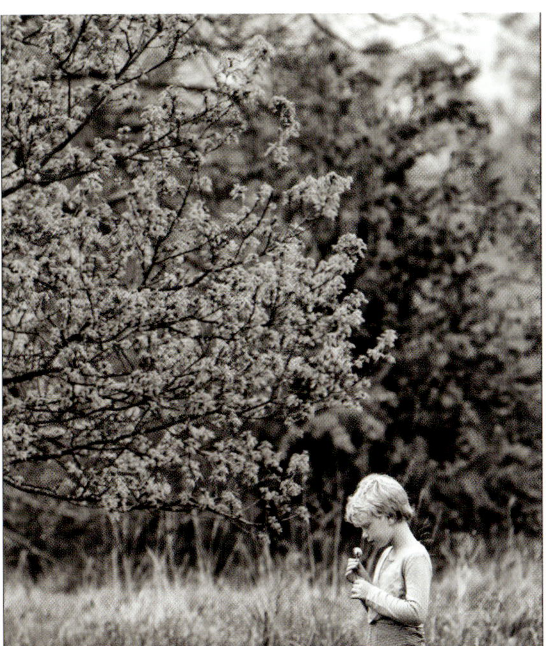

Offering something to distract or interest the child allows for the development of quiet contemplation and gives you the time to frame your image as you wish. It's often these quiet moments that produce the finest portraits – when the child slips into his world, away from the overexcitement of the build-up to the shoot. Allowing the portrait to develop like this does require patience and it is tempting to step in and 'do your job', but patience and quiet observation will pay off. This works particularly well with children aged from around three to twelve years, though you may find that a three-year-old's window of contemplation is a short one!

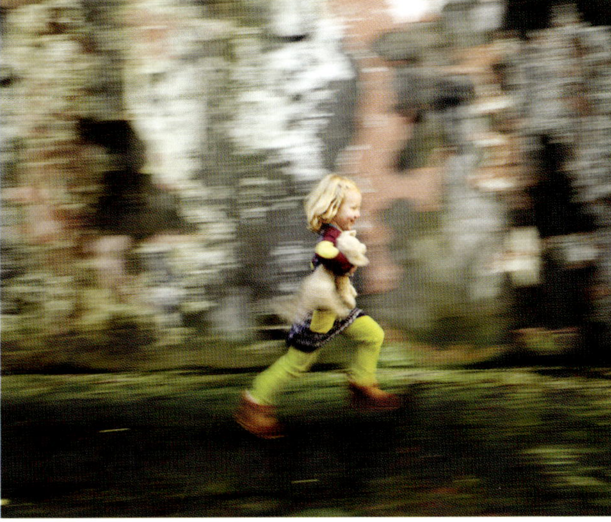

Inviting children to behave naturally, run and be at ease with you, gives you the opportunity to create vibrant imagery through use of colour, movement and expression once you have positioned yourself for the location.

to make a small, subtle adjustment. There is nothing more frustrating than having that perfect image unravel in front of you!

It's for this very reason that some photographers don't make small changes, preferring to 'get the moment'. But sometimes that compromises attention to detail and it's this attention to detail that is imperative. It can make the difference between an image which is acceptable and one that is outstanding. Make those changes in order to get the perfect image.

So how do we communicate what a small change to the placement or pose should be without creating large changes in the current set-up? Here's what we *don't* say:

'OK.'

'Could you just...'

'I'd like you to...'

'You look great but could you...'

The first thing we say is:

'Don't move. Stay exactly where you are, you are perfect.'

Then you can make your subtle changes – move a hand back, bring the eyes around slightly, drop the head, close the eyes, or whatever is required.

▶ **Fig. 6.10**
Working with babies or children who are not yet walking requires a different approach. It is still possible to utilize an interesting background and location, or you can work within the comfort of your client's home.

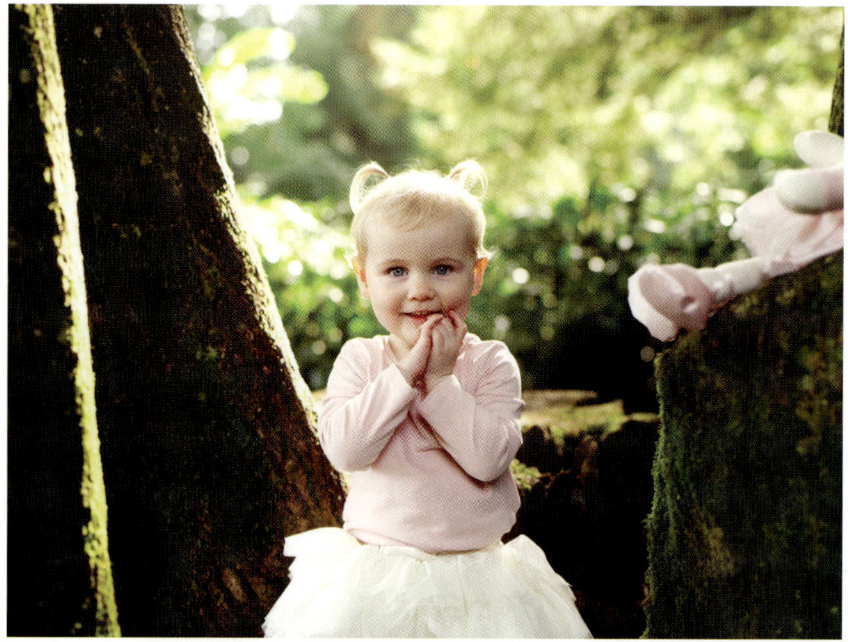

▶ **Fig. 6.11**
Taken in the early evening in the height of summer; the light coming through the tree creates the atmosphere. Placement of the subjects is just inside the shadowy area in order to take advantage of the strong rim light; being placed further out in the sun would cause the highlights around the hair to blow out. Using a diffuser here is not an option given the wide composition. A reflector is used to lift the detail in the subject. Notice the use of scale – careful composition to accentuate the tender support of the mother and then subsequent framing from the tree creating a protective structure around them. Despite being small in the image, they are still prominent. An alternative take on this would be to use the flair and create something more atmospheric. If the entire tree had been used, it may have appeared out of balance with the subject placement. Experiment with placement versus composition.

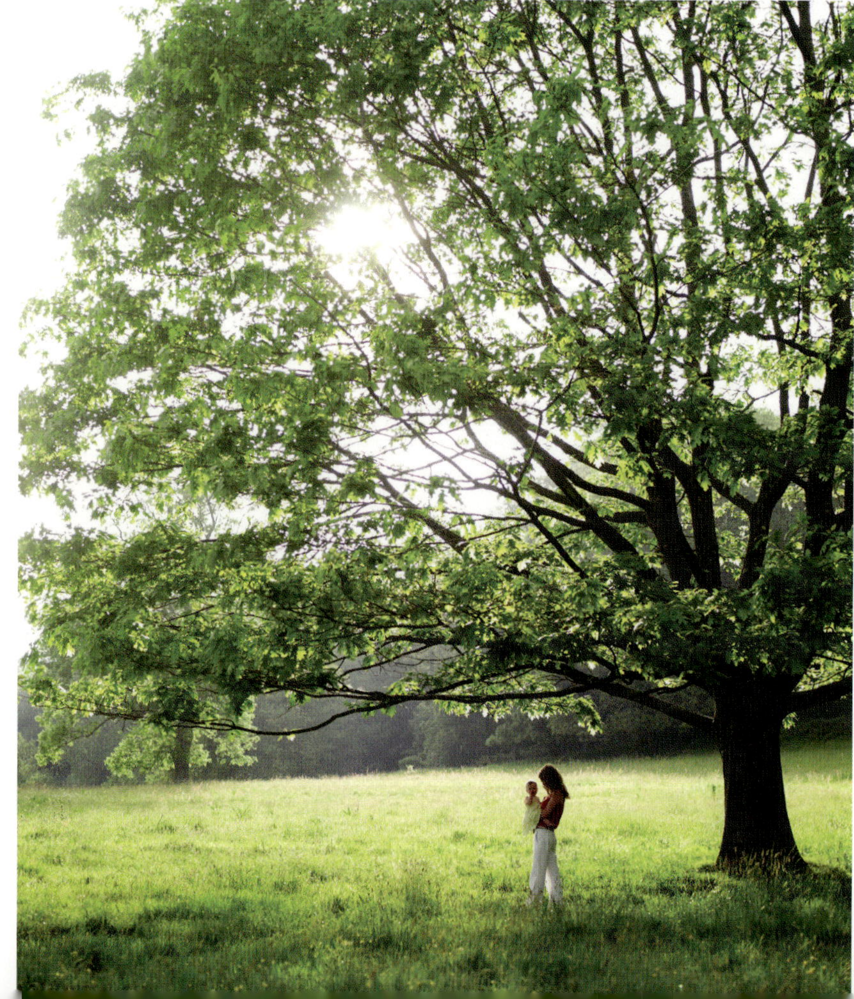

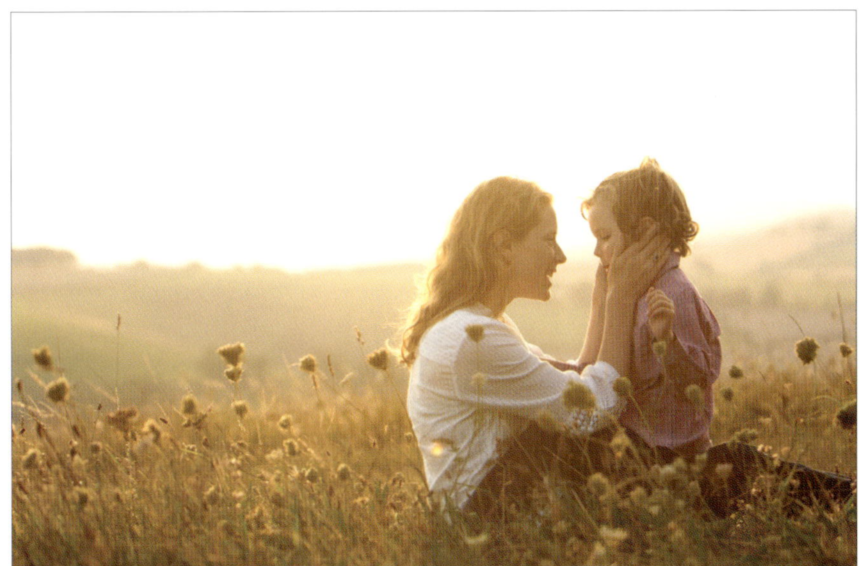

Fig. 6.12
Parents will naturally interact with their children and this should be encouraged. However, the placement, composition and use of evening backlight is paramount to the impact of the image.

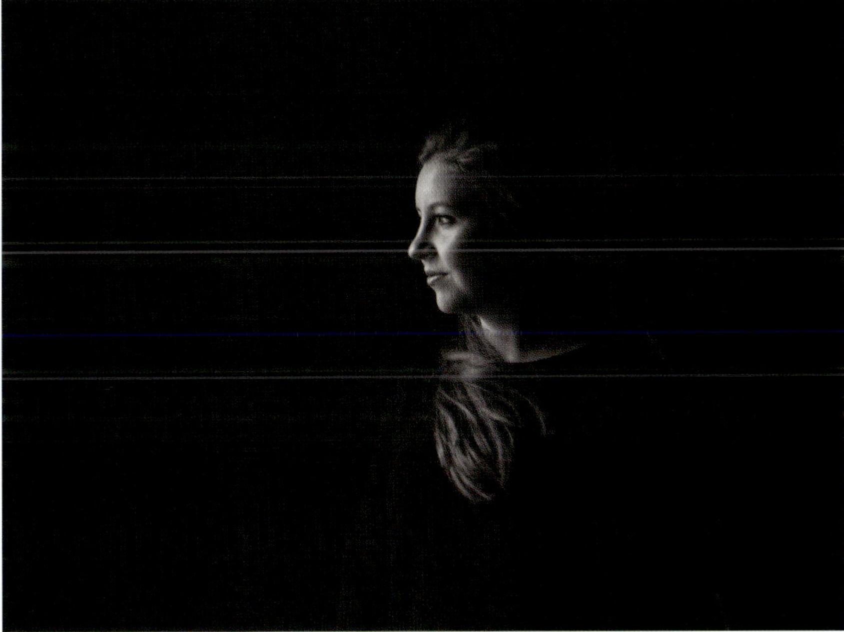

Fig. 6.13
Teenagers, with some exceptions, don't do whimsical; they do sultry, perhaps embarrassed, edgy. Different ages require a different approach. If you are a parent, you naturally develop strategies to cope with your children's different phases. It's just a matter of being on a level with teenagers, not trying too hard and above all taking an interest in them.

PERMISSION

There is little more wonderful for parents than seeing their beloved children in their pure young skin, carefree and natural (*see* Fig. 6.14). A fine line raises its head here, that between innocence and vulnerability. We can allow a child's purity to run through an image, but do we want them to look vulnerable? Sadly, it has become increasingly difficult and somewhat dangerous for photographers (in fact anyone, including parents) to be seen photographing children with no clothes, so written consent should be sought from the parents if you intend to factor this into a portrait.

We touched earlier on Sally Mann, who photographed her children nude throughout their early years and was surprised at the subsequent criticism, not understanding why this was seen as in any way exploitative. And these were her own children. So if you intend to work in this style with children in their natural form, be absolutely sure that your client understands and agrees where the images are to be used and that you have full permission to use them. If you are considering entering images into awards or competitions, be aware that you will need to allow consent for the images to be used as part of any publicity if you are successful, which will inevitably mean that the images will be accessible on the internet.

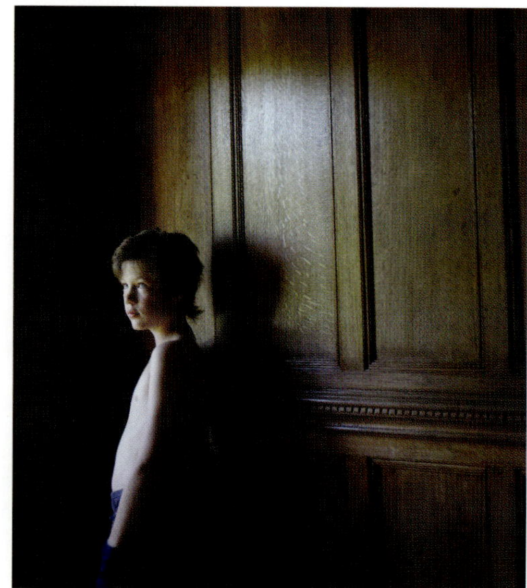

▲ Fig. 6.14

Expression and Emotional Communication

The split second of expression before you press the shutter is the final element that will wholly determine the overall feel of the image and how the viewer feels about it. It can make or break an image. Do not ask your subject to 'look contemplative' if that is the feeling you are seeking; rather, create a quietness between you which naturally results in that feel. You will find that the more you photograph children, the more you will be aware of how they react to certain situations and to the things you've said. You will become more perceptive and more tactful, knowing what to say at the right times, or even saying nothing. It is very much about your own personality and being on the same level as the child.

Remember, you are a stranger and you have to gain a degree of trust in what can be an overwhelming experience for a child. Some children are very responsive to instructions and ideas; others are more shy and less forthcoming about what you would like them to do. Here's a guide to communicating with children so that they are relaxed and at ease with you:

1   Advise parents before the shoot to try to keep the children calm, not to make a big deal of the experience, otherwise it can be overwhelming.

2   Never assume that a child is going to immediately warm to you. You may have minimal time to get your images; use the first part of your shoot to create dialogue with the child – to the point of not showing your camera too early if the child is very self-conscious. You may want to focus on other people in the family/group so that the attention is not solely on the child.

3   Be positive in your communication and be genuinely responsive and interested in children. Listen to their answers and what they have to say. Build on that conversation – it is most likely something they are interested in. Parents can be very keen to 'keep Johnny smiling' even when you aren't taking pictures. Your conversation with the child is also for the parents' benefit – part of the job of creating a wonderful portrait is the rapport that you build and it takes a little time. If 'Johnny' wants to poke his tongue out at you, you can be sure that the parents will ask him to stop. Experience will tell you that if you ask children not to do something, they will do the opposite. If you, the photographer, make demands, like asking him not to poke his tongue out, you may be creating a barrier between you. The alternative is perhaps to strike a deal, for example: 'Ok, I'd really love some pictures of you with your tongue out, Johnny. Then how about a couple for me and Mummy, without your tongue out. Can you do that for me, Johnny?' This way you are giving Johnny some control. You are asking him if he is OK with this, allowing him to be a little bit cheeky with you. You are now working as a team and not making demands on him, just giving him an opportunity to create dialogue and not to see you as a stranger, more as a friend.

4   Encourage the child to have ideas of his own for pictures. Even if you have fixed ideas, go with Johnny's too – children like to feel they are playing a part.

5   Let the child run about and feel at ease at the start of the shoot. If you go straight in, setting things up and making demands, this can be off-putting for the child as it's an unnatural environment.

6   Carry a cheap point-and-shoot camera and promise the child he can take some pictures of you once you have taken your pictures.

7   If you have an idea for a specific image, don't try this first. Gain the trust of the child, warm up the creative juices and make some 'safe' shots first. Save the best ideas for the middle of the shoot; leaving it to the end risks the child being fed up and tired.

8   Ask children if they chose what they are wearing today, talk about siblings and family – something they are familiar with and like to talk about.

9   Don't try too hard – you really can't force a child to like you and it will show in the pictures! Be yourself and project your own personality; this in turn will translate to your images.

10 If the shoot is with siblings, the older child is likely to be more confident. Start your portraits with that child so that the younger one can watch. You may also want to ask the younger sibling for some help with holding a reflector or pulling faces.

11 Sometimes, just remain quiet and allow a picture to develop.

12 By all means use bribery (but check with parents first if you are offering sweets).

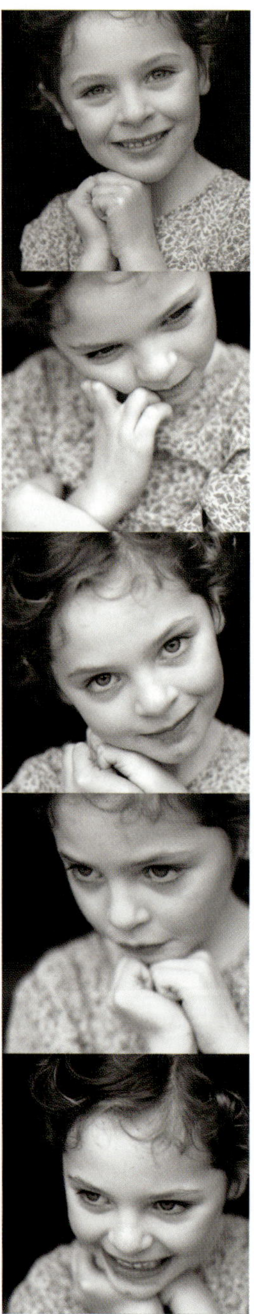

▶ Fig. 6.15
This child was vocal and carefree, so the photographer sat quietly observing her and recorded this series of expressions with a long focal length lens that put some distance between them. Patient and observant, the photographer allowed the child to express herself.

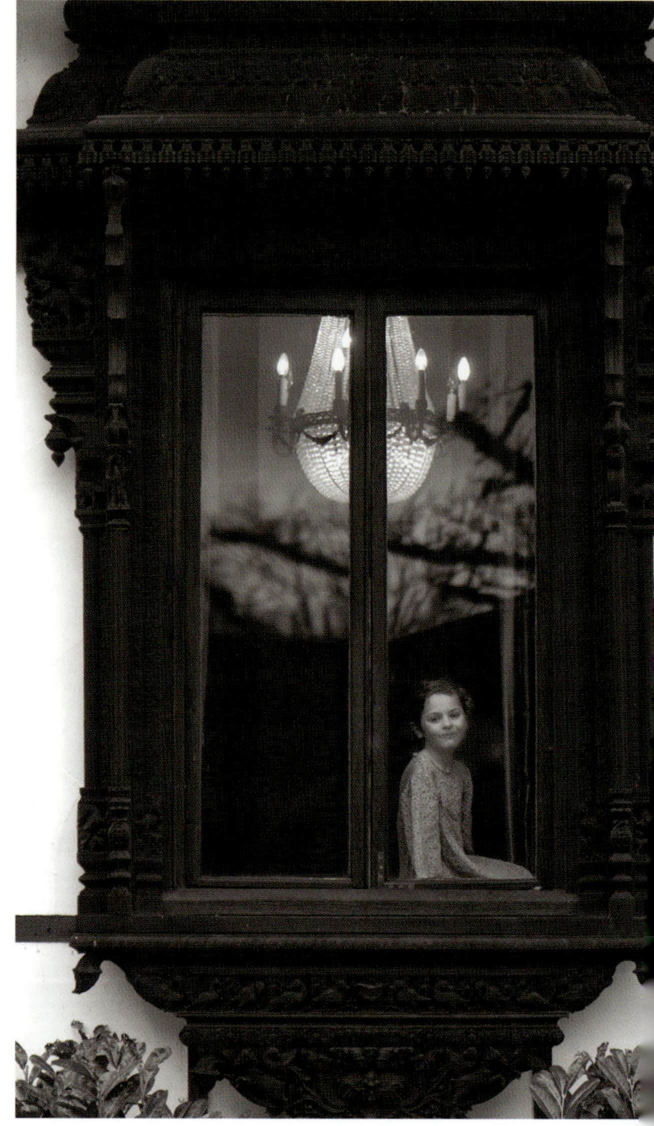

▲ Fig. 6.16
Once you have a connection with a child and have gained their trust, having verbal communication is not always necessary. Consider placement and then allow the image to take on its own character by allowing the child to react naturally. Sometimes little or no communication can be very powerful; it just takes a little patience.

Some children are desperately shy and will cling to their parents like a limpet, and coaxing them away from them in most cases will make things worse. This is the time to focus on the parents, to the point of ignoring the child. Reassure them that Johnny is fine to be clinging to them kicking and screaming, that you just want to take some pictures of Mum and Dad together. By turning the tables and focusing on Mum and Dad or a sibling, you can gently introduce Johnny to being your helper to animate others rather than him being the main focus. Children enjoy being given a role. Once he sees it can actually

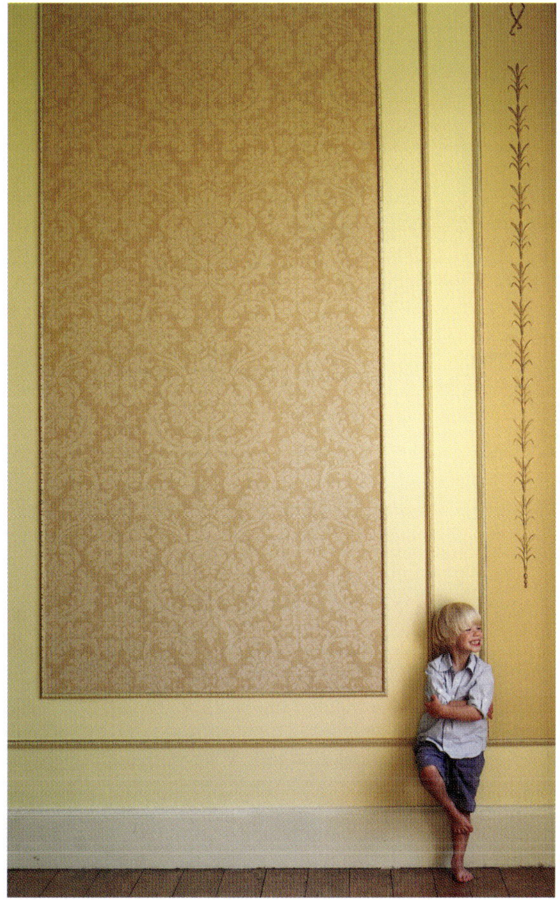

▲ Fig. 6.17

A portrait of a child looking relaxed and happy in a somewhat contrived situation. The scene was set with regard to the placement and composition – the little boy lifting his leg was a natural development on his part. The bold composition and use of negative space fills the frame with colour. Seeing a child genuinely smiling from the eyes is a wonderful image, but sometimes we can be just as moved by a child who is perhaps deep in thought, undistracted yet still content, but without the smile.

be fun, he will slowly remove himself from Mum's grasp. You will still need to factor in placement for the light in difficult situations, rely on strong composition and be wholly aware of expressions as well as changes in dynamics through the child's body language.

Of course, this method is not a hard and fast rule. Those of us who have children or are familiar with how unpredictable they can be will understand how the dynamics can change depending on how you approach the situation.

Conviction in Direction

In order for us to work quietly, confidently and to achieve a positive connection with children, how we interact with them at the beginning of the shoot is absolutely key to how the shoot will develop. Most importantly, you want the child's interest – interest in you, interest in the photographs, without him or her wanting to get in the car and go straight home. When you give direction, it needs to hold conviction and be confident, while at the same time being gentle and reassuring. Without this positive interaction, you will find it difficult to translate your ideas for an image effectively. Definite instructions or guidance directed at a child must be at their level of understanding so that a visible rapport is attained. You can ask questions and give children an opportunity to respond; you can even ask them for help in developing the image. Again, this is very much about encouraging children to feel they are important rather than just the 'subject', so talk *to* them rather than *at* them.

How you structure questions to children can make or break the response, particularly if a child is shy or a little unwilling. How we structure a question to them about what to do next can have differing results. For example, if you wish to move to another location because the light is not great where you are or you would prefer a different location, you could put it into words like this: 'Let's go over here and take more pictures,' or 'I'd like to move you over here.'

This is negative – it is about what *you* want, not their choice or about them. You are making a demand or commanding them to do as they are told, which might make children feel isolated in their decision. And if they're feeling a little insecure about their surroundings, they are highly likely to say, point blank, 'No!' Remember, you are possibly a complete stranger to them and they are rightly wary of you to begin with.

However, if you were to word it like this: 'Where would *you* like to go for *your* picture?' it doesn't matter if their answer is different from where you want

The eyes of these three siblings are all going off in different directions. Ensure that you build a direct rapport with both the children and the parents so that the parents understand that you are the main communicator, and thus the children will respond to you.

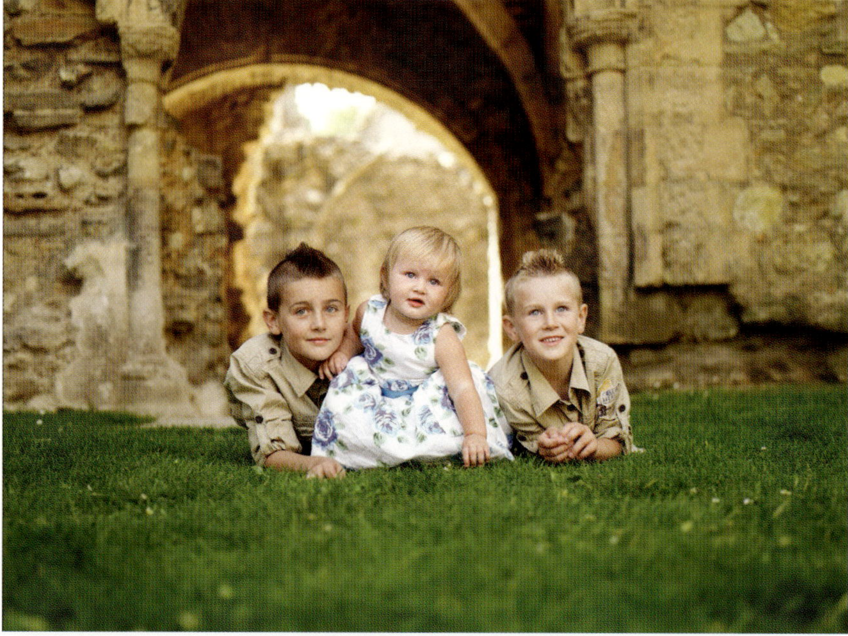

Be confident and definite in your communication to ensure a direct interest between you and your subjects.

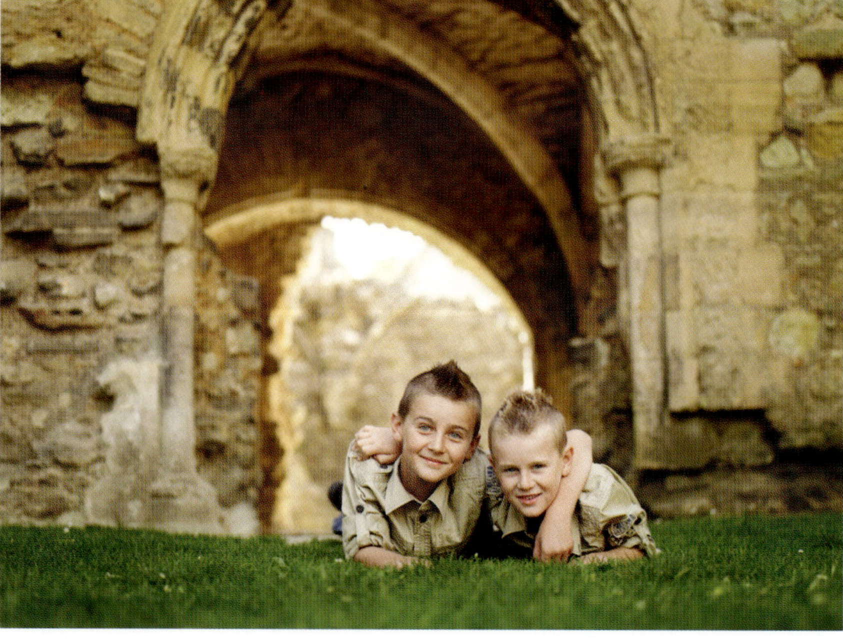

to be. Even if they suggest 'in the car', go with it at this stage – take pictures in the car and then ask the same question: 'OK, where next?' By now they will be relaxing and starting to enjoy your company and you can start making suggestions: 'How about we run along this wall?' 'Do you think your dress would look pretty against that tree? I think it would look beautiful – do you think we should give it a go and then I can show you the picture, and you decide? Is that a good idea?'

We mentioned earlier about the importance of removing coats as they can look bulky and almost

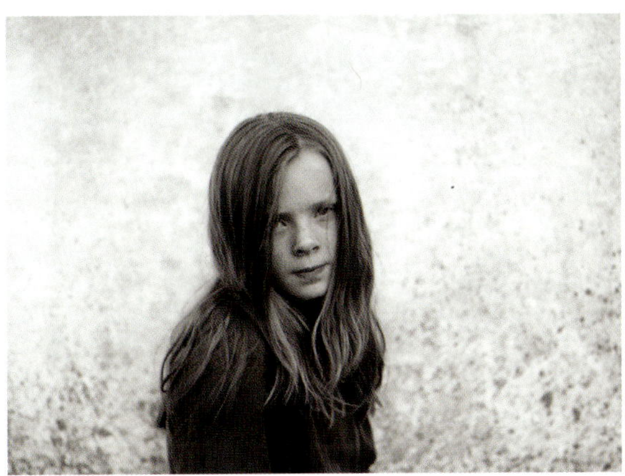

▲ Fig. 6.20
Even when a child is shy and unreactive, we can use this sensitivity – in fact, it can be incredibly powerful.

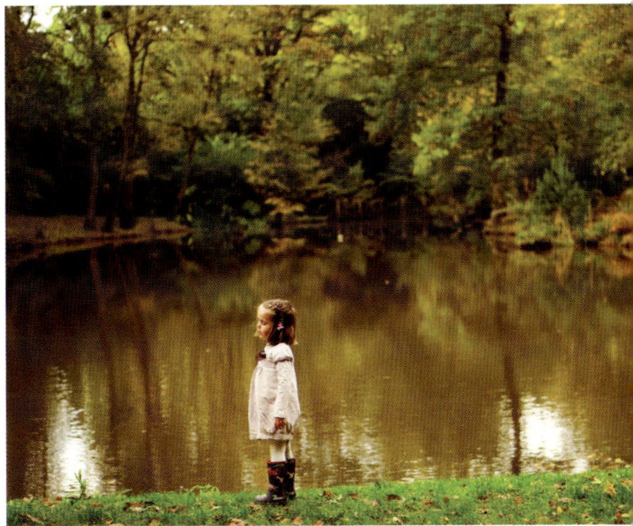

▲ Fig. 6.21
There is a very fine line between a child who looks melancholy and a child who looks plain sad. Some children actually photograph better when they are deep in thought. Occasionally you will find you are not getting the connection you were hoping for; don't battle with this for too long. You will become frustrated and it may rub off on the child. Don't hesitate to change tack: play a different game, move outside/inside.

'temporary', as if the child was just passing by. Asking children to remove their coats is a question that demands some tact. For example, we could ask:

'Would you mind taking your coat off?'

'NO!'

(You walked straight into that one!)

At this point, Mum starts to make demands, and gets cross with the child for not taking his or her coat off or doing as you have asked. How many of us have turned up at a shoot to hear mothers saying, 'Now you must do as the photographer says'...? This now becomes a negative scenario and the child will become defensive, annoyed and upset; it's not conducive to creating the right kind of emotion! We need to keep the environment relaxed, calm and positive.

So, alternatively, we could go down a more indirect route through interest and conversation:

'Did Mummy choose you a new dress especially for today? What colour is it? Is it your favourite? How about we warm up in our coats and then do some just of your dress? I think Mummy might really like that. Do you think we should do both? Your flipflops match your dress – did you choose them? Who has more shoes – you or Mummy? Mummies like shoes, don't they? They like to have a pair for every outfit, just like you have today. Do you prefer flipflops or trainers? Trainers are easier to run around in but don't look so good with a pretty dress, do they? I bet you can run faster than your sister, even in flipflops. Did mummy paint your toe nails to match your dress? I love the colour, I have some in a similar colour – which part of the dress is the same colour as your nail polish?' Off comes the coat.

In that conversation are challenges to encourage the child to be the leader, the winner. But also what is key here is that you are taking a natural interest in the child – obviously you should modify your speech to match the gender and age of the child, but listening as well as communicating verbally and taking a genuine interest are important.

It's often easier for teenagers and older children if you do the shoot at a location where Mum and Dad are not directly involved. This age group is perhaps the most challenging for a photographer. Parents with small children will most likely want to be involved in the shoot, but do give them advice as to the level of involvement so that you can put your own methods into place. For example, Mum may be

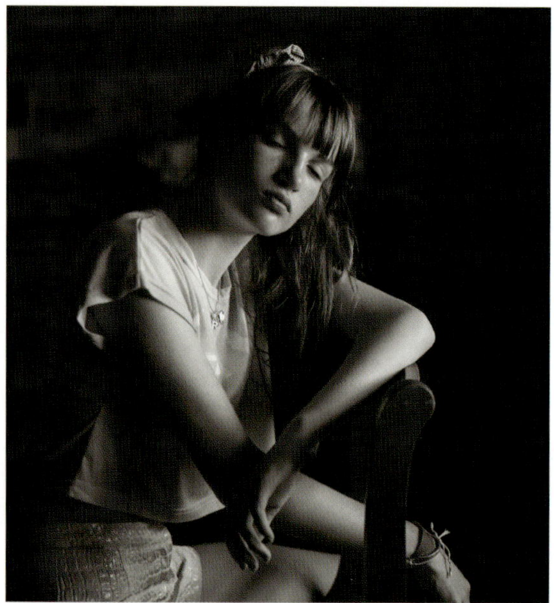

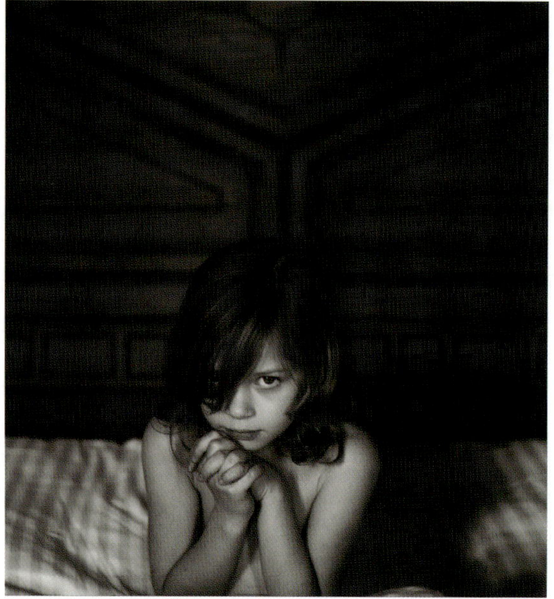

▲ Figs 6.22a–b
The low key mood in Fig. 6.22a, using just directional window light and shallow depth of field, is enhanced by the quiet, natural pose of this teenager. The girl looks entirely at ease and deep in thought, but in no way sad. In contrast, in Fig. 6.22b there is an element of sadness in the child's eyes, coupled with the protective nature of her pose. She is clenching her hands tight and there is an insecurity in the feel of the portrait. The lighting, composition and graphic content have produced a wonderful fine art or editorial piece, but as a saleable image it perhaps does not sit so well.

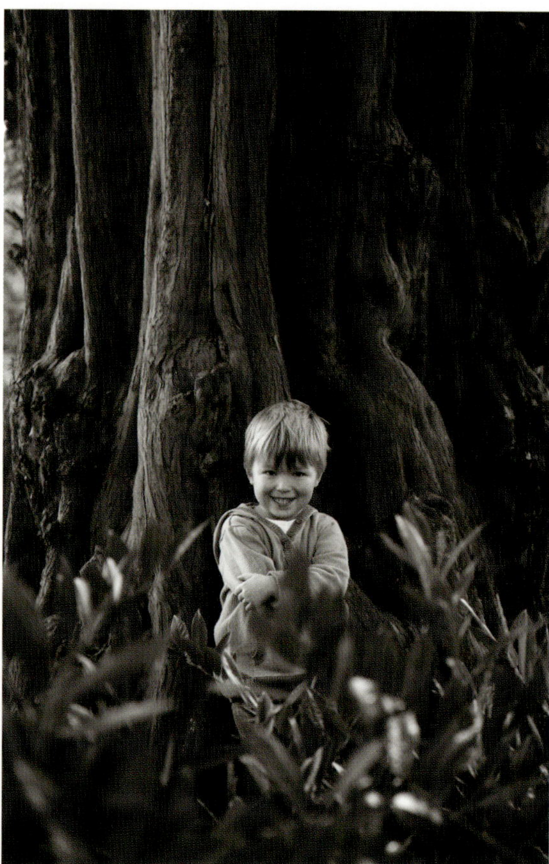

▲ Fig. 6.23
Look at adding dimension through natural framing, as here where the photographer has utilized the foliage, which contrasts with the textures within the trees.

standing behind you so that she can communicate with the child to create a response. Make sure she is at your level, her head at your shoulder height. If not, the result can be a lack of cohesion in eye contact with the camera, especially if there is more than one child.

Welcome the involvement of parents in the portrait, but be positive in your direction with children to ensure that the connection is with you. Fig. 6.19 shows the children responding to their parents behind the photographer and ultimately the eyes are all in different directions. Keep the parent close to you, and don't have more than one parent giving advice to the children.

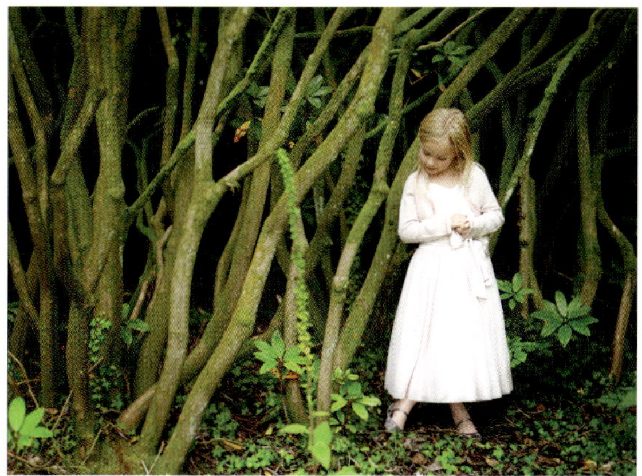

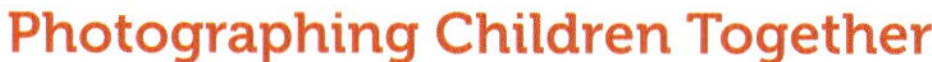
Fig. 6.24
Utilize a location to suit the mood of the image you have in mind –
a strong location like these trees will embrace something contrived
and considered, or alternatively give a contrasting, softer feel,
perhaps marrying the graphic of the trees with movement, creating
something more ghostly.

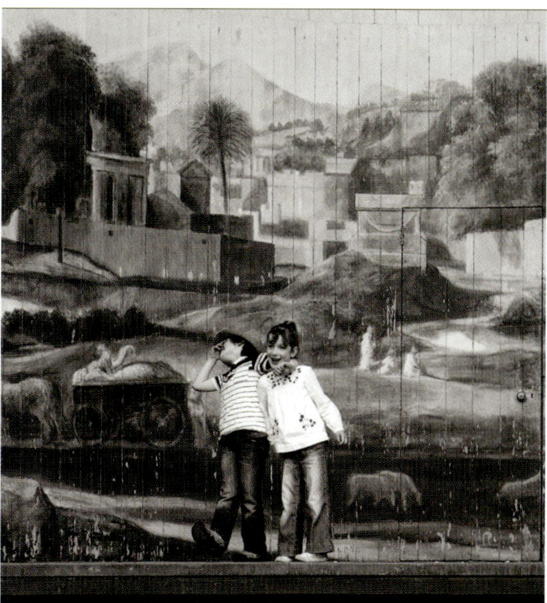
Fig. 6.25
Siblings and friends will play together naturally if you have the
patience to wait.

Photographing Children Together

As we've mentioned, photographing older children
requires a different approach. Older children tend to
respond better to posing, whereas younger children
have a shorter attention span, and it's important for
us to encourage children to portray themselves in
a way that is relevant to their age. Our perspective
on them and the angles we choose may be different
for varying ages: with smaller children we tend to
be more at eye level in order to create something
more intimate, as opposed to shooting down on
them, which can sometimes give the impression of
vulnerability.

Introducing a second person – a sibling, parent,
grandparent – can relax a child and bring context
to a picture. A second person in a shot adds another
point of interest and introduces the idea of 'relationship' into your image. It can help younger children
to be a little more relaxed through interaction and
engagement, and can distract them from you.

Try to encourage children to play and interact
together in order to capture the relationship between
them. Encourage natural posture and interaction,
which will in turn give you opportunity to 'tweak'
and create some definition in the posing. If one
child is more dominant and confident than the other
child and always putting him or herself in front of
the other, this can be frustrating when that child is
open to being photographed and the other child is
less so. However, use this child to dictate the flow of
the shoot; notice how the other child watches your
friendship build with the confident one. It is as if the
first child is giving the second the 'OK' to interact
with you and that you are not an ogre. In time, you
may find they both start competing with you for
your attention – this is the perfect scenario and you
begin to take back the control.

Symbolism

Sometimes an image can be strengthened through
removing elements as opposed to adding. An image
rarely needs anything more than great directional
light and strong composition, balanced with inven-
tive use of location, pose, colour and/or tonality.
Everything should come together to fit the desired
feel.

You may have an idea for an image which

▶ Fig. 6.26

Fig. 6.26 No price can be put on the emotive value of an image of siblings bonded – the wonderful view here, together with the anonymous juxtaposition of the portrait, opens the narrative of their future and where their lives will take them.

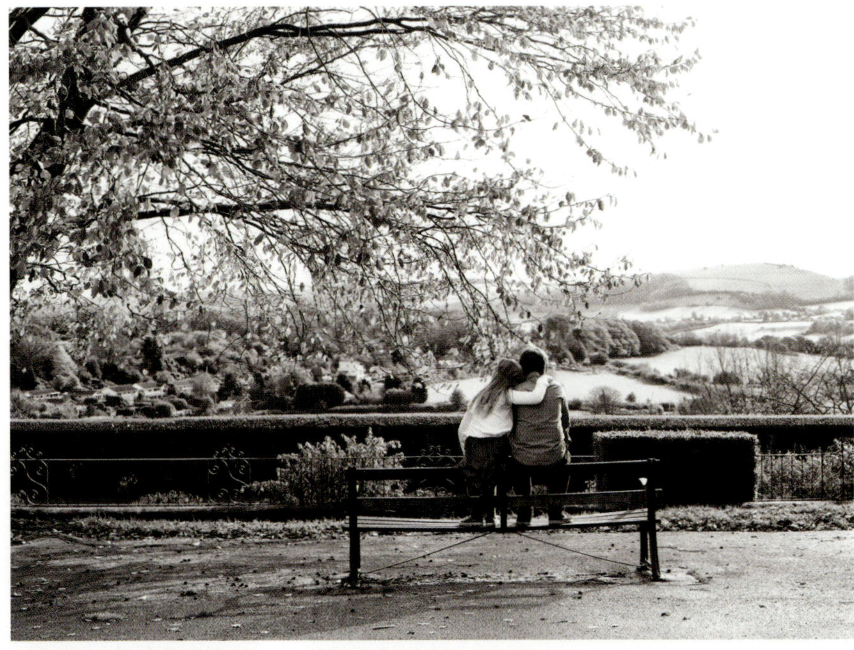

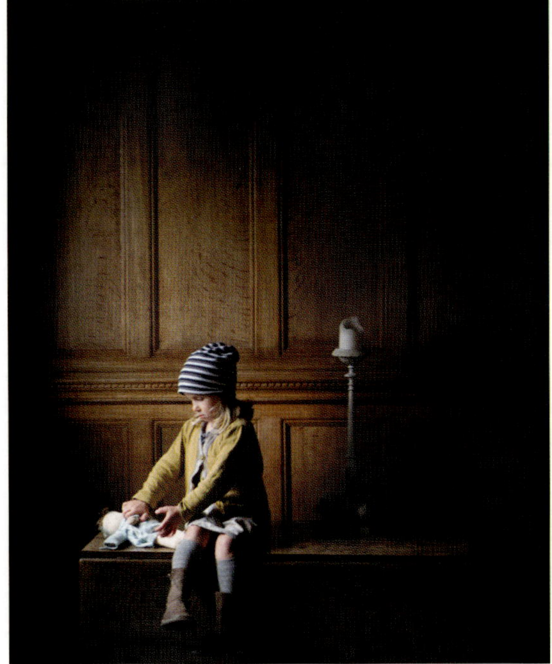

▲ Fig. 6.27a

Figs 6.27a–b
A doll was an important part of the life of this particularly shy little girl, acting as security for her. The photographer incorporated it into the portrait but not in a dominant way.

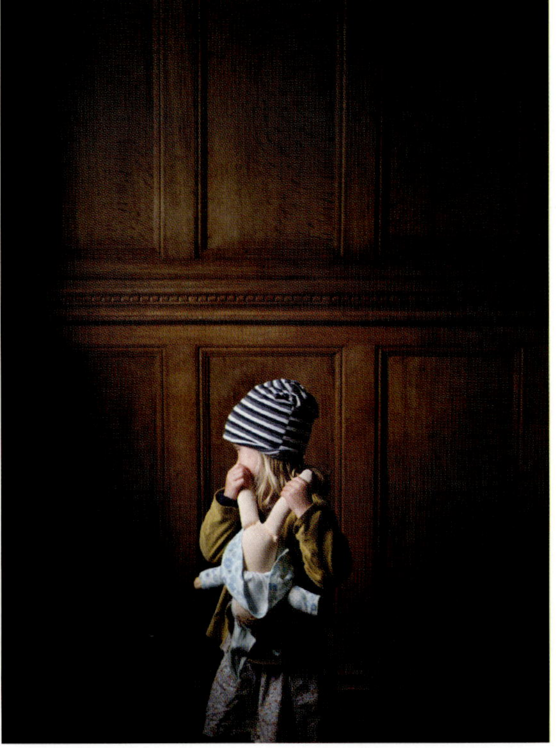

▲ Fig. 6.27b

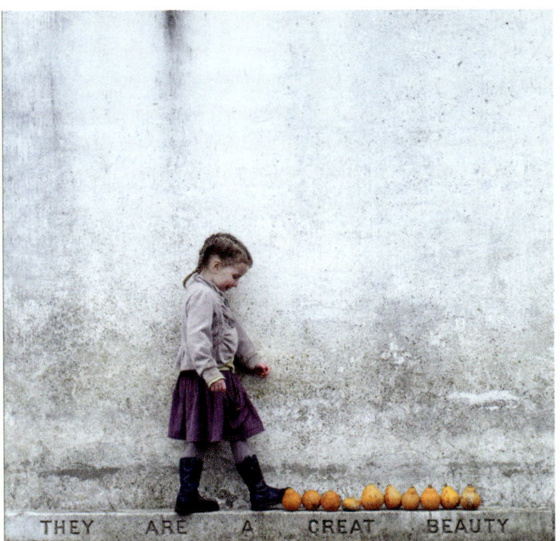

▶ Fig. 6.28
This child was painfully shy and the photographer had to use methods to distract her and keep her interested without directly communicating or asking her to respond. The use of squashes as a prop provided that distraction and they were incorporated into the shoot.

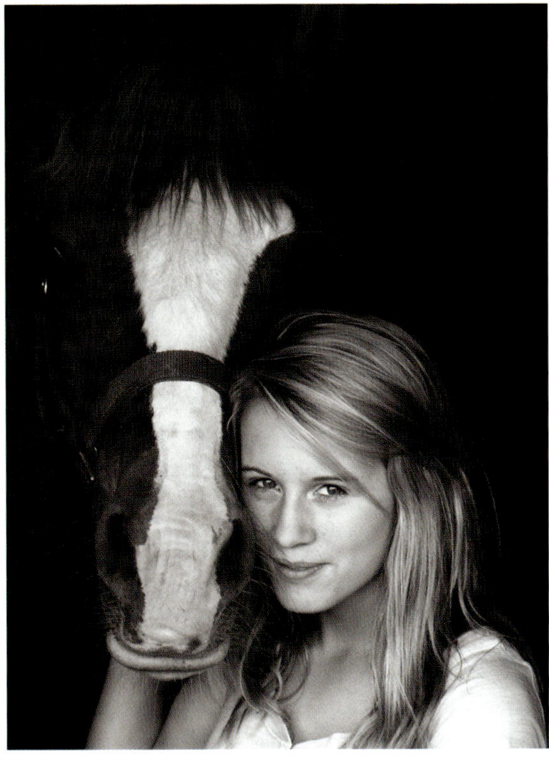

▶ Fig. 6.29
Incorporating a hobby or interest is all part of encapsulating a particular time in a child's life and takes us back to the importance of legacy and retaining childhood memories.

involves the use of some kind of prop – perhaps a toy, a hat, accessories in the form of jewellery – but ask yourself, what exactly is this adding to your image? A narrative? If so, can that symbolism that you are after be portrayed without the use of a prop? Will viewers be invited to read the image and make up their own mind rather than the image being clichéd, obvious and potentially tacky? A portrait, however, does sometimes need a little help in the form of a prop to tell the story.

Imagine your portrait on the wall in say thirty years' time. Would it still hold that nostalgia and be a talking point if it wasn't accessorized? Would it retain its timeless value? There is certainly a place for a subtle theme running through a portrait. The well-known photographer Anne Geddes is a great ambassador for the use of props in her work,

whereas you could say Sally Mann used the environment as her prop in order to add aesthetic value.

In Fig. 6.28, careful composition, use of colour and the tactful suggestion to use the plinth as a beam – to be a ballerina – has enabled the photographer to produce an interesting natural portrait with minimal interaction with the child. Having a parent to encourage and act as your communicator in situations like this is invaluable. With older children it is often not so helpful as teenagers especially can become self-conscious in front of their parents. It's a good idea to brief the parents on the type of feel you want from the portrait and explain that you may only want minimal input from them. Sometimes it just takes a parent striking a conversation with the child to put that child at ease.

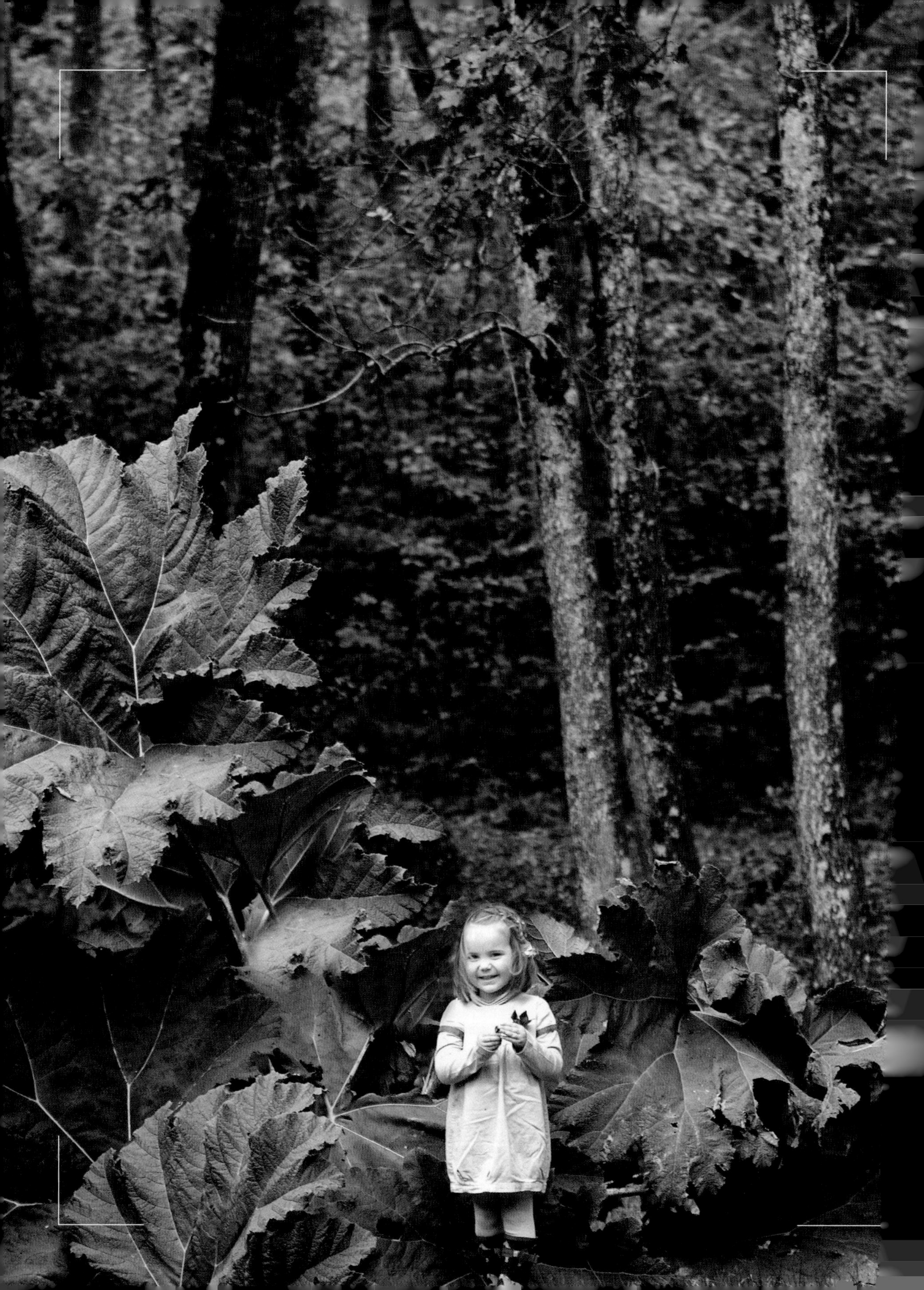

Composition, Space, Image Quality

Composition is the making up of shapes and forms to create a two-dimensional photographic image. It's the method of combining light and shapes to represent depth and space. In our case, as portrait photographers, the shape and form comes first from our subject and subsequently from the location.

In Fig. 7.1 the photographer chose to include the whole building when photographing the child. Here are a few notes on the decisions the photographer took before making this picture:

1   The placement of the child in this image is important given that the photographer has chosen to be bold with the composition and encompass the building in its entirety. If the photographer had chosen to place the child to the side, it might have unbalanced the symmetry and perhaps risked 'losing' her in the scale of the pillars. She is very much making a statement here due to her central placement.

2   The photographer has recognized that the scale and grandeur of this building, with its bold pillars, is acting almost as a protection around the child. She is tiny in comparison, but her placement and the scoop of the fabric offer almost a soft leading line into her – an element of the soft child element against the hard uprights.

3   The position of the photographer is dead central, in order to retain the symmetrical aesthetic.

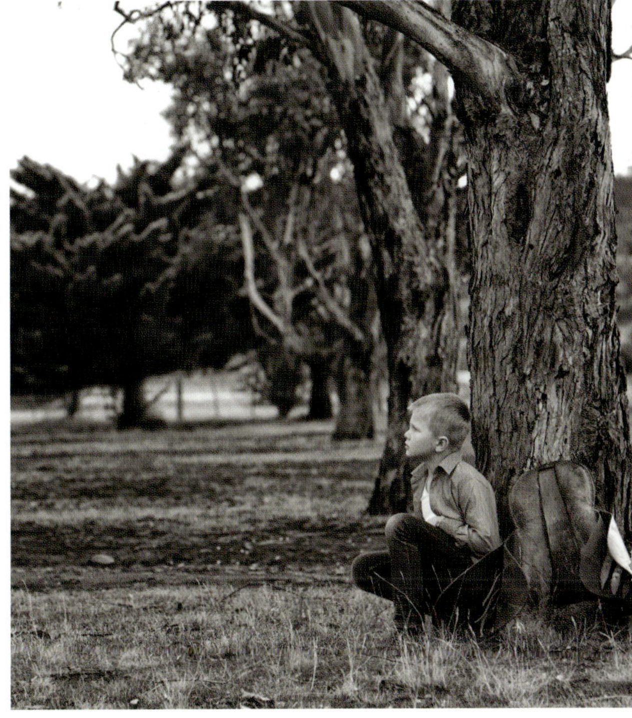

▲ Fig. 7.1
A location can offer several opportunities for composition, and it's worth considering all the variations available when you are shooting. Try to work out how many different compositions could feature in this location.

◀ Fig. 7.0
Use natural elements within the environment to add scale and depth.

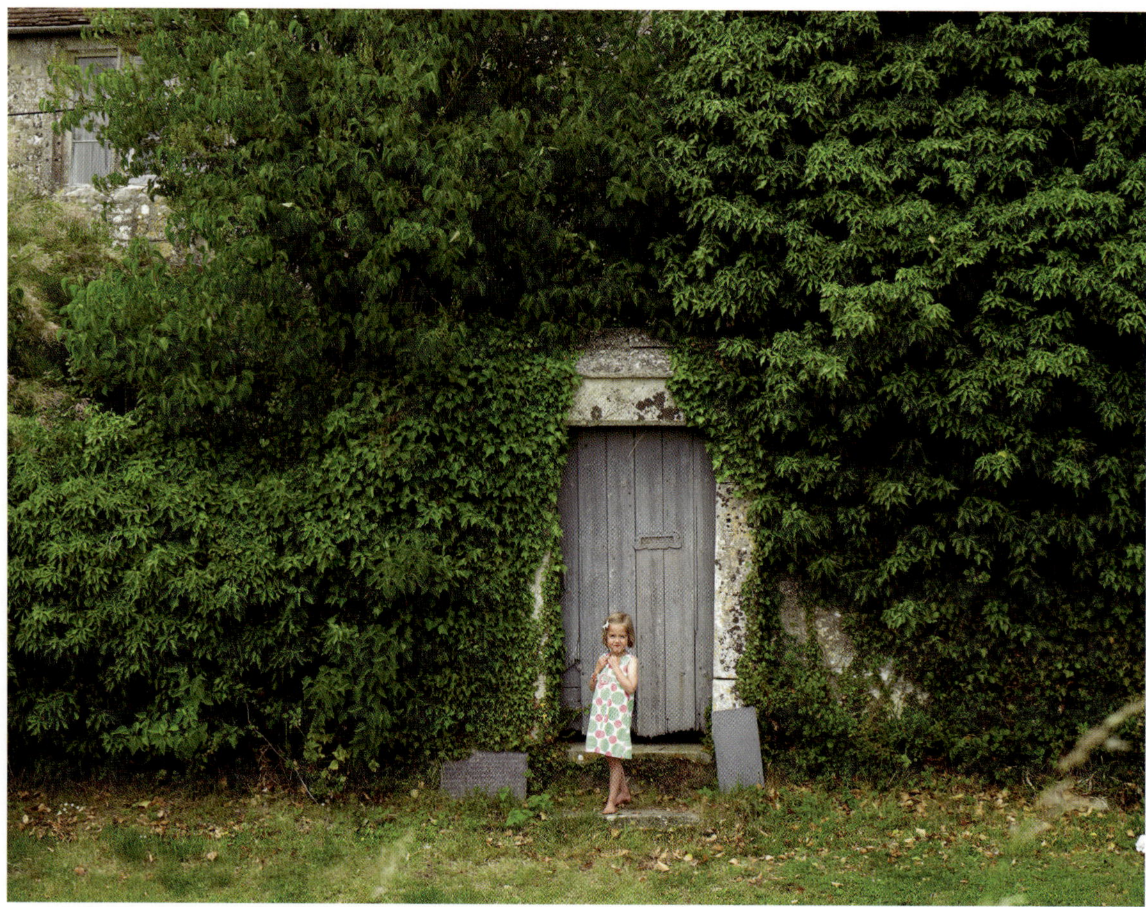

▲ Fig. 7.2
Allow space around your image to incorporate the environment and
evoke interest as well as provide natural framing and scale.

There is an innate train of thought in many photographers' minds that the only way to truly view the soul of a child is directly through the eyes, and to produce a viable 'product' they must be able to view those eyes and therefore compose their portrait as a head study. This is true to a degree. However, there are two things to consider on the subject of composition:

1   If your subject is beautifully lit, taking physical steps backwards to incorporate the world around them can encourage a story to be told. You are working with environmental portraits, so the environment should be worked as an inherent element in your images (you may as well just be in a studio otherwise). There's nothing more splendid than a photograph of a child which gives viewers the opportunity to visualize a very obvious story or to be able to make their own.

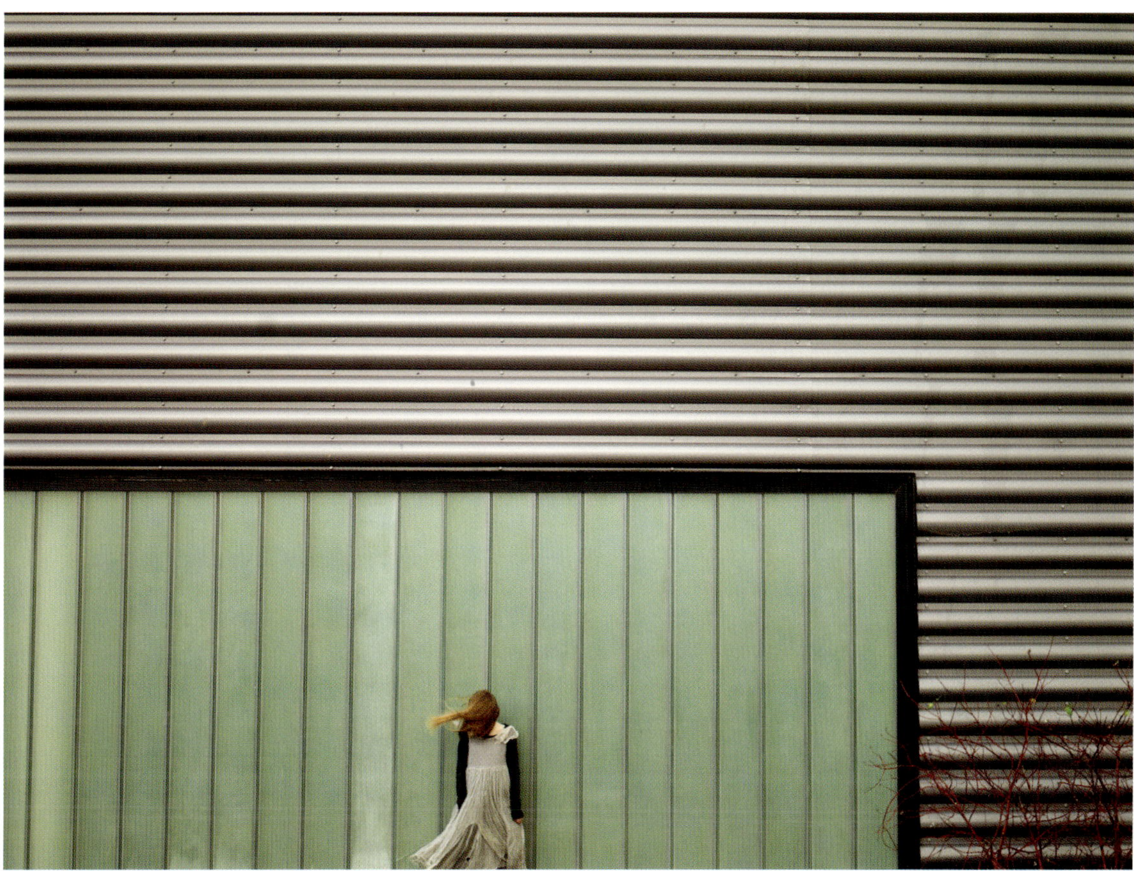

▲ Fig. 7.3
Strong graphics invite an alternative composition and placement.
In a minimalistic location such as this industrial unit, you can use
colour and movement. This is negative space that serves a purpose.

2   A photographer who owns a long focal length lens, has the ability to create expression, and can incorporate satisfactory lighting into their work will have the skills to produce a pleasing head portrait of a child. There is an element of 'seeing' in this, but it is a way of working that is accessible to all and requires minimal creativity. We can afford to take our skill base higher. To set yourself apart, you could be striving to bring architectural or aesthetic elements into your work which are either inaccessible to your peers or contain elements of composition which are unique only to your creative mind. The one thing we 'own' as photographic artists is our creative mind and no one can take that away from us, however off the wall or quirky it may be. Others may copy, but to consistently introduce new concepts and strike compositions requires individuality and in turn gives us longevity. Bear in mind that habits are easily formed in photography; often they grow from a trend or fad and before you know it, every other shot you take contains the same composition. Be open minded and search continually for new avenues of design to incorporate into your work.

▶ Fig. 7.4
An engaging head study of
a child, with direct access to
the soul through the eyes.

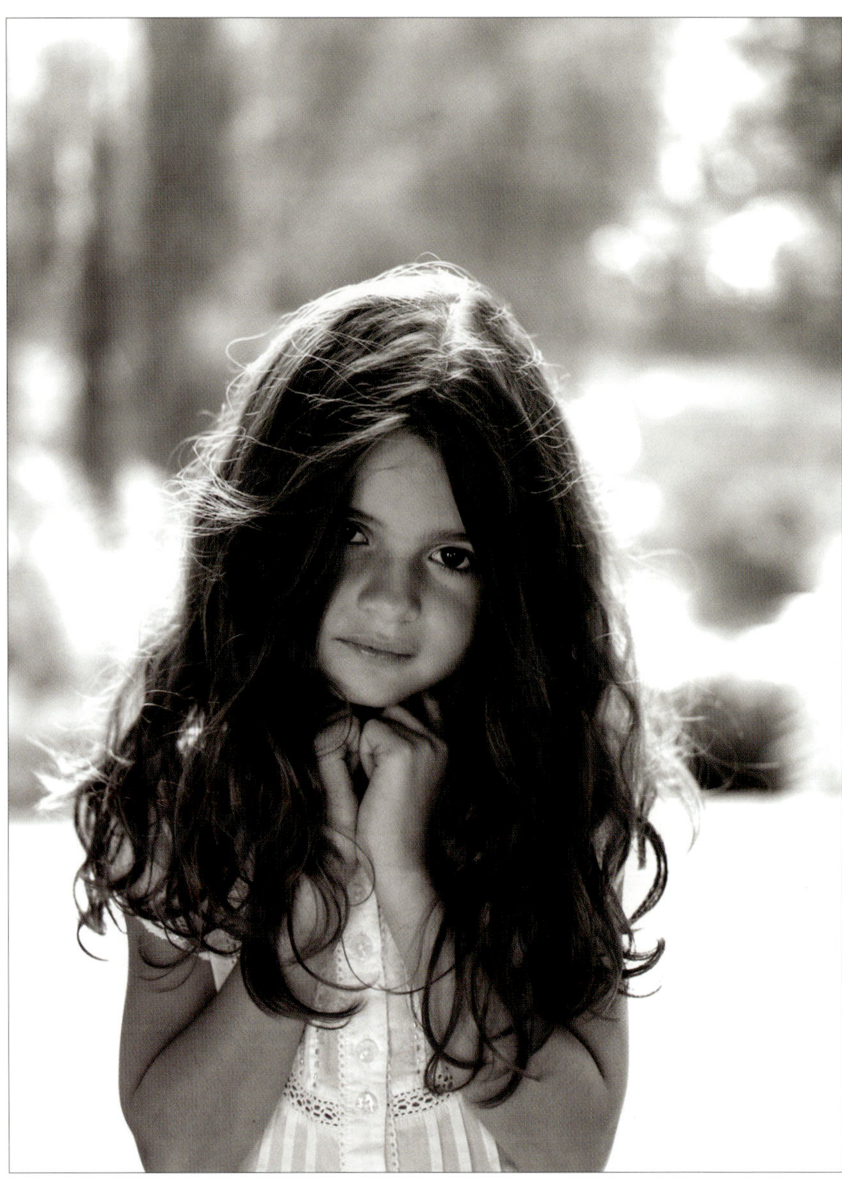

Design, Shape, Form

We can think of the natural world, architecture, the human body, as being composed from multiple intersecting shapes. If we apply this knowledge to our photography and start to view our positive space in the same way, we can learn to use shapes to guide the eye and manipulate the way in which our photographs are viewed.

Your style may be soft and whimsical with accents of ethereal beauty entwined within your portraits. It may be strong and graphic, perhaps more removed from the soft emotive value and leaning more towards graphic fashion. Regardless of how you showcase your style and how you wish it to be, shape and form still factor within the elements that make up strong portraiture, in both an organic form from the horizontal and vertical line within an environment through how you shape your subject.

Portraits with this design have a language that contains shape: a two-dimensional area that may

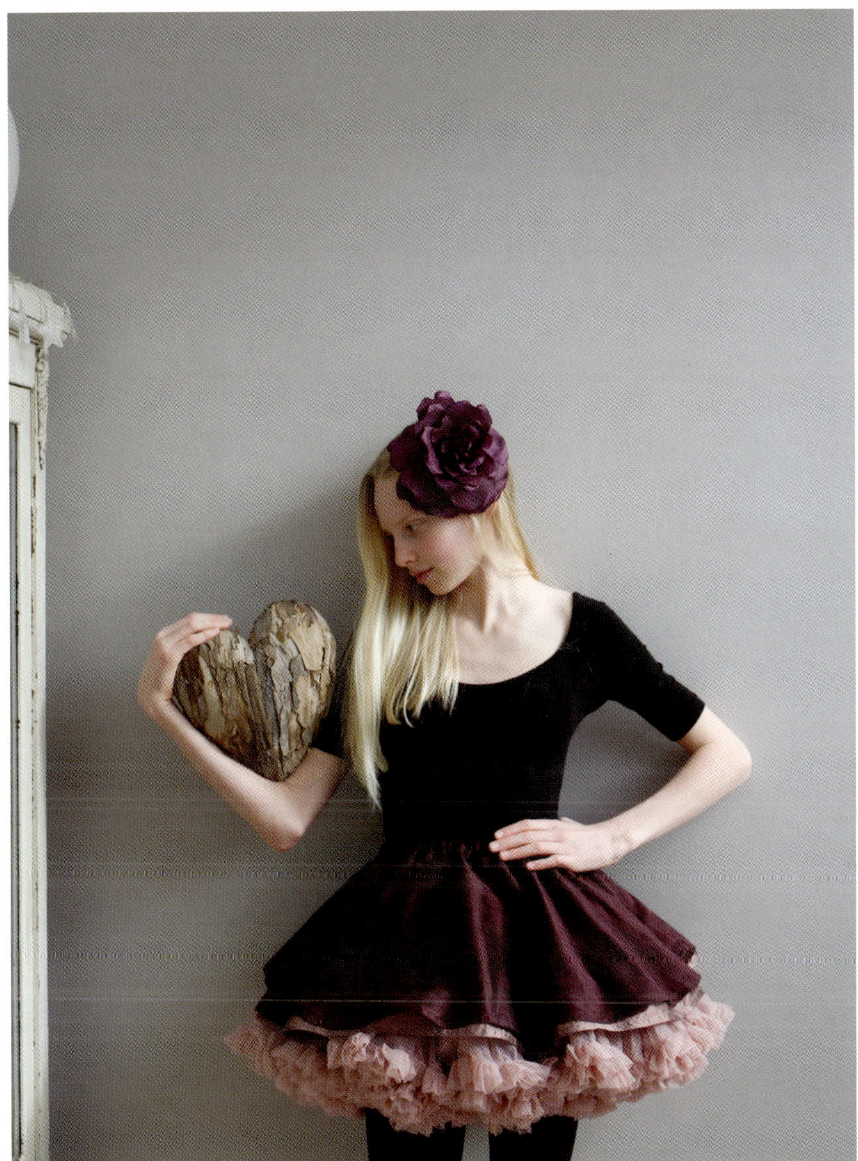

◄ Fig. 7.5
The photographer is emphasizing shape to good design effect, with the use of the girl's dress, the object she is holding, and the overall shape of her pose.

be organic or not, free-form or geocentric, open or closed, natural or of human origin. Contrary to how this may sound, this applies to all genres of portraiture and can be relevant not just to the contrived, 'man made' image, but to a fly-on-the-wall, documentary one. It is visible within the composition and the use of architecture. You need to have a refined eye for moments of shape which might occur naturally within a shoot.

Photographs are composed of positive and negative space. Things that consume space like objects and items represent the positive space, and the space in which they are situated is called the negative space. Let's imagine a simple portrait shot against a white background: the positive space would be the subject that is being photographed, and the negative space would be the white background that surrounds it. Simple, huh?

The brilliant new era of digital cameras has provided us with a tool that has changed the efficiency

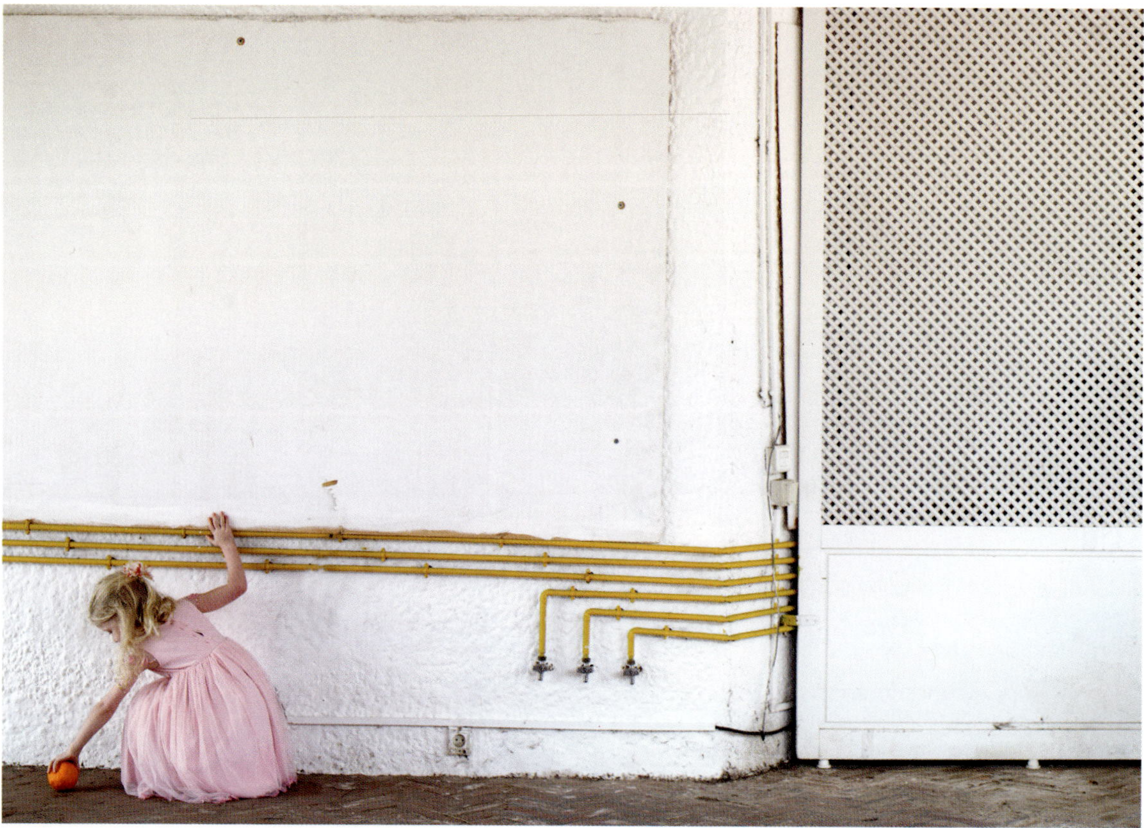

▲ **Fig. 7.6**
Bringing together shape, composition, natural placement and
perspective, the photographer has observed how the child moves
and the shapes made to compliment the leading lines and various
shapes within the location, creating perfect negative space with
graphic interest throughout.

with which photographers frame their work in
their viewfinder. It has given us the opportunity to
experiment with placement and composition and
the ability to continually introduce elements to an
image accurately and on the hoof. That tool is the
wonderful multi-sensor focusing option. Left, right,
up, down, diagonal, inside out and back to front,
you can compose and recompose in a split second.
Unfortunately (or not, depending on how you look
at it), the camera is not able to make a decision as
to the best option in a given situation, but give it
the correct message and it will obey. This takes us
back to the crucial element of photography – that of
being your own imagination and creativity.

With this tool came the fashion for using negative
space. Not a new way of working, negative space
has of course been used for years. Edward Steichen
back in the 1800s, and many other classic artists,
used it in their work to add leading lines, graphic
stability, block colour and define a story line. Now
we are seeing it in a less controlled environment.
The candid photographer can, with a flick of the
thumb, adjust and readjust on the hoof.

We should, however, stop and think before we
use an expanse of space at the top, bottom or sides
of a frame. We need to simply ask ourselves, why?
What is this space contributing to this particular
picture? Am I doing it for effect? Am I doing it just

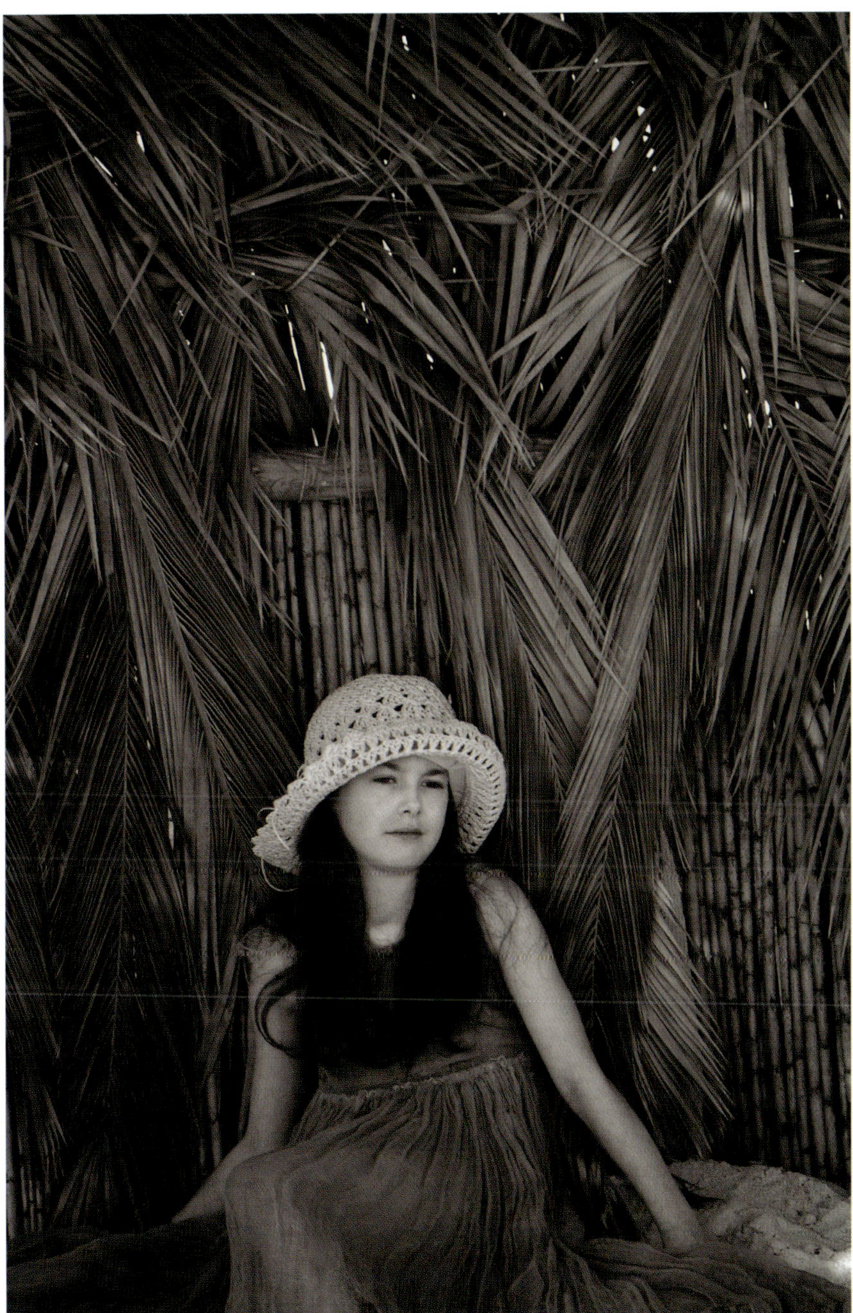

Fig. 7.7
The graphic wall of reeds on a beach adds a contrast to the softness of the child. The space this is afforded within the portrait is an intrinsic part of the make-up of the image.

because I can and I like to use every button on my top-of-the-range camera? Am I doing it because it's a trend? It would be wiser if we used our creative intelligence and looked at all the options. Might it look better with the subject dead central in the frame? Is it going to look like another clichéd picture if I use the negative space? Can you emphasize colour and tone better by using it? By the time we have asked ourselves all these questions, we may have lost the shot, so having an idea of the styling of a shoot beforehand will help us understand where we are going with it.

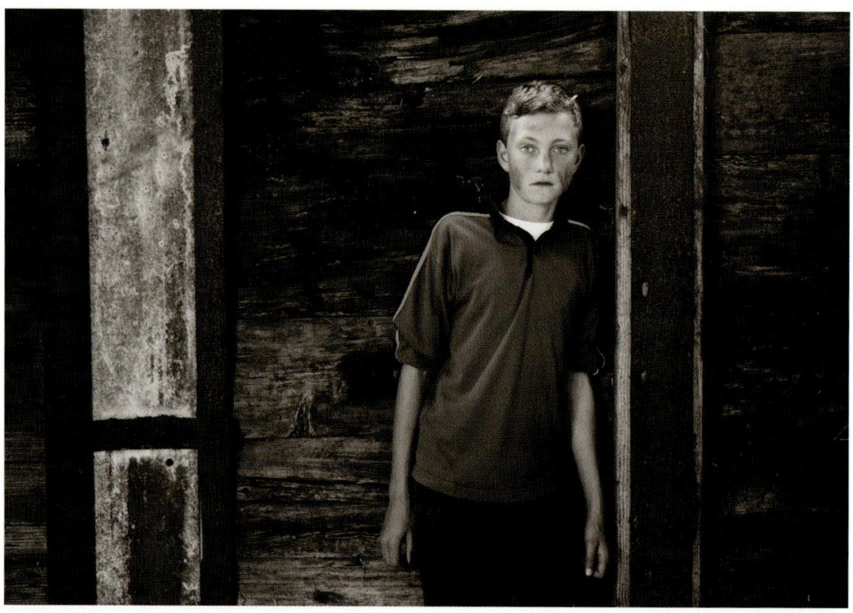

▶ Fig. 7.8
Wood and stone against the grain add texture and graphic, exposed with a narrow aperture in order to pick out detail.

There is nothing finer than a beautiful portrait, created with consideration through the use of space and leading lines which draw the eye into that wondrous pool of light and the subject. Interestingly, the viewer's thought process could be parallel to that of a portrait photographer in that we make our portraits with selectivity and by working slowly. I certainly like to take my time both when shooting a picture and when reading a picture on the wall. This comes back to slowing down and taking stock of the design and make-up of a picture. Yes, we can and sometimes have to shoot at speed and be spontaneous (especially where children are involved), but that doesn't mean we should forget about the placement of our subject or how we should compose in the viewfinder. There is a credence to the quote 'more speed, less haste' – composing efficiently in seconds, yet using part of that time to consider.

The more experienced you become, the more you will understand the limitations of your camera and that of your imagination; you will also become aware of what works for you and your style. The style of composition you use that makes your work your own is very visible and recognizable to the untrained eye. Those untrained eyes, those of your client, can tell that you have that 'something' in your work but they may not recognize what it is: your use of light, posing or a bold composition. Negative space has to serve a purpose to the aesthetic of the picture, to assist with the story telling, add graphic and so on, otherwise what is its purpose?

Perspective and Photographer Position

Before you take your shot, take a look first at where you are and ignore the immediacy of what you are about to take. Let's take the emphasis of the child away from the equation for a while; let's look at you and your positioning. How will it affect uprights if we are looking for symmetry? How does *your* positioning affect the storytelling, the view of the environment? How does taking an image and changing perspective to repeat it change the picture? If you are not happy with the angle, don't take the picture.

Lens choice, aperture and your positioning will affect perspective. For example, a head study taken with a 50mm lens, where you can be too close to your subject for comfort (noses lengthen and ears disappear) will give a different effect compared to

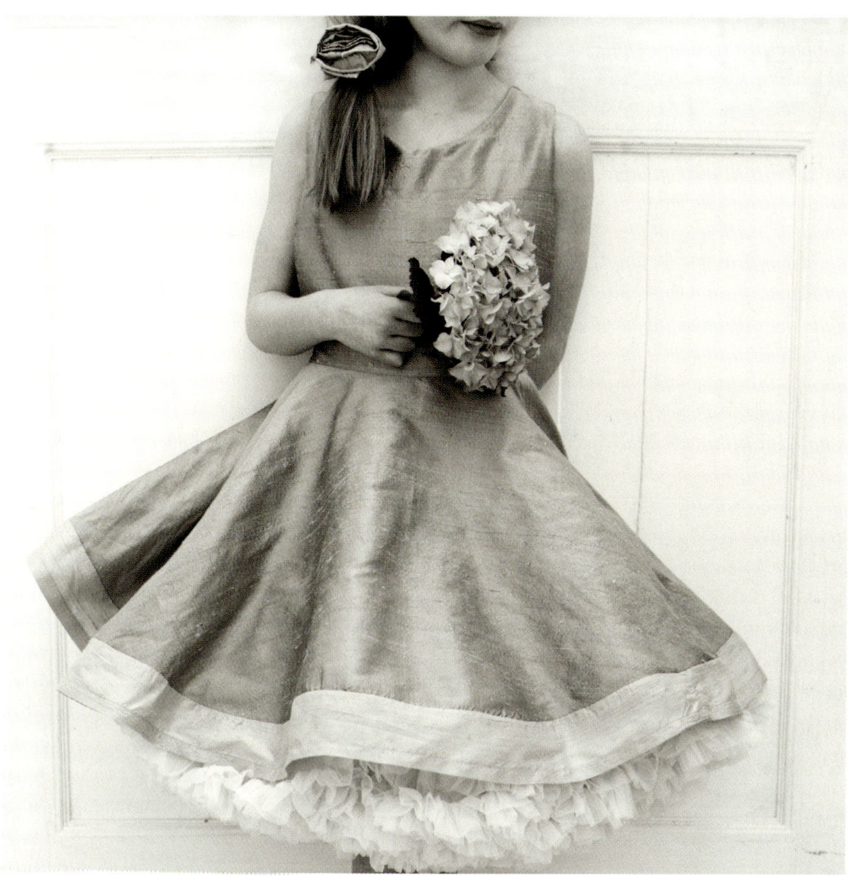

Fig. 7.9
This image would not hold its value had it been taken from a side angle. The shape, composition and crop are an intrinsic part of the design and styling.

a head study taken with a longer focal length lens. Being closer or further away renders facial features in differing ways.

Your positioning can define symmetry through your own central placement. In contrast, a portrait that is crying out for this symmetrical balance can be weakened through your own positioning being slightly off-centre. If you are searching for a balanced image, shooting the image centrally ensures vertical lines are straight. Of course, you also need to factor in the space that you have to work in. Fig. 7.11 was taken in a confined corner of a crowded room, so an ability to look at shapes and graphic and visualize cropping should be considered when choosing your location and positioning yourself in relation to your subject.

The Building Process of a Portrait

The location you choose is paramount in that it sets the scene for something special. Once all the parameters are in place, how bold you are with the way you see the final image in your head and how you translate this into your camera will be defining. Your ability to compose, recompose, check, recompose, move, recompose, change perspective, recompose, and so on, will keep the image developing without necessarily making big adjustments to the subject or even moving locations.

The temptation to fire off and hope for one good shot out of a series is tempting, of course, and indeed possible. However, the ability to be smarter in the way you work, not relying on this, will ensure that you are the one in control of the portrait, rather than the camera or merely good fortune. Being selective in how you take a picture,

DIFFERENT SHOTS IN ONE LOCATION

Learn to utilize a location: make small changes to pose, placement, depth of field, composition. An ability to recognize the weakness in a session is imperative in order to make changes as you go and to keep the set of images versatile. Notice dappled light if it starts to appear and question if it is affecting the overall aesthetic of the image. If so, move or make changes to rectify. In Fig. 7.10e the photographer is using the strong graphic element of the location, but the pose is very static, the arm being straight. In Fig. 7.10f this has been rectified, with movement in the hair and a softer positioning which contrasts with the background. The aperture has been left narrow in order to pick up the detail in the background to accentuate that contrast. However, in Fig. 7.10d a shallower depth of field on a tighter composition has been used to focus on the face with no distraction from the background. Composing and recomposing, adjusting depth of field, recognizing when a reflector is needed (Fig. 7.10c), changing your own perspective and positioning – it really is all about seeing what isn't working in front of you, rather than what is. And all this time, the light may be changing; you need to be aware of 'seeing' the physical change in light as well as watching your exposure readings in camera.

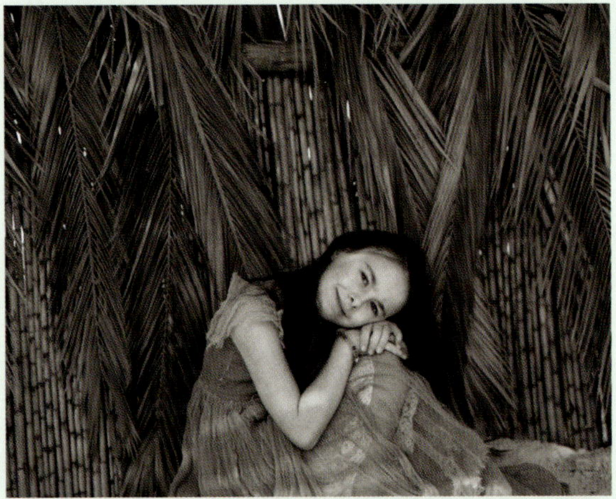

▲ Fig. 7.10a

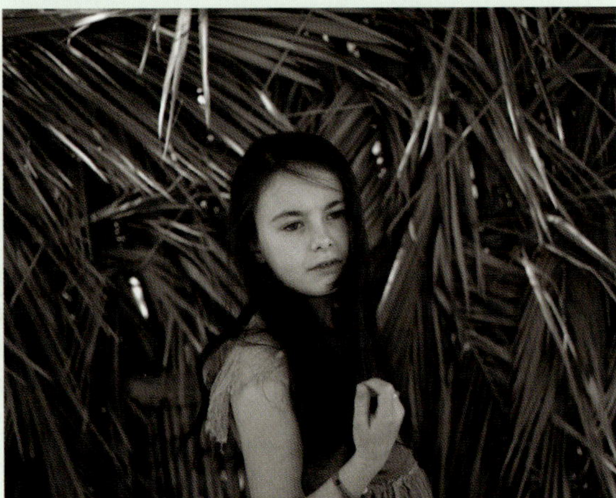

▲ Fig. 7.10b

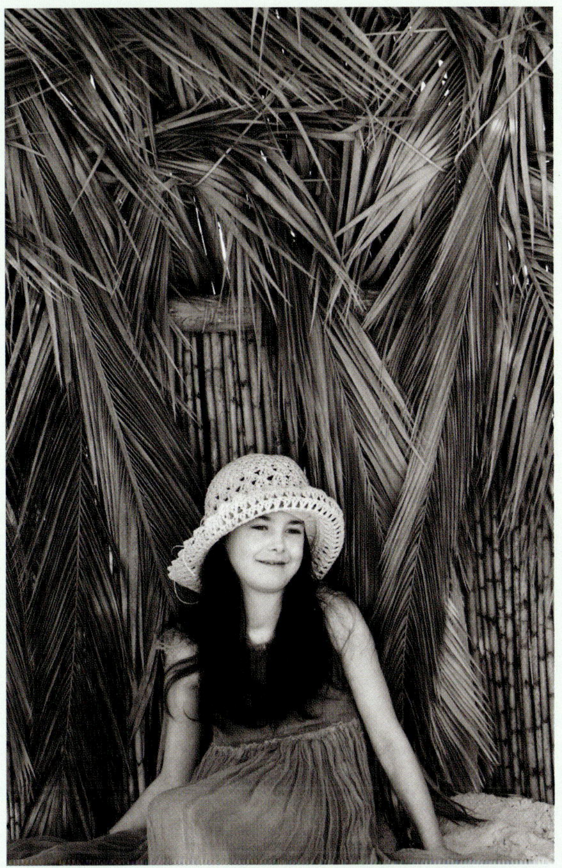

▲ Fig. 7.10c

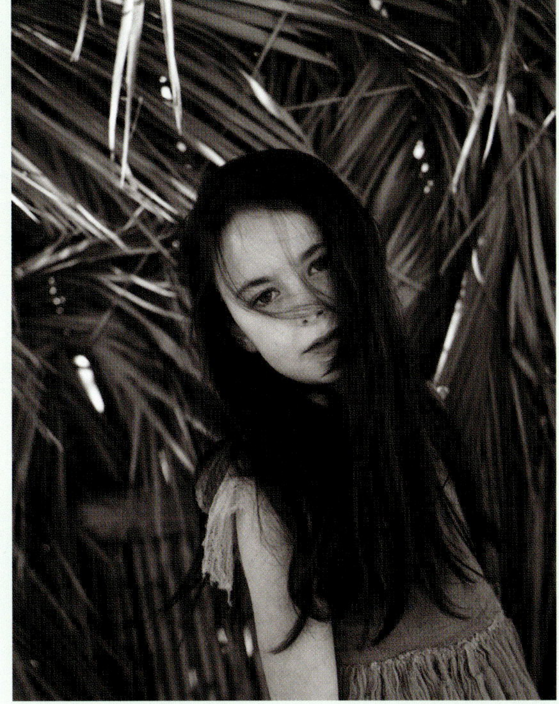

▲ Fig. 7.10d

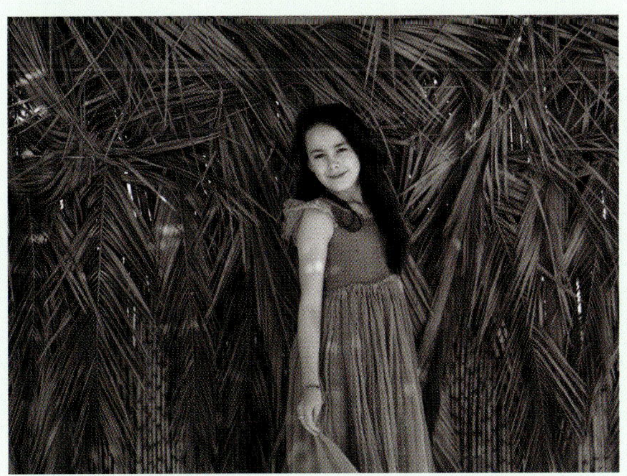

▲ Fig. 7.10e

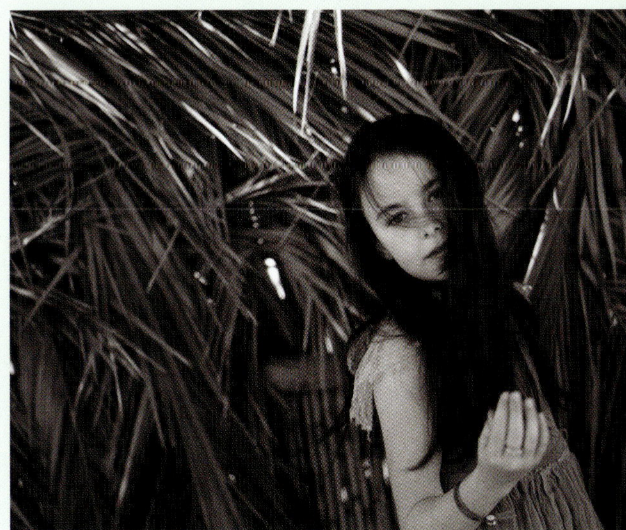

▲ Fig. 7.10f

whether it's a documentary or on-the-hoof shot or something more contrived, is a powerful way of working, and the more experienced you become in being selective, the better photographer you will be. This is important as it sets us apart: it takes us from being 'gung ho' in our photography to being specific and, not only that, it teaches us our limitations. You will soon realize your weaknesses when you try something and it doesn't work; this in turn gives us something to work on.

You don't learn much about your ability through relying on shooting multiple exposures of one scene. It's a wonderful feeling when you feel an image has come together and is working well. It's a more productive feeling when you know it isn't. Recognizing through your eyes that it's 'not quite right' is important so that you can make changes and improve.

Taking the initial idea we have in our heads and developing it slowly, perhaps removing elements that can overcomplicate it, is what helps us nurture ourselves creatively: adding movement, changing shapes, adding or taking away expression and gently tweaking to push for more from ourselves. As discussed earlier in the book, keeping this momentum going is important not only for our development, but it keeps the interest of the child. Being selective about when you push for more is paramount. For example, don't go straight in and expect that one shot to happen immediately (though sometimes it does just happen!), but develop rapport and grow the image. See an image, create it, then question it; never being wholly satisfied with the results is not negative, it's more about being hungry for perfection. It's all too easy to become embroiled in the excitement of a portrait when it is all coming together nicely and not push for more. Try to divert this excitement into 'where can I go now to make it even better?'

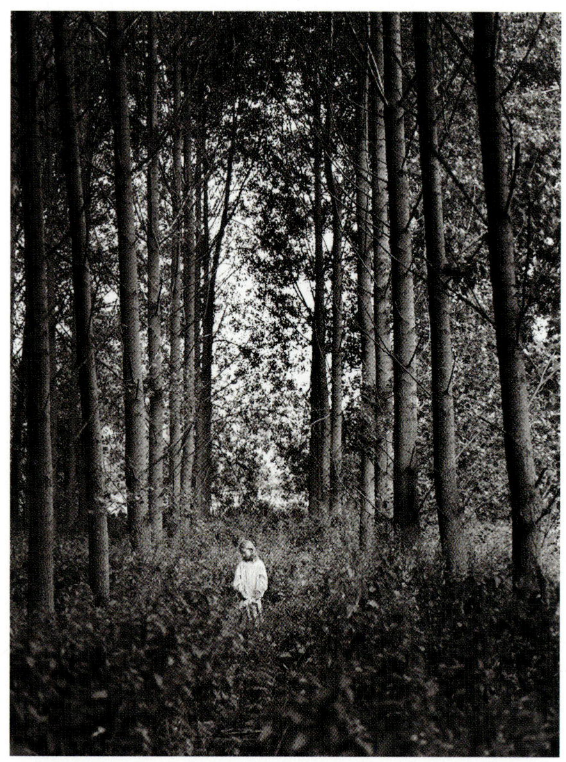

▲ Fig. 7.11

The framing of these trees forms a natural tunnel around the child, who is placed centrally yet on the bottom third, allowing for the trees to emphasize scale. There is a considerable quality of light coming through, given the time of day (late afternoon). The light is sourcing from the photographer's right but is low in the sky and therefore not creating dappling from above. The photographer's position here is important – being central keeps the symmetry of the uprights. If the photographer was positioned off-centre, the trees would appear angled and the child not central, removing the simplicity and impact of the negative space.

Image Quality

It is good practice, in fact crucial, that if you are making portraits in a professional capacity you should shoot in RAW format in order to obtain the finest detail and best quality files for your clients. Not only this, it will give you more scope for adjustments than working in the lossy format of a JPEG. RAW format retains *all* the image information recorded by the sensor and is essentially a mathematical assessment of the analogue make-up of light received by the sensor. Most modern small cameras now have the option to shoot in the higher quality format.

It may be faster to work in JPEG but, as we have

learnt in previous chapters, speed is not a prerequisite for fine art portraiture – on the contrary. Despite the extra storage space required, the main advantage of working in RAW format is the larger bit size of the file. A JPEG will give you 8 bit whereas RAW contains 12 or 14 bit, giving you higher brightness value and far more scope for adjustment on over- or underexposed files and post-processing workflow. A JPEG file being only 8 bit and with just 256 tonal values per channel means making any post-processing changes to the file increases the risk of losing details in the shadow areas.

Most cameras create both the RAW and an embedded JPEG, which is used to preview the histogram as you shoot. Using the RAW files for final output and the JPEG for client viewings can be to your time advantage, depending on how you are proofing. RAW files can be converted with ease these days in programs such as Capture One and Lightroom. For ultimate retainment of quality, work in 16 bit TIFF until you have finished processing, prior to sharpening a JPEG for print.

Working on location can sometimes mean working in low light and perhaps mixed lighting conditions, and a JPEG in these situations would be pushed to produce a file of professional quality. On occasions, when you are perhaps bracketing, over/underexposing and you need to bring something back into the image, a RAW file will allow you to do this with little detriment to the visual make-up of the picture.

Some of you may argue that RAW files take up too much time to process. If you are thinking this, perhaps you need to reassess your entire workflow strategy, including the capture stage. Are you perhaps taking too many of the same subject? We have talked in this book about individuality, precision, slowing down and essentially concentrating on refining our skills and applying them to 'an' image, singular or collection. Good photography deserves your time; just be considered and selective in what you take.

This quote from Berenice Abbott rings true, even today: 'A photograph is not a painting, a poem, a symphony, a dance. It is not just a pretty picture, nor an exercise in contortionist techniques or sheer print quality. It is a penetrating statement, which can be described in a very simple term...selectivity.' Yes, we have the opportunity to experiment today, but we must try to curb our urge to shoot on a mass scale and have some control in our thinking as well as our shooting methods. We will be far stronger image-makers for doing so.

White Balance

Some understanding of the quality of colour temperature will prove an asset in your post-capture work. In the days of film, we needed to use specific films in the studio for specific lighting set-ups (tungsten, fluorescent, etc.) along with gels in order to create the visual colour temperature we required. With digital, of course, we can either set our cameras to a specific Kelvin value, set a customized white balance (WB) using an X-Rite white balance target (recommended), or use processing software such as Lightroom or Capture One to customize our work, provided of course we are shooting RAW. Individual photographers have their own ideas about how their final images should look as regards colour temperature, contrast and brightness. Some prefer a wholly natural look as seen by the eye, in the region of 5500k, whereas others prefer a warm tone, unnatural but perhaps more inviting to view. By taking an image in situ of the X-Rite ColorChecker before we make our portrait, we can then use this neutral reading when we set our white balance in the processing software. Even if our final image is to be in black and white, we should still adjust our white balance.

By using the X-Rite ColorChecker application you can also create DNG profiles saved to your computer to streamline workflow and produce consistent and accurate colour corrections.

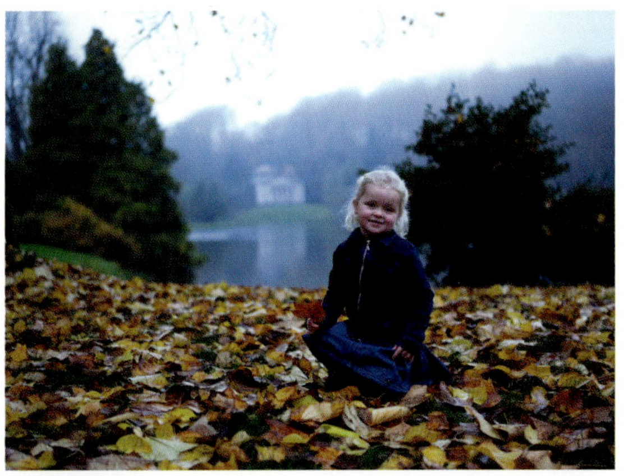

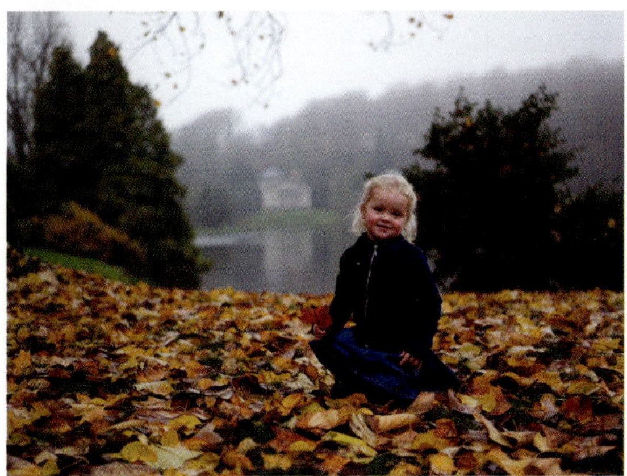

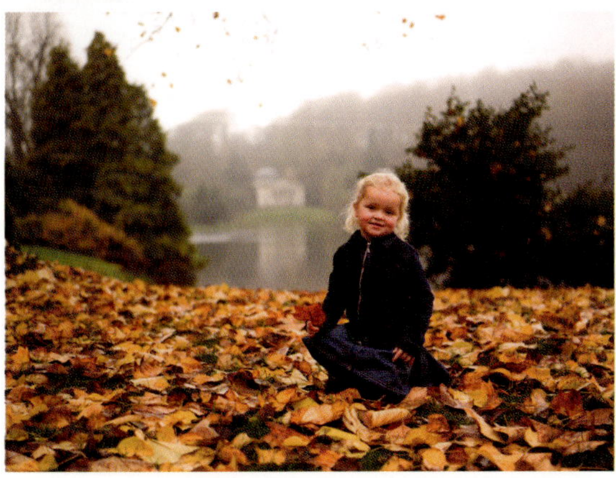

▲ **Figs 7.12a–c**
With no in-camera white balance set, this image shot in the autumn demonstrates how working in early morning light will capture the cold, blue hue that's not always recognizable to the human eye at the time (though with experience comes recognition). By using our X-Rite Col orChecker, we can select a neutral area, which will give a reading of around 5500. We then have that neutral point to work from if we choose. Fig. 7.12c demonstrates the colour temperature being taken up to 6500k. This may be too warm in some cases but here, given the richness of the leaves and the time of year, it may be a preferable choice.

Taking a White Balance Target

Leaving out elements at the shooting stage means extending the amount of time you will have to spend in front of your computer when you might prefer to be out taking pictures! So factoring these elements into your workflow will ensure a more streamlined and accurate way of working.

You can take an approximate reading from any item that is a mid-grey but it's unlikely to be a true neutral grey so there's a risk of colour casting – using a professional grey card will ensure accuracy. It's very simple to use: just photograph the grey card in situ where you plan to make your portrait, under even lighting conditions if possible and with the exposure that you will be using for the portraits. Fill the frame with the white balance target card and take the shot. To apply this in your RAW processor such as Capture One or Lightroom, use the eye-dropper tool in the White Balance tab and select the mid-grey image – you can then copy and apply this to all the relevant images in a batch. On the X-Rite ColorChecker (*see* Fig. 7.15) you will find variable options for warmer or cooler WB – whichever is to your taste.

Customizing white balance enables you to save a specific white balance in your camera, so that when you work in that environment again you can set it accordingly. This is perhaps more relevant to studio portraiture, but if there is a particular location you enjoy shooting in at certain times this may give you extra efficiency.

It's very simple: use manual focusing to target the card and set auto exposure. Using the colour checker target, the block of colour that should fill your frame when you take your sample is made up of colours similar to those we see in everyday life, such as skin tones, grass and sky, as well as representing RGB and CMYK values and the graduation of neutral greys.

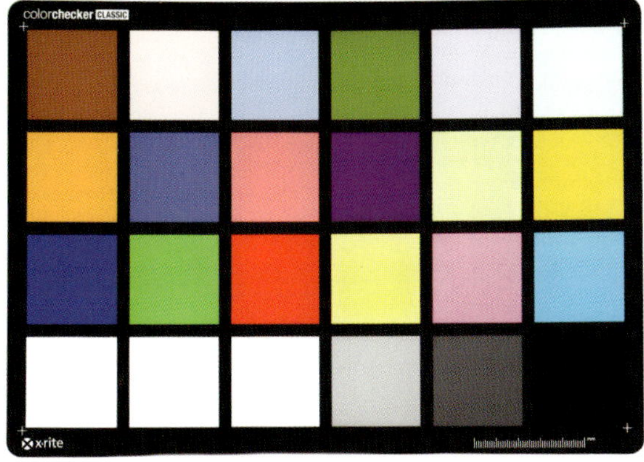

▲ Fig. 7.13

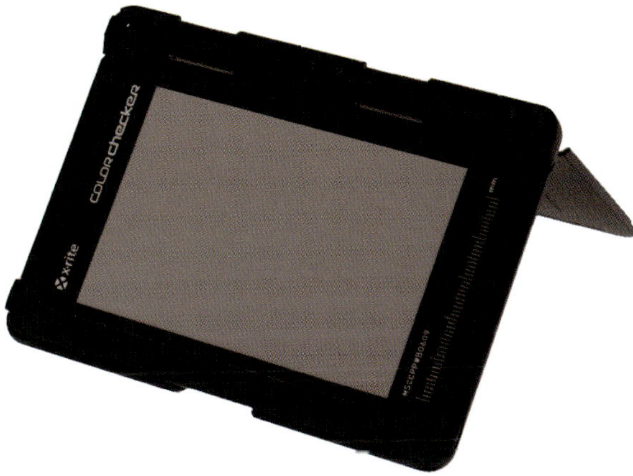

▲ Fig. 7.14
A white balance target.

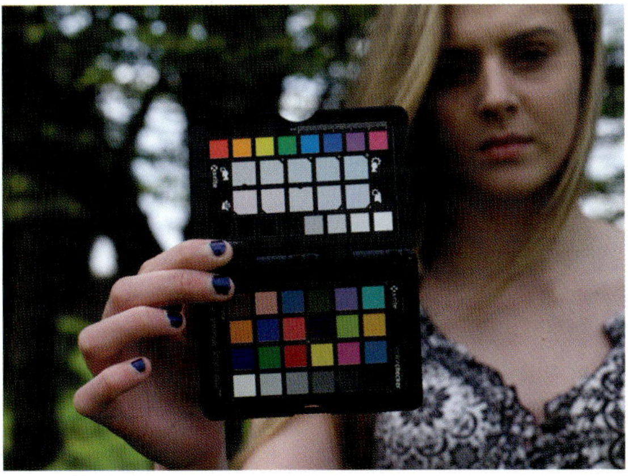

▲ Fig. 7.15
An X-Rite ColorChecker showing warm and cool options for white balance.

When you take your sample, ensure that the card is not only filling the frame but is held parallel to the lens to ensure that the light is reproducing the exact colour without drop-off, and make sure your exposure is correct or as it will be for your portrait. Strong shadows or dappled lighting will affect the quality of the reading. It only takes a second to do this and you can ask your child subject to be your 'assistant' and hold the card in front of his or her face. You only need to repeat this if the light or colour temperature change dramatically or if you move location.

There is nothing more frustrating than going through your workflow, producing colours and tones which are precisely as you envisage them on print, only to be let down at the printing stage with colour bias or flat blacks that don't match what you were seeing on your monitor. The ideal is to be able to reproduce on printed paper almost exactly what you have been working on on your monitor.

All camera brands will produce varying colour renditions, and even lenses can have an affect. If you are using two or three cameras on a shoot, you need to ensure consistency in your colours, especially if you are looking to create composites. The ideal calibration is creating a profile using the RAW image from your camera in a current shooting environment, made by using your white balance target card. For Lightroom users, there is a plug-in for RAW camera calibrating and for creating DNG profiles (these can be used in LR, or any ACR program).

Your working environment can affect how you view colour on your monitor. If you want to be completely accurate, grab a paintbrush and paint your walls a neutral grey! The ambient light you are working in can also affect how you view colours and tones; it's best to light your workspace with natural light or a daylight bulb. Being methodical with your camera settings is only viable if you also regularly calibrate your monitor. As monitors age, their performance adjusts and the display colour can change, hence the need to calibrate them. Some of the more high end (and yes, expensive) monitors are

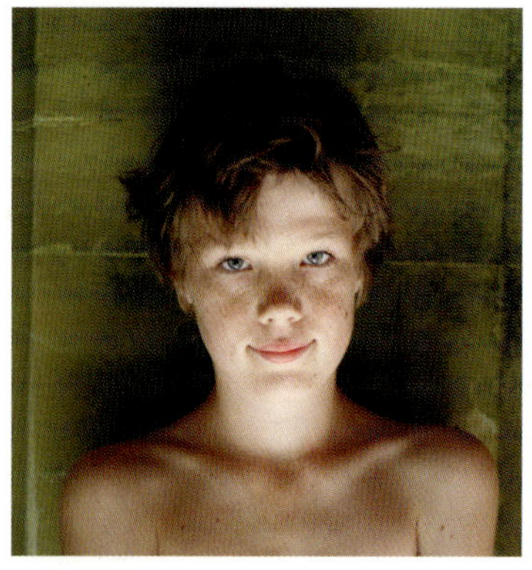

▲ Fig. 7.16a

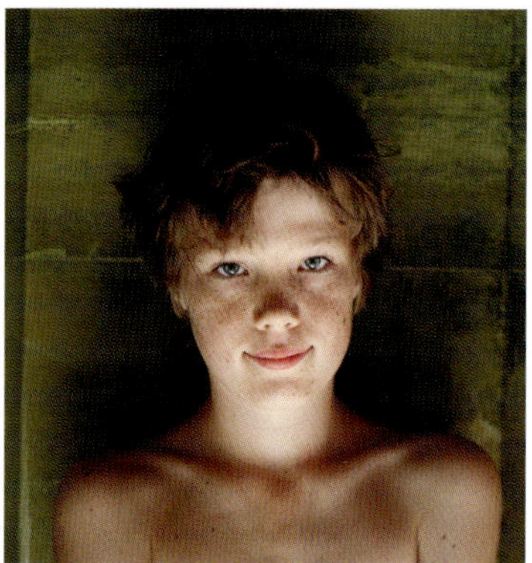

▲ Fig. 7.16b

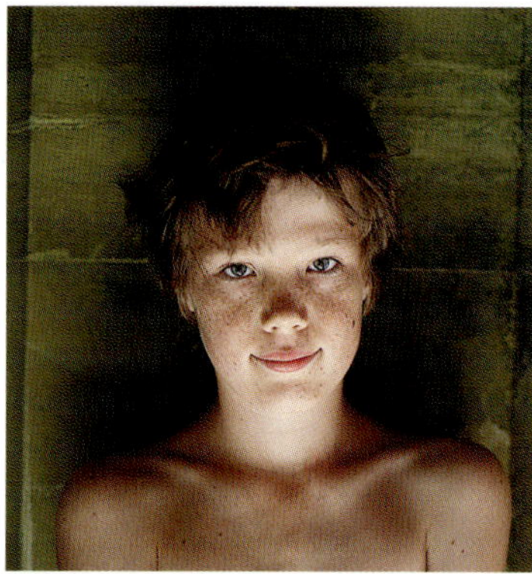

▲ Fig. 7.16c

Figs 7.16a–c
a unsharpened
b some subtle sharpening applied
c over-sharpened, showing the break-up of the image especially in the hair, eyes and skin.

self-calibrating. Prices are coming down and they are becoming more efficient, but it's not necessary to spend thousands on a monitor if you are just starting on your photographic journey. Calibrators such as the X-Rite i1 Display will help you balance what you see on your monitor with your printer. Test prints from your lab or printer will help you set this up, and when you view your prints, make sure you are looking at them in daylight or under a daylight bulb.

Sharpening

Once an image is out of focus or has movement within it, it is almost irretrievable. No amount of sharpening is going to change the make-up of those pixels. What you will be left with is an out-of-focus image which the photographer has obviously tried to salvage, leaving it pixelated. Post-sharpening will not reconstruct a soft image but, used subtly, it can create a more pronounced image.

Purposeful movement, as mentioned in a previous chapter, is a different matter but can still be affected by over-sharpening. Many of the new efficient cameras, with their automatic settings in JPEG mode, automatically apply sharpening. But be aware that image sharpening post-capture is a powerful tool, to be used to emphasize texture, but which overused can cause visually unnatural effects. If you want control of the sharpening process, turn off your in-camera sharpening and apply it in post-production.

Colour versus Black and White

The popularity of black and white has given portrait photography a new timeless insurgence, which perhaps is not as achievable with the colour image. Black and white film takes us back to the roots of where photography started and we have an affinity as humans to all things nostalgic. Those origins were the start of something special and relevant in all our lives and introduced the important process of recording history.

Running parallel to the changes in styles and trends, lifestyle photography gives us an air of documentary, as seen in newspapers. The current candid styling of imagery sits well within the realms of a journalistic style.

Similar to the styling of a portrait, taking something out of an image – in this case the colour – can change how the viewer feels about it. A beautiful, soot-and-white wash, black and white print can accentuate graphic, give a feeling of depth and emotion, and add dynamism. It can be sinister, thought-provoking and give a sense of quietness in a way that the same image in colour can't. This isn't to say colour doesn't belong in portraiture – on the contrary. How you use colour and the emotion you want to portray will affect your decision on the best treatment of your work.

Marrying colour within your location with that of the subject in a physical sense can be extremely subtle but powerful, but we need to either have a natural eye for this or educate our visual palette to visualize it. Often when you look at a print of a final image, these elements are very obvious, but at the shoot itself perhaps less so. By specializing in solely black and white portraiture you may find yourself a niche market. The market will be narrow, but this could be a fundamental strength in your marketing and also define your style, giving a very definite feel to your work simply through the use of black and white.

We can discipline ourselves to 'see' a black and white image within a given scenario or location; sometimes we can be very sure about the portrait in its entirety before we start. Being able to see in black and white takes a little practice. We all have our own tastes when it comes to tonality, and tonal range is something we need to recognize in an area or potential portrait. As with low and high key (explained in Chapter 1), a high contrast image is represented by strong blacks and whites throughout with few mid-tone or grey areas. It is conducive to strong graphic imagery with substance. A lower contrast is made up more of mid tones and can appear flat. Recognizing these tones in colour is possible through an understanding of how colour represents tone. For example, primary colours combined in an image may have the same tonal range and thus look undefined when converted to black and white.

Texture can be enhanced with black and white imagery. Colourful foliage at particular times of the year, however, can be a wonderfully vibrant element to a portrait. Much of this is down to your own personal taste, and of course your client's brief.

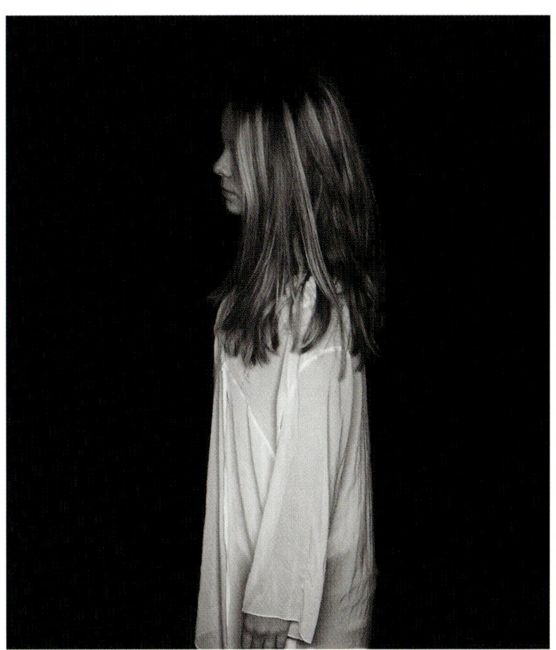

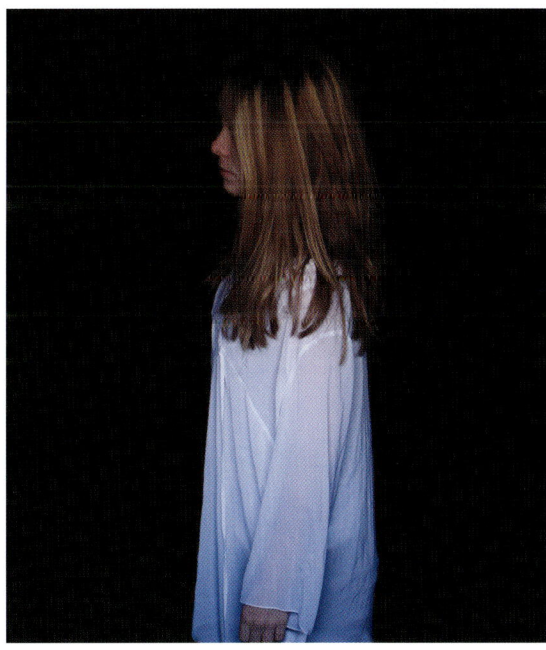

▲ Figs 7.17a–b
When shooting a scene or indeed a person, do question the narrative and the impact, if any, that colour holds. If the colour is irrelevant, or even a distracting element, remove it. Portraiture is more about taking something away than adding to it.

BLACK AND WHITE TONES

Look for shapes and shadows in an area and recognize when colour is not contributory to the aesthetic but the shadows are. For example Fig. 7.18a is fairly non-descript in colour, but look carefully at the range of tones from highlight, midtone, through to shadow. If we change it to black and white (Fig. 7.18b), those tones are emulated and we have something graphically impactive.

It would be tempting to recognize this as monotone immediately and to shoot straight into black and white – you are highly advised not to do this. The way that you process black and white is crucial to the embellishment of your work, and removing the colour from the original RAW file will eliminate this fine art quality. Not to mention the fact that, you may, for whatever reason, decide you need a colour image of this location or subject at a later date. Do not shoot black and white in camera!

Dramatic backlit sunshine streaming through smoke from a bonfire lends itself to a far more effective monotone than in colour, where the tones and richness of the file appear flat (Fig. 7.18c). This is rectifiable, of course, but the black and white holds a more mystical and graphical element (Fig. 7.18d).

Having the discipline to 'see' in black and white at capture stage can allow you to make use of a portrait that perhaps doesn't work so well in colour. Try to discipline yourself to recognize this before dismissing a location or opportunity where the colours don't work so well. The textures in the grass, the mother's hair, the leading lines of the field beyond, even the barbed wire fence, in Fig 17.18e and Fig. 17.18f are all dramatized when a black and white conversion is applied. These features make far less impact in colour.

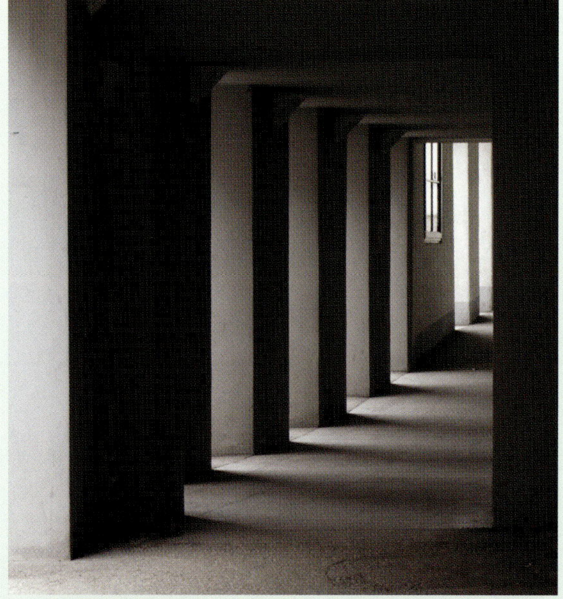

▲ Fig. 7.18a

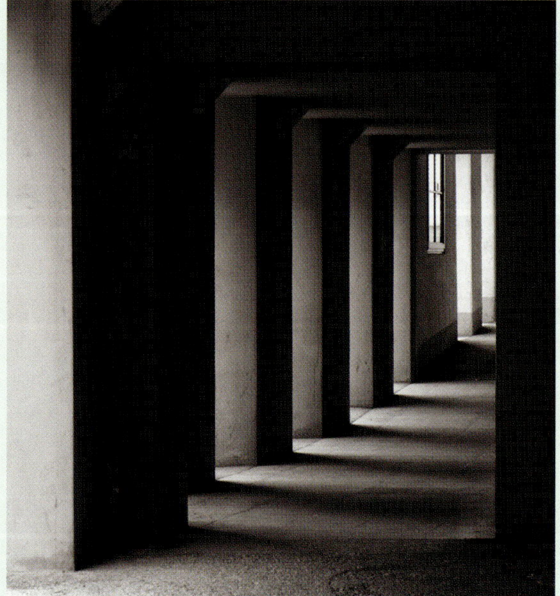

▲ Fig. 7.18b

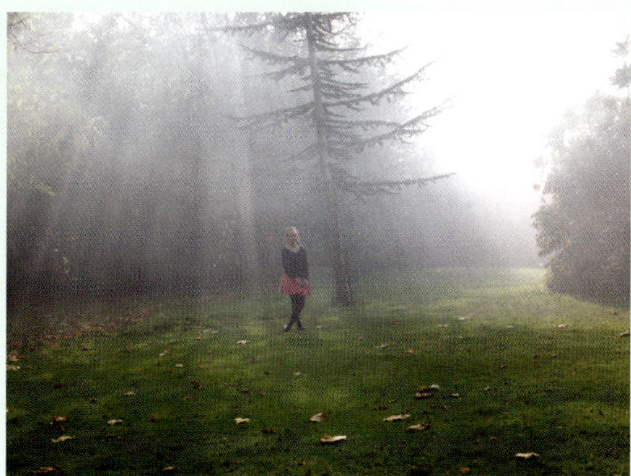

▲ Fig. 7.18c

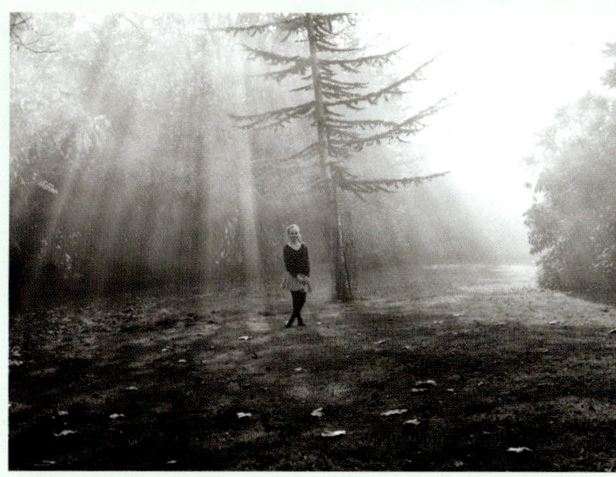

▲ Fig. 7.18d

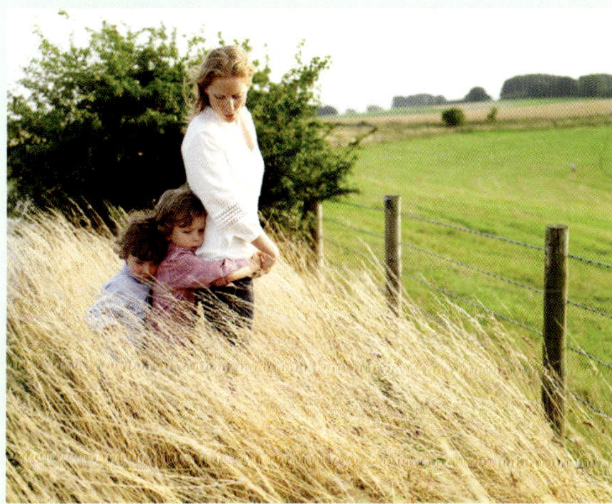

▲ Fig. 7.18e

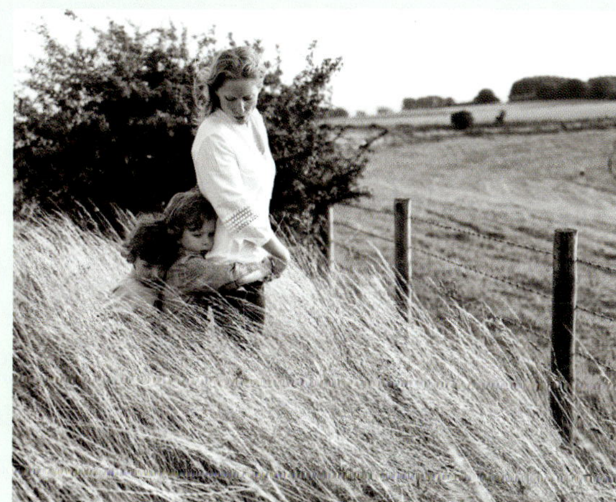

▲ Fig. 7.18f

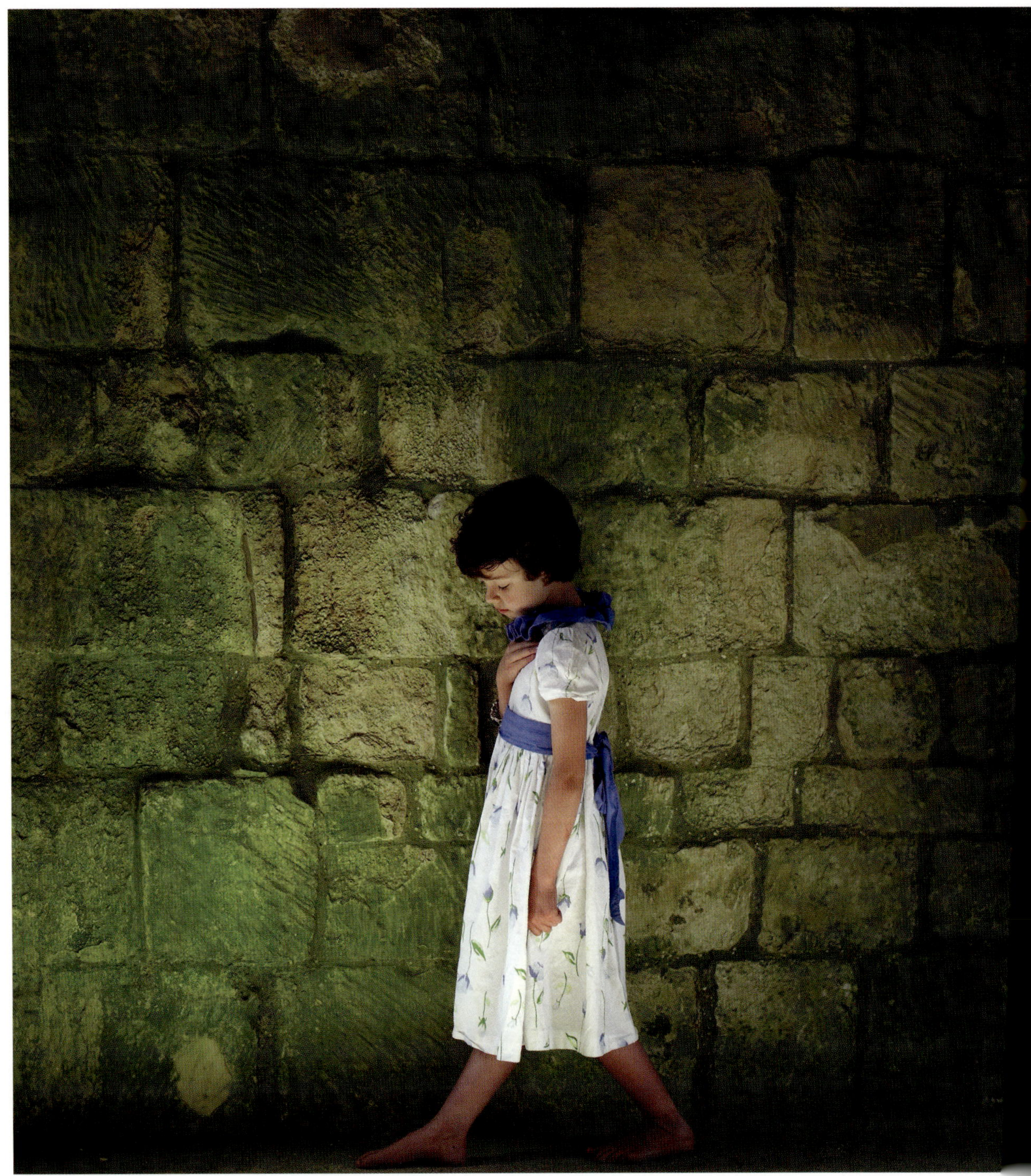

▲ Fig. 7.19
Despite a textured wall, which lends itself beautifully to black and white imagery, the dominance of the colour here lifts an otherwise quiet image sympathetically, giving it a contrasting drama to the otherwise sombre mood.

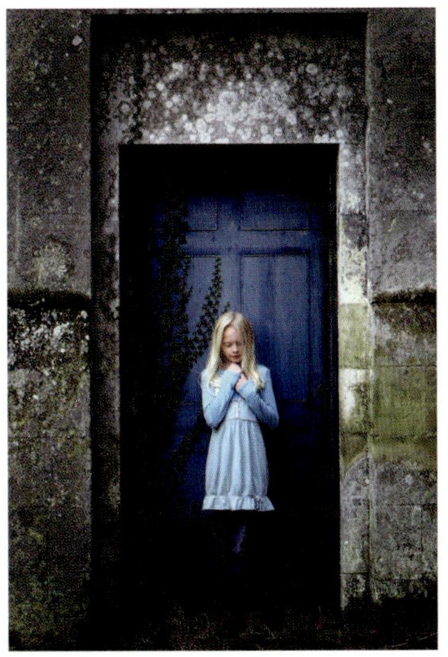

▲ Fig. 7.20a

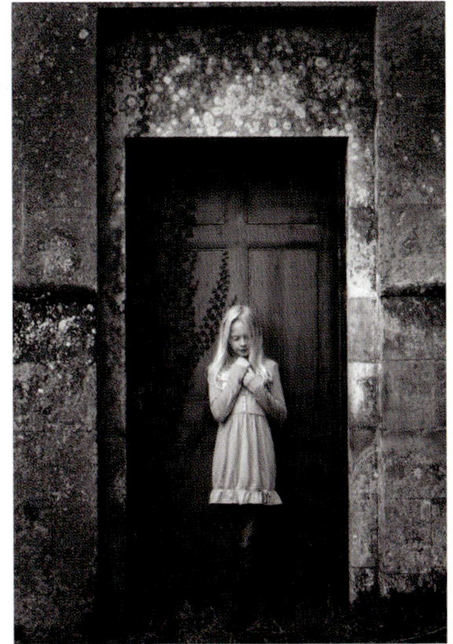

▲ Fig. 7.20b

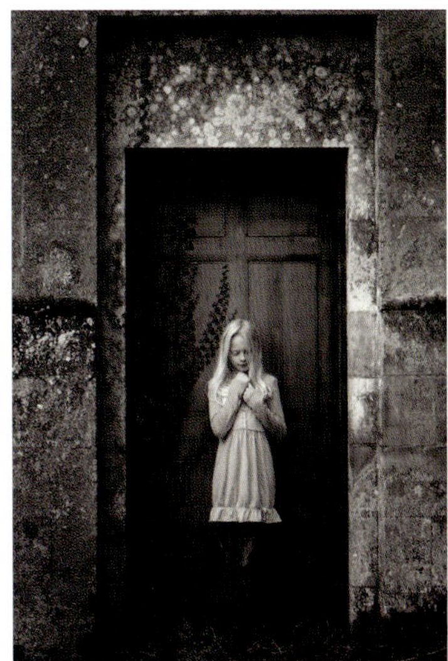

▲ Fig. 7.20c

Figs 7.20a–c
Some images work well in both colour and black and white (another reason to always shoot colour in camera). In this instance, the colour of the girl's clothes was sympathetic to the choice of location – the prominent primary colours work in cohesion with the (nondescript) greys of the wall. Those textures from the backdrop are enhanced when we remove the colour and subsequently add a tone.

The decision to add a tone (*see* Figs 7.20a–c), whether subtle or not, is up to you. By experimenting with various paper types, we can make very gradual natural changes without conversion, given that some fine art papers are warmer than others, thus giving an impression of a very slight tone. Alternatively, Photoshop plug-ins such as the highly effective and recommended Silver Efex Pro will give you variable options for tones and replica film type layers, or you can customize your own.

Cropping

We talked earlier in the book about the value of creating space around an image, to allow it to breathe, to open a narrative and to incorporate the environment for the benefit of the viewer.

One of the darkroom tools which have made the journey into the digital era, along with dodging and burning, is the crop tool. Understanding how a crop can change a picture will change the way you see your work. By recognizing the power of the crop, you will find it easier to give your portraits that extra space. Remember, you can crop in but you can't crop out. Crop at the shooting stage for the following reasons:

- To fit a particular dimension of frame, or for more creative options
- Because your client would like the subject closer
- To completely change the feel of an image
- For editorial purposes

Even a head study will benefit from being wider at the edges on the RAW file to allow for tweaking. Think about your portrait in its raw form – not just in file format, but when it's shot. It should contain beautiful light, the subject should be placed in balance with the composition, and there should be more than enough space incorporating the environment – in fact more than you need if you wish to include natural framing.

As with other elements such as symbolism, we can often afford to remove elements from a picture in order to strengthen it. Where content is concerned, however, we need to have it in place in order to be able to have that choice.

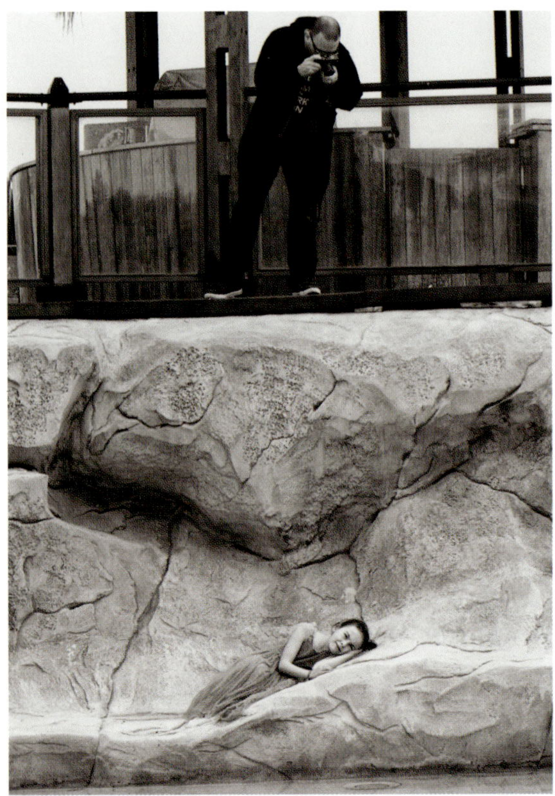

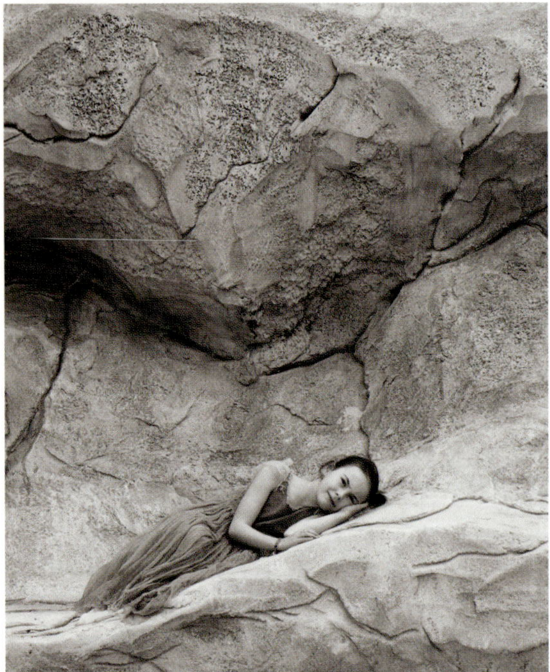

▲ Figs 7.21a–b
Cropping an image post-shoot.

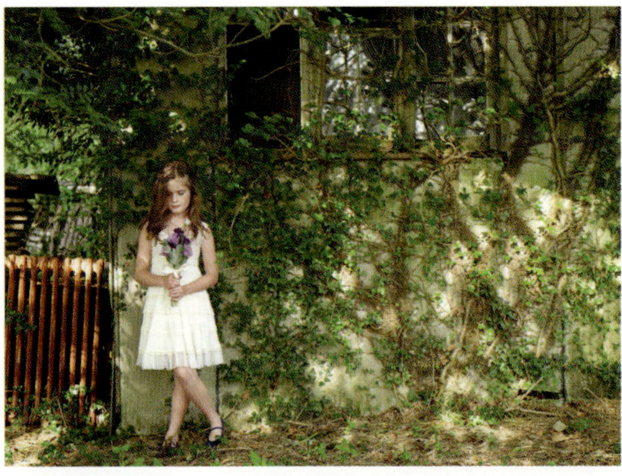

▲ Fig. 7.22a

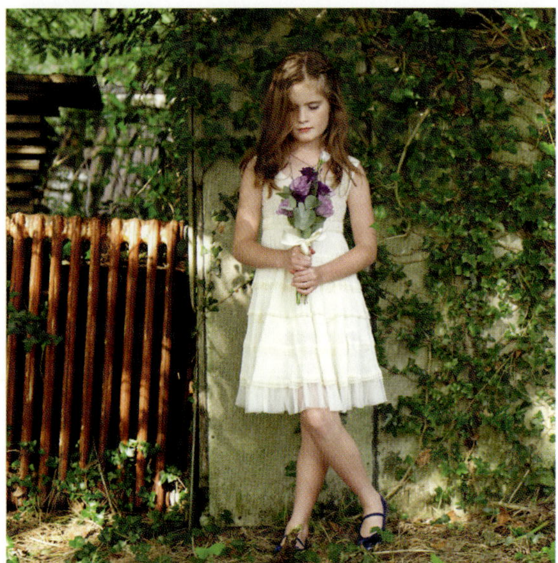

▲ Fig. 7.22b

Figs 7.22a–g
Fig. 7.22a is the original image. Figs 7.22b to 7.22g are all examples of cropping from the one image. Do bear in mind your sensor size – the larger the crop, the less detail is retained.

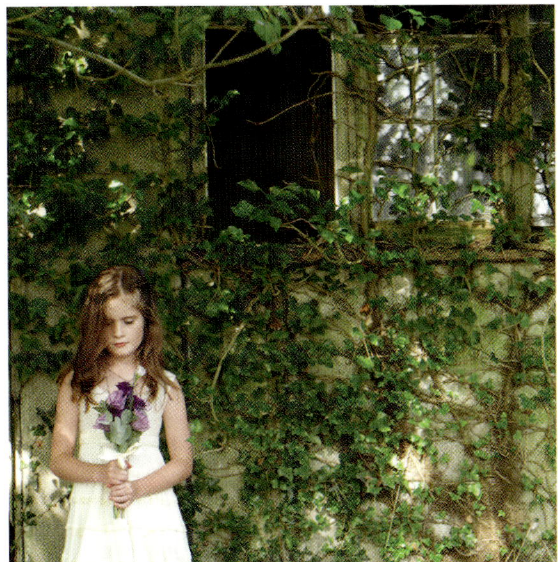

▲ Fig. 7.22c

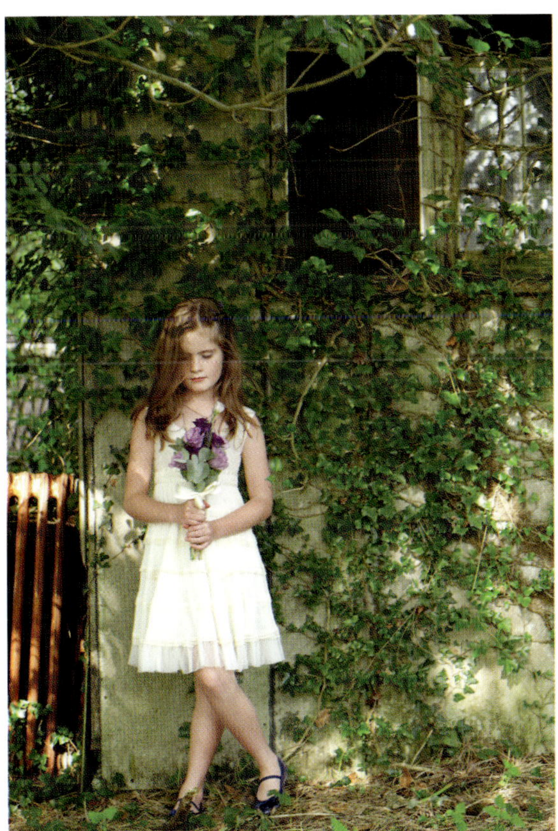

▲ Fig. 7.22e

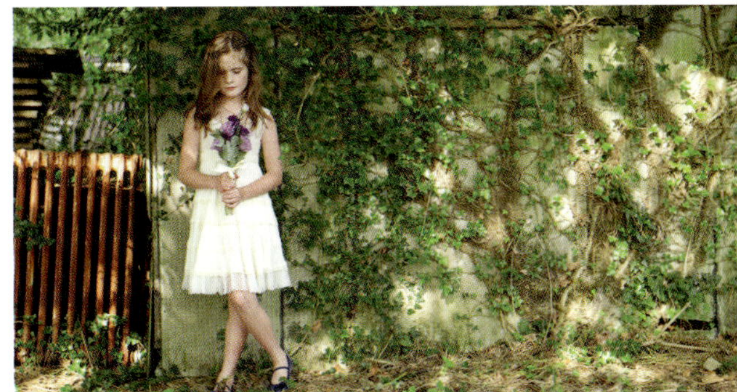

▲ Fig. 7.22d

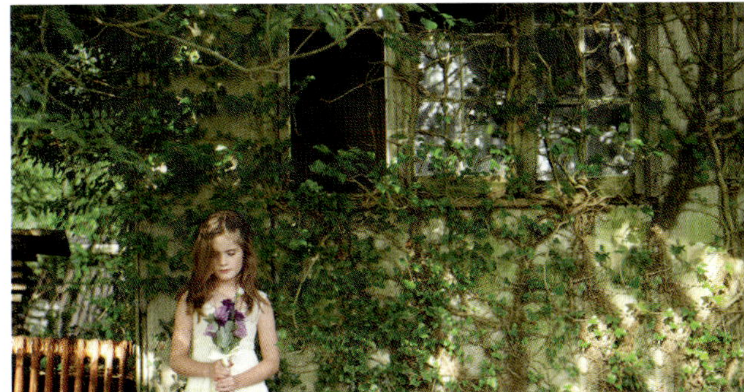

▲ Fig. 7.22f

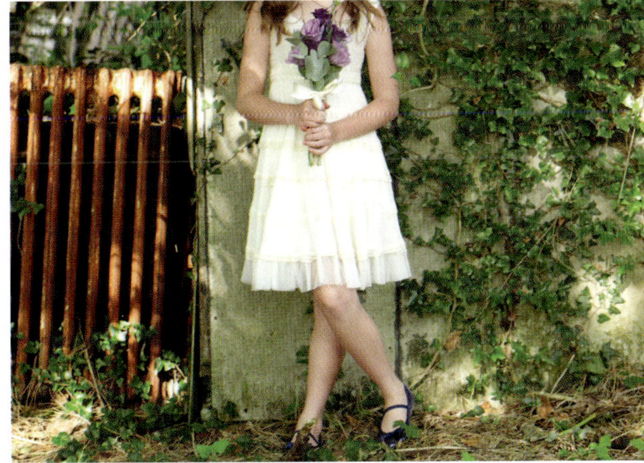

▲ Fig. 7.22g

Further Information

Cameras and Lenses
www.1stcameras.com
www.bhphotovideo.com
www.calumetphoto.co.uk
www.camerapro.com.au
www.cameraworld.com
www.canon.co.uk
www.fotoriesel.com
www.jessops.com
www.nikon.com
www.teds.com.au
www.wexphotographic.com
www.hasselblad.co.uk

Printing supplies
www.breathingcolor.com
www.epson.com
www.gicleemedia.com.au
www.hp.com
www.paperspectrum.co.uk
www.permajet.com
www.hahnemuehle.com
www.innovaart.co.uk

Production Tools
www.adobe.com/photoshop
www.adobe.com/lightroom
www.FlorabellaCollection.com
www.mcpactions.com
www.niksoftware.com
www.paintthemoon.net/blog
www.lastolite.co.uk
http://colourconfidence.com

Galleries

UK

National Portrait Gallery,
   St Martin's Place, London WC2H 0HE

The Photographers' Gallery,
   16–18 Ramillies Street, London W1F 7LW

Scottish National Portrait Gallery,
   1 Queen Street, Edinburgh EH2 1JD

USA

The Ansel Adams Gallery, Village Mall,
   Yosemite National Park, California CA
   95389

The Aperture Gallery, 547 West 27th Street,
   4th floor, New York, NY 10001

Fraenkel Gallery, 49 Geary Street, 4th Floor,
   San Francisco, CA 94108

Howard Greenberg Gallery,
   The Fuller Building, 41 East 57th Street,
   Midtown East, New York, NY 10022

International Center of Photography,
   1133 Ave of the Americas #1A,
   New York, NY 10036

National Portrait Gallery,
   F Street NW, Smithsonian Institution,
   Washington DC, DC 20560

Australia

Australian Centre for Photography, 257
   Oxford Street, Paddington, NSW 2021

National Portrait Gallery,
   King Edward Terrace, Parkes ACT 2600

Photographic Associations

UK

The Association of Photographers Ltd,
   21 Downham Road, London N1 5AA

The British Institute of Professional
   Photographers, The Coach House,
   The Firs, High Street, Whitchurch,
   Aylesbury, Buckinghamshire HP22 4SJ

The Master Photographers Association,
   Jubilee House, 1 Chancery Lane,
   Darlington, County Durham DL1 5QP

The Royal Photographic Society, Fenton
   House, 122 Wells Road, Bath BA2 3AH

USA

American Photography Association,
   Membership Services,
   PO Box 951777, Lake Mary, FL 32795

Photographic Society of America,
   3000 United Founders Blvd., Suite 103,
   Oklahoma City, OK 73112

Professional Photographers of America,
   229 Peachtree St NE, Suite 2200,
   Atlanta, GA 30303

Australia

Australian Institute of Professional
   Photography,
   Suite 5, 205a Middlesborough Road,
   Box Hill South, Victoria 3128

Australian Photographic Society,
   Suite 4, 8 Melville Street, Parramatta, NSW
   2150

Europe

Federation of European Professional
   Photographers (FEP),
   Willebroekkaai 37, 1000 Brussels, Belgium

Index